Life, Lessons, and Basketball

CHARACTER
DRIVEN

Derek Fisher

WITH GARY BROZEK

A TOUCHSTONE/HOWARD BOOK

Published by Simon & Schuster

New York London Toronto Sydney

TOUCHSTONE and HOWARD BOOKS
A Division of Simon & Schuster, Inc.
1230 Avenue of the Americas
New York, NY 10020

First Touchstone and Howard Books hardcover edition September 2009

TOUCHSTONE and HOWARD BOOKS colophons are registered trademarks of Simon & Schuster, Inc.

For information about special discounts for bulk purchases,
please contact Simon & Schuster Special Sales at
1-866-506-1949 or business@simonandschuster.com.

The Simon & Schuster Speakers Bureau can bring authors to your live event. For more information or to book an event contact the Simon & Schuster Speakers Bureau at 1-866-248-3049 or visit our website at www.simonspeakers.com.

Designed by Joy O'Meara

Manufactured in the United States of America

2   4   6   8   10   9   7   5   3   1

Library of Congress Cataloging-in-Publication Data

Fisher, Derek.
Character driven : life, lessons, and basketball / Derek Fisher ;
with Gary Brozek.—1st Touchstone hardcover ed.
p.   cm.
"A Touchstone book."
Includes bibliographical references and index.
1. Retinoblastoma—Psychological aspects.   2. Cancer in children—Psychological aspects.   3. Fisher, Derek.   4. Basketball players—California—Biography.
5. Retinoblastoma—Patients—Family relationships.   I. Brozek, Gary.   II. Title.
RC280.E9F57   2009
616.99'4840092—dc22
[B]   2009022794

ISBN 978-1-4165-8053-9
ISBN 978-1-4391-4915-7 (eBook)

To my family. To my parents for setting the foundation.
To my wife and children for everyday strength to
keep trying to live a life driven by character.

Contents

Foreword

by Earvin "Magic" Johnson

As a member of the 1980s Los Angeles Lakers "Showtime" team, I know the kind of success we enjoyed may have looked easy to people on the outside, but we put in a lot of hard work and a lot of practicing. Basketball and Hollywood go hand in hand. There's the make-believe world that appears on the court or on the screen, and then there's the reality of what it took to put that show on. I've known Derek Fisher for more than a decade, and I can't think of a better person to take this journey with as he goes behind the scenes to reveal his life in the NBA. Derek is one of the guys who appear to be working backstage while others get the spotlight; but the truth is, he's a star and has shown it on some of the biggest stages in the league and at the most critical times. His teammates and the fans understand the kinds of contributions Derek has made to the league, and I know more people will understand him and the role he's played after reading *Character Driven*.

Success is often elusive, because we set these high standards for ourselves as athletes, and the expectations we put on others can sometimes be overwhelming. I've come to know Derek Fisher as a skilled and fiercely competitive athlete. He's one of the good guys in the NBA who has taken an active role in preserving the popularity and integrity of what I consider to be the greatest professional sport in the world. He's a torchbearer for the legacy of success that is the Los Angeles Lakers, and, more important, Derek's a thoughtful and compassionate guy who cares deeply about the game and has a vision for what he wants to do once his playing days are over.

In reading about Derek's youth in Little Rock, Arkansas, in *Character Driven*, it took me back to my days growing up in Lansing, Michigan. We were both blessed with incredibly supportive parents who instilled in us the importance of giving back. It's part of everything I do with the Magic Johnson Foundation and Magic Johnson Enterprises. Our motto is simple: "We are the communities we serve." When we take care of our own communities, the ripple effects are far wider than we can imagine. Knowing that the success I enjoyed inspired Derek as a young man means a great deal to me, not only because of what's he's meant to the Lakers but also to the league and to the many lives he's touched off the court.

Derek is one of the most highly regarded players in the game today, and the respect he has earned is richly deserved. He's built a legacy on and off the court that few in the game today can match.

Whether it's his floor leadership, his presence in the locker room, or his giving back to the community, Derek Fisher is a guy who plays much larger than his size would indicate. That's one of the things scouts and coaches are always looking for in players, but in

Derek's case, what he has done off the floor as well as on the court has earned him that distinction. It's Derek's quiet example of how to live a good life and achieve success on and off the court that makes him remarkable. This is the heart of Derek Fisher. I'm glad that he's decided to share more of his life and the lessons that he's learned along the way. I hope you enjoy getting to know him as much as I have. The league, and the world at large, could use more people like Derek Fisher in it.

CHARACTER
DRIVEN

CHAPTER ONE

Putting Your Skills to the Best Use:

Performing When It Really Matters

When people found out that my wife, Candace, and I were expecting a child, more than a few of them said, "Your life is about to change." Candace and I each had a child from a previous relationship, so we had some idea of the truth of that statement. What we didn't know was the extent to which our lives would be altered several months after our twins, Tatum and Drew, were born. I don't know if having twins changes your life twice as much, but when you find out that one of your newborn children has a serious illness such as cancer, little in your life and your routine remains the same. We suspected that something was wrong with one of Tatum's eyes; after first dismissing the difference in its appearance as parental paranoia, we took her to a specialist. When we learned that she had a rare but dangerous form of cancer known as retinoblastoma—a tumor of the retina—it was as if someone had sucked all the air out of the doctor's office.

After we were initially told that there was little hope of saving Tatum's eye, we were momentarily stunned, and that pit-of-the-stomach sinking feeling could have overwhelmed us. I don't want to trivialize the situation by comparing my daughter's dire diagnosis to the game of basketball, because truth be told, thoughts of my career, the Utah Jazz's prospects for the play-offs, and any thoughts of winning a championship were very, very far from my mind. My energies were concentrated on doing whatever I could to help my daughter and support my wife, who was understandably upset and fearful. I was experiencing a lot of the same emotions as Candace, but I could sense that this was particularly hard on her. Her maternal instincts were running at their highest level, and they had been for some time prior to the diagnosis and prior to her pregnancy. Before her getting pregnant with the twins, we'd experienced a miscarriage. Losing that child was a blow to both of us, one that we'd recovered from to a certain degree, but not something we had by any means forgotten.

In the wake of that sad event, we'd decided to explore medical options to ensure a safe and full-term pregnancy. As a result, we'd seen a few fertility specialists, and we'd decided on what we were told would most likely be a safer alternative—in vitro fertilization. My whole life, I've been someone who looks at all the alternatives and choices before making a decision based on a careful risk/reward analysis. If the doctors we were dealing with felt that in vitro fertilization offered us the best chances of having a child, then that's what we were going to do. I can still remember sitting in that doctor's office talking about everything that needed to be done. I was able to block out all thoughts that in vitro wasn't normal or natural and that the procedure would be done in a lab instead of in the privacy of our home. What mattered were the results. Candace and I both were eager to have a family together, and so we were going to do whatever it took to make that dream come true.

I do have to admit to trepidation in regard to one part of the procedure. To increase the chances of having a viable fetus develop and to avoid having to repeat the painful procedure of harvesting one of Candace's eggs, we were told that it would be a good idea to fertilize and then implant more than one ovum at a time. If they "took," we could decide if we wanted to bring those ova to full term. Candace and I knew that we would of course not destroy one or more of the eggs, so we had to decide just how much we wanted to increase the odds of our successfully producing a child together. I was cool with the idea of having twins, but when the doctor said that we could go for three if we wanted to, I had to call a time-out. I looked at Candace and she looked at me. We each did some elementary-school math and came to the same conclusion. There were two of us, and if God willing Candace would get pregnant with twins, we could each handle one of the twins at a time. Two parents, two hands/arms each, two children. That would work. Any number of children above that would make the math, and the amount of work we'd have to do, that much harder. If circumstances were different and we didn't have any kind of control over the situation and God willed that we would have triplets or even more children, then we'd have accepted that also.

We looked at the doctor and said, "Two, please."

When Tatum was diagnosed, my career as a basketball player came into play in the way I handled the situation. Like many people, I believe that God never puts on our plates more than we can handle, and that everything that happens in our lives fits into a pattern of His creation. When you are faced with challenges the way Candace and I were, all the choices and decisions and experiences you have had leading up to the specific moment of having a seriously ill child fall into place. Because I'd dedicated my life to basketball, because I had been in pressure-packed situations, and because to succeed in basketball I had to understand the role of focus, tenacious diligence, teamwork, and sacrifice, we were all able to do what it took to secure a successful outcome for Tatum. Ultimately, whether Tatum's eye would be saved was out of our hands and in the hands of God. I truly believe that, but a lot of other human beings made that possible. Looking back at all those choices I made that led us to those wonderfully skilled individuals who did save her eye, I see ample evidence of the guiding hand of God at work. We asked Him to lead us and were comfortable with knowing that His will would be done, and we put the power of prayer to use.

Let me give you one example of how a choice I made in my life paid unexpected dividends down the line. We were fortunate to have a family friend who worked in a medical-school library and was familiar with all kinds of print and electronic resources. When Tatum was diagnosed and we were essentially told that our only option was to have Tatum's eye removed so that the cancer would not spread, my basketball training and God's intervention combined to make me realize that I needed to pass the ball off. This was not a shot I could take independent of the team; I needed to turn to forces greater than my own. I really believe that God put this friend in my life to be more than just someone to socialize with. He put him there because with his medical background and training, I could turn to him to do the necessary research and study to find an alternative to surgically removing my precious daughter's eye. He was able to quickly sift through much of the medical literature and report back to Candace and me.

We knew that time was running out, and the longer it took us to find alternatives, the riskier those procedures might be. Cancer has unflagging energy, and we knew that with each passing day, the tumor was growing. Candace and I could have tried to do all the research on our own, but poring through medical journals to try to understand all the complications and even just the possible approaches to treatment would have cost us precious time. Even developing a basic understanding of the options and then trying to track down doctors who either did those alternative procedures or who might be able to better explain their potential risks was not something we could do either. The clock was winding down, and we knew we needed to rely on someone who could quickly cut through the lingo and technical aspects of the treatment options and feed us the information as quickly as humanly possible. As a point guard, I have always had to assess the situation on court and distribute the ball to those who are in the best position to score. Evaluating time on the clock, the score, the opposition's strengths and weaknesses, and a dozen more factors are things I've spent nearly a lifetime doing. I had some idea those skills would transfer to life off the court, but being able to assess situations and make decisions quickly under such extreme, nonbasketball circumstances put those skills to the test in ways I had never anticipated.

That our friend found two doctors at Memorial Sloan-Kettering Cancer Center in New York who had experimented with a radical new treatment, one they'd only performed on fourteen patients, without publishing the results, is in my mind nothing short of a miracle. Those doctors had just begun the treatment in 2006—a year before Tatum was diagnosed. Another stroke of good fortune we could add to our score: When Candace and I sat in an office speaking with Dr. David Abramson and Dr. Pierre Gobin, they at first told us that the only real choice we had was to have Tatum's eye removed. I'm sure that they figured that we were parents doing our due-diligence work, getting a second and third opinion, hoping against hope that we could avoid surgically removing our daughter's eye. Of course, if removal of the eye meant preventing the possible spread of the cancer, and that was truly our only option, we would have agreed with that treatment. Something had told us, in the face of all the other opinions that lined up with Dr. Abramson and Dr. Gobin's initial assessment, that we had to dig deeper. If nothing else, we wanted to hear that dire prognosis from the best doctors in the field, and Dr. Abramson was considered the go-to guy in retinoblastoma.

Like most people, I'd heard of Memorial Sloan-Kettering Cancer Center (though I knew it simply as Sloan-Kettering), even if I'd been fortunate not ever to have had any firsthand experience with the place for myself or any of my family members and friends. I knew that this cutting-edge facility was recognized worldwide as one of the most advanced cancer-treatment and research facilities out there. What I learned as we pursued a potential treatment for Tatum was that the doctors at Sloan-Kettering had a long history of advancing treatment of the rare cancer affecting our baby girl's eye. In the 1930s, doctors there had come up with the first treatments that successfully managed the disease. Prior to that, I learned, being diagnosed with retinoblastoma was essentially a death sentence. Survival rates for the disease were incredibly low. Fortunately, thanks to the work of many doctors and researchers, the odds have significantly increased, though in most cases the patient ends up losing the afflicted eye.

The cancer is rare; only about 350 children in the United States are diagnosed with retinoblastoma each year, but it is the most common type of eye cancer among children. Worldwide, approximately five thousand children are afflicted with this cancer each year, and about half that number eventually die from it. I say "only" in regard to the number of children in the United States with the disease (compared to almost three thousand kids with leukemia for example), but for every child and every parent of a child diagnosed with the disease, that number is far too large. In most cases, the disease is the result of a randomly occurring mutation in chromosome thirteen. Most often, the affected child is the first in the family to have the disease, and only in about 10 percent of the cases is the mutation inherited from one of the parents. Candace and I weren't so concerned at that point about the cause of Tatum's cancer; we were mainly concerned with treatment options. We were fortunate to find Dr. Abramson. He was the chief of the Ophthalmic Oncology Service at Sloan-Kettering and had in the seventies trained under one of the leading experts in the field of eye-cancer treatment, Dr. Algernon Reese at Columbia Presbyterian Medical Center. Dr. Reese, an ophthalmologist, and Dr. Hayes Martin, a surgeon, had pioneered the use of radiation treatments in eye cancer in the forties and fifties. Dr. Abramson and his team continued to advance treatment options, including the type of chemoeradication (shrinking the tumor with chemotherapy) technique our friend had learned about.

When I asked them about their experimental treatment, intra-arterial chemotherapy, they seemed surprised. As Dr. Abramson later said in a *New York Times* interview, "I'm not sure how he knew about that. . . . He must have done a lot of homework." Thanks to my friend, I had been able to copy someone else's homework. Spreading the ball around, and trusting that a teammate would execute under pressure, proved to be a wise move. Dr. Abramson and Dr. Gobin stepped up for us and agreed that if Candace and I were willing to take the risk, they were willing to do the procedure. We knew that we had to do everything we could to save Tatum's eye. The decision was in that way easy. Subjecting your infant daughter to anything, even a regularly scheduled immunization, is hard. Sitting in that office, floors above the growl and hum of midtown Manhattan, we took a deep breath, trusted that the Lord had led us to this place for a good reason, and signed the consent forms and did all the other necessary paperwork.

Obviously, there is never a good time to have anyone in your life become sick, but the circumstances of Tatum's diagnosis were marked by all kinds of potential pitfalls. That spring we had only recently moved from the Bay Area to Salt Lake City. I had been traded during the off-season, but with the kids still infants and lots of loose ends to tie up, it hadn't made sense to move right away that summer. I'm sure a lot of you can relate to the problems of moving and having to find new doctors, plus deal with health insurance companies (we were fortunate to have good coverage) and all the issues of who's in network and who's not. Candace had been concerned that something wasn't quite right with Tatum's eye, but had been assured by our pediatrician that nothing was wrong. Only when we finally settled in Salt Lake City and Candace pursued second and third opinions did Dr. Katie McElligott confirm my wife's suspicions. I was at practice when the voicemail message came in telling me that we needed to get to a pediatric ophthalmologist that afternoon. I joined them there, and I was glad that we had been persistent and followed Candace's gut instinct that something was wrong. If we had waited and if we'd let the red tape of insurance companies deter us, I don't know what the outcome would have been.

Call it a mother's intuition, call it her keen sense of observation, call it the Lord moving in mysterious ways, but whatever you call it, we were grateful that we had acted on Candace's suspicions. Neither of us had ever heard the word *retinoblastoma* before, and I'd never even thought that people could have cancer of the eye. In most ways, Tatum was a typical ten-month-old child. Being fraternal twins, Drew and Tatum were going to be subject to a lot of comparisons, maybe more so than other siblings. When they were born, Tatum had darker skin than Drew, whose coloring was more cocoa. Drew had a lot more hair than Tatum, though now that isn't the case, and he was always a lot less patient than her. When Drew was hungry, everyone in the house, and probably the surrounding neighborhood, knew that he needed food. He had to nurse or get a bottle immediately, and we could do nothing to persuade him to just hold on for a minute. Tatum, on the other hand, would wake from a nap and assess the situation, come fully awake and alert, then eat. Even from her earliest days, she seemed quite playful and mischievous, more capable of demonstrating a bit of an attitude.

Candace had noticed that sometimes when she looked into Tatum's eyes, something didn't seem quite right. She couldn't articulate exactly what was wrong, and each time I looked into my little girl's eyes, I was so in love that I couldn't imagine there being anything wrong with her. I felt the same about Drew. They seemed to me to be God's perfect little creations—even if they did fuss and cry a bit. But sometimes when light shone in Tatum's eye, Candace thought it didn't seem to reflect back the same way it did from her other one, or in the same way it did from Drew's. In the more than ten years that I'd known Candace, I'd learned to trust her instincts. If she thought something was wrong, then something had to be wrong.

Candace noticed that in some photographs of Tatum, depending upon the angle, one of Tatum's eyes reflected back a white light. That white light, visible in the pupils of children with retinoblastoma, is known as leukocoria or the cat's-eye reflex. Just as a cat's pupil appears white in certain lighting, so will that of a child who has retinoblastoma or other eye conditions including Coats' disease. That white reflection in photographs does not always indicate those serious conditions, but it is definitely worth checking out with a doctor. We learned all of this only after Tatum's diagnosis, and our doctors told us that it is a good idea to take a monthly flash photo of an infant and child to check for that telltale marker of a potential problem.

After the examination, when the doctor told us that he'd detected some abnormalities and what he suspected was a tumor, I felt as if all the air in the room had been sucked out. I remember grasping Candace's shaking hand, and my mind rushing. The sensation was like what happens when you are driving a standard-transmission car and you think you're in gear but you're in neutral. You hit the gas and you can hear and feel the vibration of the rapidly racing engine, but you don't increase your actual speed. Thoughts were bouncing all around my head, but I wasn't making any kind of positive steps toward coherence.

Looking back on it, I now realize, how could it have been otherwise? I'm not a real worrier by nature, and despite the difficulty Candace and I had experienced in having lost a child previously, I didn't fixate on the list of possible bad things that could happen to the twins before or after they were born. I had lost some people close to me, usually after a long and protracted illness, as with my grandmother. I'd lost a few older relatives, but they had lived what seemed to me then to be long lives. Nothing could prepare me for someone telling me that my daughter had cancer. It was a life-altering moment, like a kind of sign being driven into the ground indicating that was *then,* and next was *now.* Facing the prospect that she might lose not just her eye, but that we could lose her, was unimaginably difficult to process.

In a way, hearing that news was also as if I'd instantly done some mental spring cleaning and thrown away anything that wasn't needed and put everything else neatly into order. As clichéd as it sounds, I knew in that moment that very little besides my daughter's health and my family's safety mattered. All the little gripes and complaints I might have had about how the season was going, even though things were going well—any nagging pain from overuse or injury, any thoughts about upcoming games, whom I'd be matched up against—just neatly took their place in line behind—a long ways behind—one overriding concern: what were we going to do to help our daughter?

The next day, Tatum was given an MRI exam that confirmed the diagnosis. We had a play-off game that night against Houston and I would suit up. At that point, no one except Jazz owner Larry Miller, General Manager Kevin O'Connor, and trainer Gary Briggs knew the specifics of the situation. They told me that I was under no pressure to play that night or any other during the play-offs. They agreed that Tatum's condition and our privacy was what mattered the most.

I had been making such a mad rush from practice to doctors' appointments to the hospital for tests that the reality of what was going on with our child hadn't really sunk in. We'd won the game, and only when I sat in front of my locker after the game did the truth hit me, and it hit me hard. I sat staring blankly ahead of me, a towel draped over my shoulders. A few minutes later, reporters were allowed in, and they were just doing their job, but the last thing I wanted to do was to talk about the game, the series, or anything to do with basketball. All I could think of was what my daughter potentially faced. I didn't want anyone to see the anguish I was experiencing, so I went into Briggs's office and broke down. In some ways the game had been good for me, a distraction, but it only delayed the inevitable. I was devastated. That private moment of despair was good for me, helped me get it out of my system and refocus on the task at hand—how to overcome the dire diagnosis and what seemed at the time the absolute certainty that Tatum's eye would have to be surgically removed.

The day after we met with Dr. Gobin and Dr. Abramson, on Wednesday, May 9, 2007, Tatum would undergo the procedure at NewYork-Presbyterian Hospital.

Dr. Abramson knew about the play-off game the Jazz had that night against the Golden State Warriors. As a former alternate on the 1960 men's Olympic swimming team, he knew what an athlete's life was like. He suggested that we could hold off doing the procedure, until after the game. A delay of just a few hours would have no effect on the prognosis for Tatum's eye.

"Absolutely not," I told him. "Just do what's best for my child. How many games I miss in the play-offs is totally irrelevant." I meant every word of that, and even when Dr. Abramson suggested some possible adjustments to the schedule, I remained firm in my commitment to Candace and to Tatum. There hadn't been any real need for discussion—Candace and I both knew that as difficult as the circumstances were, our decision on Tatum's care was easy: spare no cost, leave no stone unturned, and put basketball where it belonged on my list of priorities, well below my family and its needs.

Doing the right thing came so easily because of the values that my mother, Annette, and my father, John, had instilled in me from the beginning. They made every sacrifice they could to enable me to be where I am today, and they demonstrated every day that you put your family members' needs above your own. Dr. Abramson was simply trying to accommodate me and my needs, figure my career into the scheme, and I appreciated that, but I never questioned whether we should do the procedure as soon as humanly possible. This was an aggressive and risky treatment, and the two men who pioneered it gave off an air of quiet confidence that I'd always appreciated in teammates. Not that they needed any more motivation, but just to show how the Lord does truly move in mysterious ways, Dr. Gobin, who grew up in France, had lived for a time in Los Angeles while working at the University of California at Los Angeles medical center. He was a die-hard fan of the NBA team there and remembered me from my days with the Lakers. Score another bucket for the home team.

I felt confident in the team we'd assembled. Dr. Gobin and Dr. Abramson were realistic but confident. I liked that about them both. They were as personable as could be without seeming smug or fake. They were clearly brilliant men, but their compassion and consideration for us as people, and not just as an opportunity to test a procedure that could make them famous or wealthy or both, really impressed me. They didn't push us to try something; instead, they only agreed to do it when we brought up the possibility. Their confidence and calm helped to settle our nerves a bit, but nothing could still them completely. Dr. Gobin, who specialized in something called interventional neuroradiology, was a highly respected medical pioneer, primarily known for advanced treatment for stroke victims. In 2001, Dr. Gobin joined the Weill Cornell Medical College as professor of radiology and neurosurgery, and the New York Weill Cornell

Hospital as the director of the Division of Interventional Neuroradiology.

I didn't know this at the time, but there was a third member of
the medical team, Dr. Ira Dunkel, a pediatric oncologist who also
worked with Dr. Abramson and Dr. Gobin to come up with this
treatment. A tumor-killing drug would be injected through a tiny
blood vessel in the eye. Within fifteen seconds, the drug is directly
on-site in the tumor. It either destroys the tumor entirely and it dis-
appears, or it becomes calcified.

I've been anxious before games before, but nothing compared to
the jitters I experienced that night. Prior to surgery, from our hotel
room, we could see Central Park spread below us, and I envied the
imagined emotional ease of the runners and cyclists I saw circling
that great expanse of green. I'd heard that some people consider Central Park Manhattan's lungs, providing a breath of fresh air squeezed
out by the concrete ribs that surround it. I wished I could exhale,
heave a great sigh of relief, but as daylight turned to twilight and
then into full darkness, I found myself drawn to that window and
knew that for me there was a very different reason that New York is
the city that never sleeps.

In some ways, Tatum's being an infant was a blessing. We didn't
have to explain to her the risks, and she didn't have to deal with the
anxiety of knowing that she had cancer or that she faced a surgical
procedure the next day. Unfortunately, we had no way to communicate to her that because of the procedure, she couldn't eat. Normally,
she was a happy and satisfied baby, but being forced to go without
food had her especially fussy that night and the next morning. Candace and I had both flipped a switch in our minds the instant we got
the diagnosis. We'd been in caregiver and protection mode all week
and were especially alert that morning. It tore us up to hear Tatum's
wails, and to see her in distress was gut-wrenching. We made a few
calls back to Utah to make sure that Drew, my daughter Chloe, and
my stepson, Marshall, were doing okay. Once Tatum finally fell
asleep, we made a few more phone calls to family members to let
them know what was going on. My mother assured me that the

prayer circle at Eighth Street Church back home in North Little Rock was complete and doing the necessary work. Until that night I'd never really thought of the significance of the name of my hometown. A rock can be a weapon or a refuge, and as Jesus told St. Peter, it was upon that rock He was going to build His church. Home and family have always been my rock, my touchstone, the place on which the foundation of my life was built. I could add that to the list of the many blessings I've received. Hearing my mother tell me that those prayers were going out, I knew that we had a whole bunch of folks on the sidelines and in the stands doing their best to help my family get through this difficult time.

We knew that waiting while Tatum was in surgery was going to be the hardest part, but showing up at 7 a.m. for a 10 a.m. scheduled start was difficult. When one of the surgical-team members was called away by a separate emergency and Tatum's procedure was delayed, our already protracted period of anxiety went into overtime. Though we weren't guaranteed results, we had been encouraged by the success rate among the few patients who had previously undergone the treatment, and we had a lot of faith in the doctors. Knowing that any kind of invasive procedure was risky, and knowing that with an infant, and with the veins and arteries in such a delicate part of the anatomy—the eye—the operation required great precision, Candace and I were both on edge. We'd read up on the procedure, knew that this was the best chance we had, but still the thought of having toxins injected into our child's system to attack a tumor was unsettling at best. I tried to stay focused on the positive and was grateful that my years in the league had taught me how to fight off distractions. Prayer made that task much easier as well.

By the time we were instructed to put on masks and gowns so that we could escort Tatum into the operating room, a steady diet of adrenaline had begun to take its toll. Tatum too had exhausted herself, and I was grateful that she was asleep when Candace laid her down on the table. We both kissed her and told her that we loved her. I've faced some tough assignments in my life, but nothing compared to having to walk out of that room. I trusted the doctors and have faith in God, but leaving your child to face any kind of uncertainty or pain had me feeling as if a brick were lodged in my throat. When I turned back to catch one last glimpse of Tatum, I was struck again by how small and vulnerable she looked surrounded by all the adults in the room and the various monitoring devices. Walking out of that operating room was the toughest part of this ordeal yet.

Most days when I have a game, I take a short nap to restore my energy before heading to the arena. We'd been told that the procedure would take a couple of hours, and I spent nearly every second of that time on pins and needles. I was grateful that our friend was there with us; he and I spent most of the time talking about what we imagined the progress was and counting down the minutes until someone came out to give us the promised midsession report. That report never came, but when one of the team members at last reported that the procedure had gone well, I was enormously relieved. When we saw Tatum being wheeled past us in a kind of incubator, my heart did skip a beat—seeing her in that device, alone and isolated, had our hearts aching for her as we walked alongside her to the recovery room.

I was glad that we had a job to do while Tatum was in recovery. A tube had to be inserted through her femoral artery in her upper thigh. The doctors didn't want the incision to tear open, so we were given the job of keeping Tatum still. As each minute passed postsurgery and she came out of her anesthesia-induced slumber, she grew more and more active and agitated. Another concern was that she keep down any fluids or food she was fed, so Candace and I worked together on that. It felt great to contribute to Tatum's well-being and comfort. I don't like to give up control, and the feelings of helplessness that I'd experienced during the operation had started to work on me. Just being able to hold Tatum in our arms made us feel as if we'd been given some powerful medicine to calm us and soothe the aches in our hearts.

With the procedure completed and the early prognosis good, all we could really do was wait—both for Tatum to recover from the anesthesia and for the three weeks to lapse before we returned to see if the chemotherapy had had the desired effect. With Tatum's immediate safety and condition seemingly well in hand, I had a few moments to think about all that had happened. Through the week we struggled with Tatum's health concerns, I'd been in close contact with the Utah Jazz organization, and they couldn't have been more supportive. When Tatum was in recovery and sleeping again, I called Kevin O'Connor, the team's general manager, to let him know Tatum's status. I followed up that phone call with one to our coach, Jerry Sloan, simply to let him know how Tatum was doing. No one asked me if I'd be able to make that night's game, no one pressured me in any way to commit to anything. They both simply were glad to hear that things had gone well for my daughter. That meant a lot to me. Though they were my bosses, work was something fairly far from their minds.

During my phone call with Coach Sloan, I'd let the team know that as much as I wanted to remain on the active roster for that night's game, I understood that it really wasn't my decision to make. Basketball, and our series with the Warriors, diminished in importance compared to taking care of my family. That said, I still felt a sense of responsibility to my teammates, the organization, and the fans. We were, after all, in the play-offs and needed to maintain our home-court advantage with a win that night in Utah. The Jazz organization and fans had high hopes that we could make a run deep into the play-offs and win an NBA championship, which had eluded them.

I had my priorities straight, but knowing that Tatum's chemo treatment was an outpatient procedure, we had scheduled a return flight for that day regardless of the game back in Salt Lake City that night. The Jazz had helped us out greatly by securing a private jet to take us back and forth. Our only concern about flying so soon after the treatment was Tatum's leg. We needed to keep her still. We wanted to be back in Salt Lake City to be with our large circle of supporters and to restore as quickly as possible some semblance of normalcy in our lives. Even though Drew was too young to fully understand what was going on, I'm sure that he and Tatum both were picking up on the worried vibes that Candace and I were putting out despite our best attempts not to. Marshall, Candace's son and my stepson, had been affected as well. He was well aware, at age twelve, of everything that was going on, and I knew from conversations that I had with him, that he was both worried about his half sister's health and his mother's mental state. He hated seeing her worried and upset, and the sooner we got back home to him and to our life and its routine, the better it would be for all of us. I also put a call in to the mother of my daughter Chloe. Though she was much younger than Marshall and couldn't fully comprehend what was going on with her baby sister, I wanted to let her know that things were okay.

Once we got permission to leave the hospital, we got back to Salt Lake City as soon as possible. If we had any indication from the doctors that it would have been in our best interest to remain in New York, we would have done it. They assured us that nothing more was to be done except to wait to see if the drugs had the desired effect on Tatum's tumor. We were also reassured because our friend with the medical background was a former registered nurse, and he could monitor the incision on Tatum's leg and take all the steps necessary in case something happened. The doctors kept telling us that we were in good hands and were comfortable in having us leave.

In our minds, the major challenge was over—the procedure was done—and the rest was out of our hands. That wasn't the most comfortable place for either Candace or I to be in. We're both take-charge kind of people, but we'd trusted in what our friend had told us and then the doctors. Everything had worked out as well as could be expected. We just had to let go and trust that we'd done the best we could, prepared ourselves and executed the game plan to the best of our abilities. We put our faith in God, comfortable in knowing what a prayer warrior Candace had been throughout this time.

Despite the many times I'd played in either New York or New Jersey and my having lived in Los Angeles for much of my early adulthood, the drive through the west side of Manhattan to the Lincoln Tunnel didn't do much to settle my nerves. I couldn't help but think of Tatum's delicate physiology and be amazed that these potent drugs had worked their way through her veins and arteries. In some ways I wished that when we came out on the New Jersey side of the Lincoln Tunnel that we'd be on the other side of this crisis. In some ways we were, but it felt like being in the waiting room prior to the procedure, with little we could do to help Tatum. More waiting was ahead of us, but something told me that I could do more.

Once we reached our cruising altitude and were making our way west, thoughts of our play-off series crept back in. I'd done the right thing by my family, and I had another job and another group of people I was beholden to. If I could help that second group out, I wanted to. I wasn't certain if I was capable of shutting out everything that had transpired in the previous few days, but if nothing else, maybe by being there I'd lend an emotional hand to my teammates. I had placed a second call to the Jazz's front-office personnel to let them know I was heading home. No one asked if I was coming to the arena, and I hadn't volunteered any further information. I appreciated that no one in the Jazz organization put me under any kind of pressure to play that night. I still wasn't certain as we flew over the darkening fields of the Midwest if I was even on the active roster for that night.

Another "coincidence" played in my favor. Our series was against the Golden State Warriors, a team I had played for from 2004 to 2006. I'd been traded just that off-season, and while some of the personnel had changed, I was still familiar enough with their tendencies to feel comfortable playing against them. I had missed the first game of the series, a game we'd pulled out after trailing by 3 at halftime and by 5 going into the fourth quarter. The Warriors up-tempo style and the performance of their guards Stephen Jackson and Baron Davis, who had combined for 40 points, made me think that I might be needed. Our guards Dee Brown and Deron Williams had done a great job in my absence, but play-off pressure was a whole different thing. We needed everyone on the roster to contribute, and I had no idea if I was on the roster or if I could contribute.

The flight home was quiet, each of us lost in private thoughts. Candace and I had decided not to reveal any of the details of what was going on in our personal life. While I was up front with the team, I'd been so busy attending to Tatum's needs and keeping close family members posted on what was going on that I hadn't had time to even consider what I might do that night, and the furthest thing from my mind was what anyone outside of that small circle knew about the situation.

When we saw the Great Basin and the Great Salt Lake below us as we banked into our final approach, I still had no idea what I would do if the team called on me to perform that night. Everyone wants to feel needed, but that night I was hoping the Jazz would have the game in hand without me. Once in the terminal, we were all met by my friend and assistant business manager, Duran McGregory. He said to me again how he was thrilled to hear that the procedure had gone well. He told me he had a message from the Jazz. I was on the roster and the team wanted me there if I felt up to it. I discussed things with Candace, and she was all for me heading to the arena. She understood that I had a job to do there as well as at home. With my responsibilities taken care of on one front, it was time for me to do my job. Duran would take me to the game, and a car service would take Candace and Tatum home.

I was surprised to learn that an unmarked police car was going to escort Duran and me from the airport, which was about ten minutes from our residence in Salt Lake City, to the arena. I was eager to find out how the game was going, and when we turned on the radio, I learned from Hot Rod Hundley that things were not going anything like I'd hoped. Dee Brown had been hurt and taken to the hospital with a possible neck injury when our own six-feet-eleven-inch Mehmet Okur fell and landed on him. Five minutes into the game and the Jazz were down to only ten players. I said a prayer that Dee was going to be okay. I also learned that Deron Williams had picked up two fouls within one minute in that too eventful first quarter. We were forced to use a forward, Andrei Kirilenko, at the point for a few minutes. When I heard all that, my mind started racing. All of this information was coming at me so fast, and I was listening to the game instead of being on the court or courtside participating in it. As the police car's Mars light strobed the scene inside and outside the car, I had that peculiar sensation of being both in the car and outside of it looking in on the situation as it evolved.

To make matters more surreal, when we pulled into the players' entrance and I got out of the car, teams of cameramen and soundmen and photographers were there. With flashes going off and guys hustling alongside me as I strode quickly into the arena to the locker room, I was doing everything I could to keep my mind focused on what I needed to do. I wasn't exactly certain of what that was, but even getting undressed and then dressed in my uniform helped me filter out some of the distractions. I'd put on a game jersey thousands of times in my life, but that night I had to slow myself down and really think about left arm and right arm, right-side out and inside out, frontward and backward. I wish I could say that a calm descended on me, but I was more like numb, relying on muscle memory to do even the simplest things such as tie my shoes.

I was surprised by the sea of noise that washed over me when I came out of the tunnel and onto the arena's floor. I heard a few people shouting my name, and I looked up and was impressed by how many fans had worn baby blue to the game.

Anytime you come up out of the tunnel, you see the court fully spotlit and gleaming, but that day I really felt that I was walking toward the light. Making my way to our bench, I saw a few of our guys looking at me. I could see a mixture of concern and a happy-to-see-you look. I glanced up at the clock; 3:18 remained in the quarter. Carlos Boozer had just been fouled and was making his way toward the free throw line. I felt as if someone were massaging my tense limbs, easing some of my anxiety. I was much more at home here, stepping out onto the floor of a basketball court, than I was sitting in a hospital waiting room or a doctor's office. New York City literally and figuratively felt a thousand miles away, and yet in other ways it felt as if I were still there.

I said a couple of words to Ronnie Brewer, Paul Millsap, and Jarron Collins, letting them know that things had gone well. I didn't have much time to talk. I heard assistant coach Phil Johnson call my name, letting me know that I was going in for Andrei Kirilenko. Boozer hit both his free throws to extend our lead to 84–80. I walked toward the scorer's table, and I could hear and feel vibrating in my chest the outpouring of affection from the Utah fans. In the days to come, I would learn more about the amazingly supportive fans and how they embraced my family and me with their show of faith and support. In Salt Lake City, family and faith come together in a unique way all the time, but this was different and special. I can never repay the people for their outpouring of support for the rest of that season. A thank-you can never really be sufficient, but I want them all to know how deeply grateful I am to them and what a cherished place in my heart they hold.

New York and doctors' offices and waiting rooms and the fans were out of sight and out of mind as soon as I stepped across the sideline. I immediately went into game mode. On our first possession after the free throw, Carlos Boozer captured an offensive rebound, and the ball was kicked back to me. I fed Carlos for a bucket and was feeling pretty good even though everything seemed to be happening in a blur of motion and emotion. I tried to focus on just merging with the flow of the game. The Warriors made a basket and then we turned the ball over. They converted to pull within a point at 86–85.

I threw a bad pass a few seconds later; fortunately, my former Golden State teammate Jason Richardson rimmed out a three-pointer at the other end, and we ended up leading at the end of the third quarter 90–89. Jason had gone out of his way to let me know that he was thinking of me and rooting for my family, but like any true competitor, he would have put the proverbial dagger through our collective hearts if he could by hitting those long-range jumpers of his. This was give no quarter and ask for no quarter, as it always was, especially in the play-offs. Stephen Jackson and Baron Davis also expressed their concern, and only later could I fully appreciate how much those words meant to me.

Despite how numbed I was by the events of the day, the extensive air travel, and the far-out-of-my-routine journey to the arena, I felt the electricity in the air. Not all the buzz in the building was a result of my being there under those circumstances. This was a definite play-off atmosphere, which seemingly soaked in through our pores and fed our adrenal glands. The game was definitely on.

Those three plus minutes went by in a flash, but when I sat on the bench during the quarter break, I once again marveled at Jerry Sloan's game-management skills. Getting me in there immediately wasn't just an act of desperation. He knew that if I had time to sit on the bench, I had time to think. While it's important to be aware and alert on the court, it's often more important to react to what you observe while in the flow of the game than it is to ponder things. If I had sat on the bench, my mind might have wandered a bit—I'm only human. By being forced into the action immediately, my body was jump-started and my brain instantly switched to basketball mode. No premeditation, just action. I also marveled that Deron Williams, who seldom got into foul trouble, had earned his fourth. It all seemed part of a larger plan.

Back on the bench at the start of the fourth quarter, I was better able to focus on the ebb and flow of the game instead of wondering whether I could play and actually contribute. With that question answered, my mind focused more on how to slow down Golden State's offense. With our guards in foul trouble, the Warriors' Baron Davis and Jason Richardson were taking it to us with a mix of threes and dribble penetration. With just under eight minutes left in the fourth quarter, we were ahead 99–96. Right before the TV time-out, Baron Davis had converted a layup for his thirty-third point of the night. When one player has a little more than a third of his team's total output, you know he's having a night. We had to figure out a way to put the clamps on the guy.

Following that time-out, we went on a bit of a run. At the 4:52 mark, our center Mehmet Okur hit a three to put us up 106–100. Things were looking good, but with the way Golden State was hoisting up and hitting the three, it was still really just a two-possession game. Just as I suspected, Stephen Jackson hit a trey. Next, Jason Richardson fired up a three, was fouled, and hit two of three free throws. He followed that up by hitting a three, to put Golden State up by a point, 108–107, with just a little more than two minutes to play.

I went to our assistant coach, Tyrone Corbin, and said, "I can play defense." He nodded. The competitor in me came to the surface at that moment. I wanted in there, feeling that I could do what we needed to turn the tide. Tatum and my family were in my heart, but the game was on my mind. With 1:13 remaining in the game, Coach Sloan had me reenter. We were down 110–107. A few moments later, the Warriors scored again, and we trailed by 5 with less than a minute to go. On our next possession, Deron made a great pass to Carlos Boozer for a jam. We put the Warriors on the line, and we were fortunate they missed a couple of free throws. With two seconds left, Deron made a runner to tie the game at 113. Overtime.

The rest, as they say, is history. We jumped out quickly to a lead, but the Warriors scrambled back into it. I forced Baron Davis into a critical turnover just when we needed a stop. With just over a minute to play, we were up by 3 when Deron Williams found me open in the corner. I got the ball in rhythm, got in good bent-knee position, and rose up with my eyes locked on the rim. The shot felt good leaving my hand, but I'd had that feeling before and had been disappointed, but this time my faith in myself proved good—as did the shot. We were up by 6, and I followed up that shot with a pair of free throws in the waning seconds, and we pulled out the W.

I did something a bit uncharacteristic for me following that three-pointer. As I headed back on court during a time-out after that shot, I pointed to the sky. My faith in God is something personal to me, but at that moment I had to acknowledge that I didn't make that shot on my own. A higher power, God, had helped me make that shot. Jesus Christ was there for me in that moment in ways that allowed me to find within myself the strength to do my job and do it well. I did another atypical thing for me. After the game, TNT's Pam Oliver wanted me to do the postgame interview. Normally, they go to the star of the game, the guy who had the most points or hit the game winner. Instead, they came to me because of my family situation. Candace and I had agreed to keep things within the family, but when Ms. Oliver asked me about what had been going on, my gut told me that I needed to open up.

With tears in my eyes and an enormous sense of relief, I told her, "It was very, very serious. My daughter's life was in jeopardy. She has a form of eye cancer called retinoblastoma. And the only reason I'm saying this now is because there are kids out there that are suffering from this disease, and people can't really identify it. It's a very rare disease. And I want people out there to take their kids to the ophthalmologist, make sure they get their eyes checked, and make sure everything's okay, because we could have lost my little girl had we waited any longer."

I knew that I had a message to deliver. I had to do the right thing, and if I had to feel a little uncomfortable by sharing a personal slice of a sometimes too public life, then I was glad to do it.

This book is, in a lot of ways, a product of those experiences. I don't know that if we hadn't gone through what we did and received such enormous support locally and nationally, I would have wanted to write a book. I've never felt particularly special just because I am a basketball player. I am more reserved than most people and truly felt that what I did in those days dealing with Tatum's health, and in the days and weeks following when I asked to be released from my contract so that I could work someplace where Tatum could receive the kind of follow-up care she needed, was simply what most fathers, most parents, would do for a child or other family member. I was somewhat taken aback by all the attention the things I did or the choices we made as a family received. I was, and continue to be, enormously grateful for the outpouring of affection and am humbled by the media attention and people's view of me. On many levels then, this book is payback. Not only do I want people to know about retinoblastoma (Candace and I have started a foundation to promote education about the disease and possible treatments), but I want them to know that what took place in those few weeks was the product of an upbringing, an environment, a long list of influential people, and an agency with capabilities far beyond what we humans can muster.

As I stated before, I realize that everything that came before the moment when Tatum was diagnosed was preparing me to deal with that crisis. And as uncomfortable as it can sometimes be to have a light shone on me, I feel it's my duty and my privilege to share with you more of those moments that led to our victory on and off the court. I don't feel that my life has been in any way extraordinary, but I do believe that I have something to contribute, and giving back in this way is one form of giving thanks for the many blessings my family and I have received. In the pages that follow, I'm going to share with you some of the many lessons I've learned that have enabled me to succeed and stay sane in this sometimes crazy game of basketball. I didn't get here alone, and I'm glad to have you along with me on the journey.

I also know that in the most rational sense, my having spent thirteen years in the league is in a very real way less a product of anything that I've done than it is a product of some large plan laid out for me. I'm going to share with you some of the fundamental lessons I learned on the court and off that have enabled me to succeed beyond what most people who saw me play the game could ever have expected. I've always had a quiet confidence in myself and my abilities as a basketball player. I'm also realistic enough, analytical enough, to know that confidence alone wasn't what got and kept me here in the NBA. I also know that I've been blessed beyond all measure—the success of Tatum's procedure is just one small example of that. I've been provided with opportunities and the ability to recognize them when they present themselves, and the skills and faith to seize them.

I don't know that I go out of my way to be a nice guy, it's just a part of who I am because of how I was raised and because of all the reinforcement I've gotten for sticking with some of the fundamental truths about how to live my life—whether that's been the Golden Rule of doing unto others as I would want them to do unto me or understanding the fundamental truths of how the triangle offense should be run. It took me some time, but I've come to understand that the two selves—the basketball player and the man, husband, father, friend, and brother—that I sometimes felt I had to keep separate actually work together as a team. Who I am, what I do, and how I conduct myself are all bound together in ways that I've only lately begun to understand. Just as there's no sound reason that a guy who is six feet one and not the fleetest of foot can play in this league and contribute to the degree that I have, there's no logical reason that now, at the age of thirty-four, I should be enjoying one of my best seasons ever as a professional. I should be on the downside of my career, but as I see it, things have never looked brighter, my future never more certain, my love for my family never more a source of contentment and pleasure. In no way am I ready to hang it up, but this seems like a good point at which to stop and take stock of where I've been and how I got here. I love playing this game, I love my family and the life I'm privileged to lead. In my mind, my NBA career is only going to lead me to halftime in my life. What's to follow will likely be as fulfilling and rewarding, mainly because of what I've learned about myself and the world during this thrilling ride.

CHAPTER TWO

Practicing the Fundamentals:

Building a Solid Foundation

o to any court, gymnasium, or college or professional arena, and you're likely to hear shouted from the bench or by one of the players, "Box out." Even though we're often encouraged to think outside the box, sometimes tried-and-true conventional wisdom serves better than innovation. As in most sports, in basketball you can only score when you have the ball in your hands. On a good night, a team will score on about 50 percent of its possessions. When you factor in that when you have the ball, the other team can't score, you can better understand why each possession matters so much. That's where boxing out comes into play. When a shot is in the air, the ball isn't in the possession of either team. It is literally up for grabs. The cliché states that possession is nine-tenths of the law, but in basketball it is everything. The more possessions you have in a game, the greater the number of opportunities you have to score. A simple truth that we sometimes forget.

That's why you hear coaches stressing that players must box out when the ball is in the air following a shot. By putting yourself in good position to rebound the ball, and by preventing your opponent from getting access to the ball, you're increasing the likelihood that you will either retain or take possession of the "rock." Many games turn on those transitional moments when the ball is not in the hands of a player from either team. When you understand that basic truth about possessions, when you really have a firm understanding of that important fundamental, you see things from a slightly different perspective. While statistics such as points scored, rebounds corralled, assists made, and turnovers committed say a lot about the outcome of a game, the things that don't appear in the box score on your favorite Internet sports site or in your local newspaper often really tell the tale of W's and L's. Coaches will frequently talk about those "intangibles" and the "little things" in their postgame press conferences, but sometimes even we players forget the things that determine the razor's-edge margin between going home happy and replaying repeatedly the moments when the game slipped away. I've been in both positions, and believe me, I'd much rather look back on what went right than on what went wrong.

Chalk it up to genetics, to good teachers, or what have you. The thing that has kept me in the game of basketball for thirteen professional seasons isn't my blinding speed, my stunningly quick first step, my prodigious hops that allow me to take a quarter off the top of the backboard, or my possessing the wingspan of a jumbo jet. Instead, what has made me a valuable part of three different NBA teams and what brought me back to the Los Angeles Lakers, where I was privileged to be on three championship teams, is my ability to execute the fundamentals of the game. Whether it's putting a body on my man to box him out, taking a charge, or doing any of a dozen other "little things," those are among the skills I bring to the court each night. As all coaches will tell you, your shooting touch will come and go from night to night, but the energy you bring, the intensity with which you compete, and your ability to focus on doing the little things shouldn't vary from game to game.

So many people focused on the three-point shot I hit in overtime in the game the night following Tatum's procedure; what I remember, and what many of my teammates and coaches recalled, was the turnover I forced in overtime. That little thing produced big results. Similarly, the eighteen-foot jump shot I hit in the 2003–4 Western Conference semifinal at the buzzer to beat San Antonio still looms large in people's imaginations. Some people referred to me as the Fish That Saved L.A. for making that basket. What they don't remember is that in that game I grabbed a couple of rebounds that led to opportunities for us to score. Regrettably, I also missed one of two free throws—and making free throws is another of what I consider to be the game's fundamentals. Not that I'm hard on myself and demand perfection, but that missed free throw stands out in my mind almost as much as those made shots—more on how I deal with that tendency later.

Just as important fundamentals must always be kept in mind on the basketball court, similar kinds of fundamentals exist in life. I've been fortunate that from my earliest days I was surrounded by people who instilled in me the values and beliefs—and showed me how to put those intangible things into action—that have led to success in all phases of my life. The most influential people in my development as a human being also happened to be devoted to basketball as well. Had I been born into a family of mathematicians, musicians, or mechanics, I would likely have succeeded in those fields and been much the same person I am today. It just so happens that my career is basketball.

Well, maybe "just so happens" isn't the best way to put it. My mother, Annette, played basketball all through school, as did my father, John. He played for a couple of years at Southern University, but then he left school and joined the air force—more on that bit of influence in a while. My father was a Lakers fan from the beginning, and my earliest memories of growing up in our house on West Twenty-second Street in Little Rock, Arkansas, are the sounds of radio and television broadcasts of various games. Those were the Magic Johnson years, and he was my favorite player. My dad was also a huge Oakland Raiders fan. Why the California connection I have no idea, since Dad was originally from Louisiana. Because we had no pro teams in Little Rock, and the Lakers and the Celtics were the top teams in the league back then, it made sense that we'd root for one of the perennial powerhouses. I followed my dad's lead and became a big Lakers fan. That I would later be drafted by the team I rooted for as a kid is just another example to add to my list of events that have fit into the larger pattern that was not of my design.

Despite his affiliation with West Coast teams, Dad introduced me to the marvel that was Julius "Dr. J" Erving of the Philadelphia 76ers. By the time I was born in 1974, Dr. J had just led the New Jersey Nets to their first ABA championship. Later, when the two leagues merged in 1976, Irving joined the NBA as a Philadelphia 76er. I was too young to remember all of that, but my dad told me about Dr. J's standing up to the Nets owner and demanding that he be traded because the Nets had reneged on a promise to redo his contract. Dr. J was one of the league's most important stars, had been the ABA's Most Valuable Player, and was a charismatic figure who helped the NBA emerge from the shadow of Major League Baseball and the National Football League to become a huge and profitable industry. My dad reinforced the idea that what was right was right, and Dr. J's demands weren't out of line or greedy. He was simply expecting to be treated fairly and honestly.

More than those elements of his off-the-court dealings, my dad held Dr. J in such high regard because of what the man could do on the court. His incredibly athletic "above the rim" style of play ushered in professional basketball's modern era. His spectacular dunks were legendary and inspired many future pros. As talented as those 76er teams were, they couldn't win the championship with Dr. J until the 1982–83 season, when they beat our beloved Los Angeles Lakers in four games. I was only eight and a half years old at the time, but I still have vague recollections of those games and the conference finals against Boston leading up to that championship. The Dr. J vs. Larry Bird rivalry and later Bird vs. Magic Johnson set the tone for the NBA's marketing of marquee matchups. I don't remember many of the specifics of that championship season, but I'm sure my dad could recap all the games, and especially how torn he was to see one of his personal favorites go up against his favorite team.

My mom still has a photograph of me, no more than two years old, wearing a tiny Dr. J T-shirt. In the photo, I've just released a shot at a mini-basketball hoop, and I don't mind telling you that my form even at that age was really good. Dr. J and I couldn't have more different types of games, but in the years since I've been in the league, I've come to understand that Dr. J was someone worth emulating for what he did off the court as well as what he did on it. Following his retirement, he put his business savvy to work as an owner of a Coca-Cola bottling plant. He also worked as a television analyst, became a part owner in a NASCAR team (he saw that African-Americans were underrepresented in that profitable enterprise). He has also served on the board of directors of Converse (prior to their 2001 bankruptcy), Darden Restaurants Inc., Saks Incorporated, and the Sports Authority. In 1997, he joined the front office of the Orlando Magic. I've always felt that it's important to have a plan for your life, and clearly Dr. J was looking beyond his years in the game to the rest of his life.

As much as my dad idolized Dr. J and impressed upon me how the man conducted his life, there was always Magic in my life. For as many pictures as we had of Dr. J around the house, we had more of Earvin "Magic" Johnson. That I would one day wear the same uniform that he wore, that I would one day meet him and have him serve not just as a distant role model but as a mentor and as a friend, was something I could only dream about. That it all, and then some, became a reality is again part of that larger plan that I could not have put into motion on my own. When I came to the Lakers, I knew about the transition that Magic had made from basketball superstar to entrepreneur and advocate. As much success as he earned on the court, he has achieved even more off the court. Magic Johnson Enterprises and the Magic Johnson Foundation are two parts of that success. The first is an enormously successful business organization, and the second is a charitable foundation that has done incredible good work. What unites them is Magic's sense of community and empowering those in ethnically diverse communities to take charge of their futures. As a two-year-old, of course, I had no sense of the possibilities that were open to me.

Many years later, I was proud that Magic recognized something in me. Magic had no way of knowing this, but during the first month of my first season in L.A., as I stood on the balcony of my apartment in Marina Del Rey—I was alone, and the city lights sprawled out beneath me—I said to myself, "One day, I'm going to be big in this city, big like Magic." At the time, I didn't fully understand what an affirmation was in the way that I do today. Thirteen years have come and gone, and there are certainly bigger stars in the L.A. firmament than me, but something close to magic has happened in that time. Dreams are powerful things, and the Lord has moved more than mountains it seems since I was that two-year-old kid with the good shooting form.

I'm not sure who instructed me in the good shooting technique captured in that photo of me as a baby, but it could have been my half brother, Duane. My mom had previously been married, and Duane was ten years old by the time I was born. He was already playing on various school teams and at the local Boys Club when I came around. I can't say I idolized Duane, but I did want to go to the gym with him. Today, I understand that when he was fifteen and sixteen, the very last thing he wanted was to have a little brother tag along. My mom and dad insisted that he take me to the Penick Boys Club in the Boyle Park section of Little Rock or to the gym at Parkview High School, where he played.

At first he resisted the idea, but not for long. My mom and dad, my dad especially, knew how to lay down the law. They did not put up with any back talk. That was part of the reason Duane moved out of our house to live with his biological father for a short while. At the time, I didn't really know what was going on. Duane was there one day and gone the next. A few months later he was back. Whether it was the military that instilled a sense of discipline in my father that he carried over into his family life, or if his own father was a no-nonsense man, I'm not sure. All I know is that my backside was on familiar terms with my father's hand. Divorce is never easy on a kid, and I suspect that Duane had some issues to deal with—the "you're not my real father" kind of thing that would surely have upset my dad. I remember my mom saying once that Duane needed some discipline in his life. I think that my mother's soft side must have taken over in the wake of the divorce.

Of the two, my mom was definitely the softer touch. What do you expect of a woman whose people came from a place called Sweet Home, Arkansas? I can't think of a better word to describe my mother than *sweet*. She could be strong, too, when the situation required. That sweetness carried over to her cooking as well. I can remember eating a lot of meals with one of her specialties—minute rice with sugar and butter sprinkled on it. I know it doesn't sound like much, but even today those simple flavors can stir up all kinds of pleasant memories. With my mother's family nearby and my father's in Louisiana, we spent more of our time with her family than his. We were a tight-knit bunch, and that was reflected in our Sunday-afternoon, postchurch family dinners. All my aunts and uncles and my cousins would gather at my Grandma and Grandpa Johnson's house. He insisted we call him Papa, and my mother got her pleasant disposition from the two of them. That was also where she got her grounding in religion.

My mom's home away from home was the Eighth Street Baptist Church. She still sings in the choir there, just as she did all the years I was at home. Sunday meant three things in the Fisher household: church services, Sunday school, and that family dinner. Sunday wasn't the only day devoted to the Lord, however; when I was young, we were at the Eighth Street Baptist Church four or five days a week. Today, the minister there is Jamal Wesley, who was two years behind me in school and also played on the basketball team. Back in the day, though, the Reverend Mr. Sawyer was the congregation's spiritual leader. As a kid, I thought of him as a black version of Colonel Sanders. Instead of having silver hair though, his was salt-and-pepper, and he had a full beard. As a kid, I thought the man must have been positively ancient to have hair of such a color, but he couldn't have been as old as I imagined since he remained the minister there for years after I left Little Rock.

The great thing about my hometown and that neighborhood is that not a whole lot has changed. Many of the deacons and associate pastors and ushers are still there, according to my mom. I like knowing that they are still there, just as I like knowing that my sister, DeAndra, who is two and a half years younger than me, now lives with her husband and two kids in the house I grew up in. There's something reassuring in my boyhood home still being home to some members of my family, in my mother still attending the church where I spent so many hours of my youth, in some of those men who served as examples to me of the proper way to live still being there. As an NBA player, my life feels as if it is constantly in motion. I like knowing that I am still anchored to some places, that one of the fundamentals of my life, my root system, the places I frequented as a youngster, still remain, reminding me of the lessons I learned.

I enjoyed Sundays, but I wasn't a deeply spiritual kid. I went to church because that was what you did. I grew up doing it, and it was part of the routine, part of the almost ritualized life we all led. Before I started playing on school teams, Saturday was youth-league basketball games, Sunday was churchgoing and family dinner, Monday was laundry day, etc. In my family, every day seemed to have a purpose, a center around which the other activities revolved. Growing up with that sense of orderliness had a profound effect on me, I realize now. That's probably why I adapted so easily to the structured life of an athlete. As much as people might like to imagine that my life mainly involves sitting around at home in anticipation of playing a game and is a far cry from the nine-to-five routine that most people experience in the corporate world, the truth is far from that. Having a place to be, having obligations to be met, and adhering to a somewhat strict schedule took hold as a necessity when I was young.

I don't mean to suggest that churchgoing was strictly an obligation, something to be checked off on an invariable and rigid to-do list. What I mean is that I found some comfort in knowing what to expect. It's funny to think of it now, but one of the most vivid memories I have of my brother Duane was when he jumped out from behind a door and screamed at me. I can still recall that bladder-burning sensation of fright that electrified my system. That current must have flipped the switch at the waterworks, because I burst into tears. I think I was only three or four at the time, still at an age when a chest-heaving, I-want-my-mom spasm of crying could go on for minutes. I still don't like surprises, still don't like being caught off guard, but at least I've developed better resources to deal with the many things none of us can fully anticipate in the game and in life. Turning around after hearing a teammate yell, "Help!" and coming face-to-chest with someone the size of Shaq bent on getting to the basket might make you want to cry, but you know you have to develop a better strategy than that. I guess I owe Duane a nod of gratitude for helping me realize that lesson early on.

One of the other lessons I learned at home that translated well when I began playing organized basketball was that hard work and staying focused on a task can take you a long way. My father worked for the U.S. post office as an administrator. My mom worked at Worthen Bank. My father had a late-afternoon starting time, so he was home with us during the day before we entered school and was around before and after classes when we began our formal education at Wilson Elementary School. My dad felt that we should always be doing something—preferably something quiet so that he could get his rest. When my dad started at three and my mom didn't get off work until four thirty, he'd take DeAndra and me over to the bank so that we would not be left alone.

We were under strict instructions to behave ourselves and not to draw too much attention to ourselves. My mother's coworkers thought we were cute and always remarked on that and on how well behaved we were. Of course, being kids, we'd sometimes get restless, and it was fun to wander into the bank's lobby among what seemed to be velvet ropes used to keep the customers in an orderly line. More than once, I pulled down one of the stands that held up the ropes. The ringing sound of metal on tile startled me and brought my mother out from behind her desk beyond the tellers' windows. My heart fell each time I saw the look of embarrassed disappointment on her face. Seeing that would have been punishment enough, but her telling me that she couldn't trust me and that I had to stay by her desk until I could prove I was capable of behaving like a decent young man deflated me even more.

Having both my parents working and sharing child-rearing instilled in me at an early age the idea that you did whatever you had to do to make a life for your family and for yourself. We weren't poor—I wasn't raised in the projects or anything like that—but we certainly weren't wealthy. I never lacked for any necessity, but that was because of my parents' hard work. We had a nice brick, split-level, three-bedroom house on a corner lot with a decent-size yard in a neighborhood filled with similar modest-size homes. My neighborhood friends and the kids I went to school with all seemed to be in similar circumstances to mine. I didn't compare myself to them or the circumstances of my life to theirs, but I don't remember any notable exceptions to what I would now identify as lower-middle-class lives.

Not all the mothers in the neighborhood worked, but a lot did. I never thought of myself as a latchkey child or anything like that. I just knew that Mom and Dad both worked, weren't always home at the same time during the week. I never really heard either of them complain about their jobs or their situation. They devoted a lot of their time to us and to church, but like most kids I never gave much thought to the sacrifices they made, never wondered why they didn't go out to dinner together, go to the movies, or do any of the things that the adult couples I associate with today do. Their lives seemed to revolve around work, tending to us, and church.

Even though I wasn't consciously aware of all these things at the age of six, the message was clear. You have a job and you do it. You get up in the morning (or in the middle of the day in my dad's case), and you get out the door to do what you're supposed to do. I don't remember ever thanking my mom and dad for doing the things they did for us, and I'm sure that they didn't expect us to fall all over ourselves in gratitude. I'm sad to state that, but like blocking out in a basketball game, the seemingly little things they did for us all produced good results. We had a comfortable home, were well fed, and had clean and neat clothes and a few nicer things to keep us happy and having fun.

My dad was good with his hands, and in my elementary-school days I saw the Arnold Schwarzenegger movie *Conan the Barbarian.* I loved that film and in particular the swordplay. This wasn't the dazzling display of swordsmanship with whippy épées and foils of the Three Musketeers. It was the basic and brutish hefting of a broadsword. I was a fairly thick-shouldered and stout-legged kid, and that kind of battle seemed to suit me. Dad made a sword out of wood for me, just like the one Conan used. Though it was far duller than the steel ones used, it sharpened my imagination. I loved to just wander around in our yard, wielding that sword and twirling it overhead, bringing it down on imagined enemies and the trunk and low-hanging branches of the few trees around.

Having that sword helped ground my "Derek the Barbarian" fantasies in the real world. Truth be told, that sword was an exception in my life. I wasn't often carried away by flights of imaginative escapism. I was a down-to-earth kid even in my play. I think that was why I was drawn to sports. They were played by an established set of rules, conducted on spaces with defined boundaries, and you kept score so that you knew where you stood at all times. Within the confines of those games, I did allow my imagination some freedom; I frequently imagined as I shot baskets at my friend Clarence's hoop that I was playing in some imagined championship game in either the NBA or the NCAA. Like most kids, I narrated the game's progress in my mind, heard the imagined roar or groan of the crowd at each critical turn of fortune. Most frequently, we won. Despite my Conan infatuation, I did not imagine myself to be the tragic figure, the wounded warrior who stepped out of the hospital room and onto the court to pull out a last-second victory. Instead, I was the steady if sometimes spectacular player who could always be counted on to produce good results. When the game was on the line, I was the one who everyone in my imagined games would turn to. I won time after time, coming through in the clutch, with no chest-humping, trash-talking, in-your-face reactions. I'd just calmly walk off the court after another buzzer beater, pick up my lunch pail, and head home after another day at work.

When I began playing organized basketball, a lot of what I'd learned worked to my advantage. I'd been hanging out with Duane's friends at the gym for a while. I knew that I couldn't act out and give him a reason he could use with my parents so that he wouldn't have to take me with him. I wanted to be at the gym, as much as I wanted to be with him, and I really wanted a chance to play basketball. I didn't whine or cry or run around. I had some skills, and a lot of Duane's friends and teammates liked, or at least tolerated, my presence to a greater degree than Duane did. In time, I won him over. I knew my place. Just as my mother and father told me how to behave in church, at my mother's workplace, and at home, I knew how to conduct myself early on while on the basketball court.

I didn't enjoy being my brother and his crew's gofer, but if running down errant shots or passes, and helping rebound and return the ball to someone practicing his free throws, earned me some goodwill and a chance later on to work on my dribbling or to put up a few shots, then I would do it. Paying my dues didn't bother me, but not being treated fairly did. If I did all the things that I was supposed to do, then those other guys had to hold up their end of the unspoken bargain we'd entered into. I could tag along, do my duty, and earn my reward. That was how the world was supposed to work, and I had a strong sense of that necessary and equal exchange of effort and reward instilled in me from my earliest days. In seeing my parents collectively working long hours, rising early on Saturday mornings to get me to my games, and doing the same on Sunday to get us all to church, regardless of the weather, their mood, or what had to be their collective exhaustion, then I should do the same thing. In a way, what I saw as their reward was that Sunday dinner.

I don't mean to suggest that my parents lived a life of unending drudgery and walked around like automatons doing one task after another. But for some reason, they really came to life on the weekends or at one of Duane's high school games. My mother was an energetic and vocal fan, and she cheered her children on during whatever game she attended with a kind of ease and joyful purity that I didn't witness much at other times. My dad was a bit more reserved, but he often volunteered to be one of our coaches, and I saw a light in his eye, and an intensity and energy in his every movement on and around the basketball court, that I didn't see in him elsewhere. For my mom, singing was the other great joy in her life, and seeing her swaying and clapping with the rest of the choir filled me with a similar kind of spirited energy. But I took more of my cues from my dad and sat or stood more or less impassively, not letting much of my emotion show. That was how a Fisher man was supposed to behave. Don't let yourself get too worked up over things. Keep it steady.

My father would sometimes get wrapped up in watching games on television, but he was also a close observer of teams' tendencies, and he watched the ebb and flow of the game with more of a studied seriousness than a fan's emotional involvement. I'd hear him say more often, "Do you see that? Look at what he's doing there," than I would any other exclamation of joy or dismay. I knew he enjoyed watching the game, and I enjoyed being with him, but I can't really say that his watching games was fun in the same sense that most people might use the term. They were learning experiences and a bit of a bonding experience, but what we did had to have some purpose beyond its being just a source of entertainment or a way to fill up some idle time.

All those observations and picking up on some subtle and not so subtle cues (my dad was not averse to using his belt on our behinds when we seriously violated a rule) put me in a good spot when it came time to play for the 76ers in my first year of Penick Boys Club basketball. I was of course excited to get out on the court and play. I'd witnessed up close and personal the adrenaline rush of a basketball game. I was one of the ball boys for the varsity basketball team when Duane was playing. That meant that I did what I was used to doing when I was in tag-along mode—gather the balls that got loose during warm-ups, assist with some rebounding, and distribute balls to the shooters. In addition, I was handed a towel, and whenever a sweat-coated player fell to the floor, one of my fellow ball boys and I rushed out onto the court and mopped up the spot the referee pointed out.

Even in that limited capacity, I sensed the energy in the gym, and I'd sometimes charge out there with such vigor that I'd overshoot my mark a bit and come to a screeching halt. You would have thought that I was polishing one of the floors in the White House in advance of a visiting dignitary's arrival the way I attacked those wet spots. I'd dash back off the court and kneel along the sideline, not so secretly hoping that it wouldn't be too long before I was called upon to do my duty again. I don't remember thinking that I wanted to be out on the court to be the center of attention. I just wanted to be of use. Sitting in the stands and watching the game take place in front of me was okay, but being involved, even tangentially, in those high school games was important to me. Being just a passive, or even an active, spectator was not something I sensed my family did. We were doers and not just watchers.

To that end, Mom didn't just go to church and attend services, she was a part of the services. She also performed other functions within the church community. My brother was on the basketball team, a valuable and contributing member of the squad and not just someone who bought a ticket or rode the pine and was lucky to see a few minutes of on-court action during what some people refer to derogatorily as "garbage time." We were active. We were doers.

And just as you conducted yourself a certain way in public while at your mother's workplace, in church, at Sunday school, and in the neighborhood, you understood certain expectations governed your conduct and performance on and around the basketball court. I was told that as a ball boy I had certain responsibilities. My dad stressed that I shouldn't look around and make faces or scan the stands for friends. I should watch the game so that when called on, I could go into action immediately and without being asked twice. I wasn't to dash out there of my own volition either. I could anticipate when I would be called on, but not make those decisions myself.

I don't want to make too much of those early experiences on the basketball court, but they were formative, and the lessons I learned as a ball boy, while watching the game on TV with my father, and while hanging out with the older kids have never left me. My dad stressed that my mopping up the floor wasn't just for cosmetic reasons. Someone could slip on that wet spot and be injured. That injured player could have made the difference between winning and losing. My dad wasn't trying to burden me with worry. He was trying to make clear something that I know a lot of young people struggle with: the relationship between cause and effect. My mother's yanking me by the arm and tugging me out of the bank lobby and telling me to sit still was just one of many lessons I learned about consequences. Right action earned you a reward. Wrong action earned you a punishment.

That didn't mean that I was immune from childhood acts of rebellion and indifference to cause and effect. With my friends I built ramps and jumps out of scrap lumber we salvaged from one another's garages, discard piles, and garbage-day derelicts. I suffered more than my share of scraped knees and scabbed elbows when one of my attempts at turning my regular old bicycle into a BMX or stunt bike went awry and I spilled to the ground while practicing my daring jumps. I was learning lessons about risk and reward in those moments, and they were kinds of extra-credit, outside-the-curriculum activities that supplemented my education. What I learned was something like equations: Ground = hard. Boy = fragile. Pavement = rough. Skin = shreddable. Stupidity = painful.

However much I might have acted out away from my parents' watchful eyes or away from the basketball court, I can't recall a time when I didn't listen to my coaches, act sensibly, and try to put into practice their instructions. I can still remember my first practice with the 76ers and being amazed at how incapable many of my teammates were of even getting into a straight line and performing a simple layup drill. Many of them had to be reprimanded or reminded that they needed to focus. I didn't. I was intent on learning more about the game and refining my skills. Maybe that early photo of me with the fundamentally sound follow-through is an indication of the genetic link that connected me to my father and mother. More likely it was also a product of osmosis. I was picking up on the current of athleticism and performance and execution that permeated the air.

Parents frequently instruct their children, "Do as you're told." In most houses, the emphasis is on the *told.* In mine, it seems to me now, the emphasis was on the *do.* I wasn't very different from most children in one regard. I wanted to please my parents. Much of the pleasure we took in our family revolved around basketball, so naturally I wanted to excel at it, earn my parents' attention and praise. That's not to say that they withheld those things from me; far from it. Neither did they pressure me into playing the game. I developed a passion for the game, but I was also involved in a lot of other activities and sports. Experts tell us that we don't really choose whom we fall in love with, but that some kind of chemical attraction brings two people together. I can believe that when it comes to basketball; on some subconscious and perhaps chemical level I must have felt a magnetic attraction. The hollow ringing sound of a ball being dribbled on a hardwood floor, the squeak of basketball shoes on a highly polished court, the feel of the pebbled grain of the ball in the grasp of my fingers, and the sight of the ball arcing in the air, its backspin seeming to pull me toward a simpler time in the past, still entice and enthrall me.

I didn't think about those things then. I'm not even sure I felt them. I had a lot to learn and was an eager and willing student, but I wasn't ready to fully commit to the game, to declare my abiding love. A sturdy foundation was being laid, but it wasn't as if my family and I had a blueprint for what the structure would be like. My parents were great believers in our doing things, as I said, and much of that belief was founded in the old line about idle hands being the devil's workshop. More than that though, my parents believed in the value

of sports and how they could contribute to a young person's development as a human being, a well-rounded and respectful human being
who understood sportsmanship and the benefits of hard work and the
reliance on self and others. Sounds pretty basic and by the book, but
that was our reality back then.

Even if I hadn't demonstrated any real competency in the game,
I'm pretty certain my parents would have still encouraged me to participate. They wouldn't have pushed me in a direction I clearly didn't
want to go, but they would have made certain that I found something
else to do with my time. I *know* this next point: my parents had no
desire to live out their dreams through me. Even when I was in college, we didn't really discuss a possible NBA career for me. I was in
college to get a degree, to do well in the game, and to learn something about how the world operated and how to get along with a
wide variety of people. Basketball was a means to an end, not an end
in itself. That was true when I first laced up my shoes in a league
game in 1980, and it's just as true today. Fundamentals are fundamentals because they are less likely to change than anything else.

What I like about the idea of boxing out is that it doesn't really
require a tremendous amount of athletic ability to be good at it.
All you have to do is understand a few things about your body—to
lower your center of gravity and to use the strongest muscles of your
body, your legs and your butt—to help you move someone the way
you want him to go. To succeed requires mostly focus and desire, a
willingness to put the effort into something for which you won't
likely earn attention. Even today, in the sophisticated world of the
NBA, with our love of statistics and the endless hours of video players
watch, blocking out is mostly noticed only when it doesn't occur. Just
as we sometimes take for granted the love of others and feel its absence more than its presence, the same is true of most of the fundamentals in the game and in our lives.

Paying attention to even the simplest things, the most ordinary of
things, can help us reap substantial rewards—first among those is the
satisfaction that comes with knowing that you've done the right
thing. That simple lesson in cause and effect shaped my early experi-

ences in the game and with my family. It has never left me. It helped me to take possession of the things I value most and eased my transition from one level of the game to the next.

While these fundamentals have served me well, some of my most vivid memories are of the times that I failed to put them into practice. Sometimes we learn best from our failures rather than our successes.

That lesson was hammered home at my first varsity basketball practice at Parkview. We were running a basic three-on-two fast-break drill. As we crossed the half-court line, the ball was in my hands. A defender came out on me to cut off the passing lane, so I fired a precise behind-the-back pass to the cutter. The pass was on the mark, but it went right through the guy's hands and out of bounds. Even before the ball was past him, I could hear Coach Ripley's shrill whistle echoing in the gym.

"Everybody stop!" he shouted. "Take a knee right where you're at."

I've since come to know that educators refer to these instances as teachable moments. All I knew back then was that I wished I could have not just taken a knee on the court, but that I could have melted through the floor and crawled right on out of there.

"Everybody but you, Fisher," coach added.

I knew enough to make certain that I looked coach directly in the eye when he addressed me.

"Look at your jersey, son. Does it say Patriots or Globetrotters on there?"

Coach reminded everyone that there was the Parkview way of doing things, and I'd just demonstrated the way not to do things. As he said to all of us, why make a fancy pass when a good, old-fashioned, tried-and-true bounce pass would have done what was needed? He admitted that the pass was on the mark, but because I'd done it behind the back, done something unexpected, I so surprised the receiver that he missed it. Coach concluded, "It was pretty, but it wasn't useful."

The message came through loud and clear. That wasn't the last behind-the-back pass I threw in my life, but it was the last one I threw at Parkview, where, like at home, I received the kind of grounded training in the fundamentals of the game and of life that have gotten me where I am today. Only when it was the best alternative did I ever resort to a "fancy" pass again, and even then only after giving all my options careful consideration. That's the benefit of being trained in doing the right thing. You're more careful, more deliberate, and you "know" when it's time to think and when it's time to react and let your training take over.

CHAPTER THREE

Developing Other Skills:

Becoming Multi-Dimensional

From the time I first played the game until now, every coach I ever had has stressed that the little things make a big difference in the success of a basketball team. That's one of the reasons I started with the fundamentals. As I wrote, I really do believe that everything in my life has happened for a reason. Not only does that help explain why I was able to deal with my daughter's health crisis so well, but I also believe it answers the question that has been on my mind and is on many people's tongues: how did I make it into the NBA and have a career that has lasted so long? Certainly, a lot of players out there are taller, stronger, faster, better ball handlers, purer shooters, more tenacious rebounders, and are as astute about the game as I believe I am. Maybe they don't outperform me in all of those categories, but at least in some of them. So how have I lasted into my thirteenth NBA season? How is it that the average length of a career in the NBA is five years and I've more than doubled that number?

What's funny to me is that I believe something over which I truly had no control initially got me driving down the lane toward success. If I feel special in any way, other than that I've reached the top in a select occupation, it's that I'm left-handed. Estimates vary, but only somewhere between 7 and 13 percent of the people in this world have a dominant left hand.

Why do I attribute some of my success on the basketball court to being left-handed? When I first started playing the game, few of the kids I played against were quick enough to figure out that I dribbled the ball in a different hand than they did. They were so used to seeing other right-handed players that they expected a player they were guarding to go right, shoot with the right hand, etc. I was able to blow past a lot of defenders just because I was doing something they didn't expect. Anticipation is key in any sport, and my being left-handed gained me the upper hand immediately. In many of my first games, I was the top scorer. I can remember some games when our team had 22 or so points and I had either scored all of them or the vast majority of them. I don't want to leave you with the impression that I was only successful because I was left-handed—my passion for the game, that I was naturally strong and stout for my age, the genetic influence of my parents, also chipped in big-time to help me.

My early success on the court gave me confidence. So much of success in sports and in life generally is a matter of attitude. I had a natural passion for the game, and I had early success at it, so that motivated me to get better. I'm no different from most people. I enjoy doing things I'm good at and avoid things I'm not successful at. I can't say that if I hadn't had that early success or that if I were right-handed, I might not have succeeded to the degree that I did, but I sometimes wonder just how large a role that "choice" I made to be left-handed figured in what I see as someone else's master plan. I put quotation marks around *choice* because, of course, I didn't choose to be left-handed. That characteristic was handed to me by someone or something other than me.

I never considered myself the da Vinci or Michelangelo of basketball, and though I enjoyed that early success in youth-league games, eventually things mostly evened out. Maybe because I was more conscious of handedness and its effects, I was always aware which was the stronger side of my opponent. If I was hustling back on defense, I anticipated better which direction a player was likely to drive. One of those small things, but I believe that since the majority of players in the league are right-handed, they didn't think as much as I did about it. When you are the majority, you simply assume that everyone else is like you. Having to think about hand dominance is just one small example of how I had to think differently and more often than kids I was playing against and with. Being more thoughtful on the court could sometimes be a disadvantage of course. In sports you want your body to take over, and in time most of my thinking would submerge into my subconscious, but from the very start, having to think out there, having to pay attention to those little things, paid immediate dividends.

When I say "developing your other, or off, hand," I mean that in a couple of ways. First, I mean it in the basketball sense of having to learn to use your nondominant hand to dribble and to shoot. That was one of the first things I had to learn and to practice in youth leagues, but don't think mastery of that comes easily or is a minor element of the game. Going into my senior year in college, when I had more firmly set my sights on a possible NBA career, I devoted a lot of time to refining my right-handed dribbling. I walked to and from classes and practices dribbling with my right hand exclusively. I also use "developing your other hand" to refer to learning other skills and developing interests outside of basketball. I was not just a little basketball-playing machine. I had other interests: other sports, music, video games, television. I was also a good student and eventually attended a fairly progressive arts-oriented high school. Finally, I use "developing your other hand" to refer to working on parts of your character and temperament that don't seem to be your natural inclination. We all have strengths and weaknesses, but it often takes someone else to help us to refine our personality and to bring out elements that we may not see in ourselves.

Another distinct advantage that I had, though I didn't always appreciate it, was my father. As an ex-military man, my dad was old-school in a big way. He believed that if you were going to do something, it didn't matter what, you should put everything you possibly could into doing it well. The work ethic that he and my mom exhibited was instrumental in my development, and my dad also did more than just lead by example. He pushed me in certain ways that I can never forget or thank him enough for. I was a typical kid, and sometimes, if I had been allowed to, I might have chosen to just hang out. Yes, I loved playing basketball, but I wasn't the most driven person in the world back then. I also wasn't the toughest kid either, and standing up for myself wasn't something that came naturally to me. I needed someone to push me to develop the personality traits necessary to succeed at the highest levels.

I use the word *push,* but just as I had a natural inclination to be left-handed, I had a natural inclination toward basketball. My father never demanded that I play. He simply recognized that I had chosen to play that sport, so he wanted to make certain that I did whatever I could to be successful. Some of the ways my father influenced me were subtle. By the time I was playing organized ball, shoe companies such as Adidas, PUMA, and others had come along and transformed the world of athletic footwear, with all kinds of trends and fads and newfangled innovations. To put things into better context, the first Nike Air basketball shoes came out in 1983, when I was nine years old. That groundbreaking achievement represented a refinement in the concept of basketball shoes—a much needed and appreciated advancement.

The first basketball shoes I wore were Converse All Stars, the basic Chuck Taylor high-tops. Canvas uppers and rubber soles. White. No stripes. No swoosh. Unadorned classics as plain as white bread, and now that I know better, about as supportive as that sandwich staple. I still laugh a bit whenever I see old photos from those days. I look as if I'd stepped out of a photo shoot with Elgin Baylor and Bill Russell— which had interrupted my practicing my set shot. At the time, I didn't think much about it. I was just glad to have a new pair of kicks and to be out on the court. Those shoes are representative of where we were as we entered the 1980s. Baby boomers were really coming into their own in the 1980s, and the "me generation" label that had been applied to them didn't really fit my dad. I also realize now that he was also probably concerned about some of the influences that preyed on urban African-American young people. I'm not talking just about the gang violence and the number of kids killed for their Starter jackets, but the number of young people who felt a sense of entitlement. My dad was part of the "me-ager" generation. He had grown up, by some standards, poor in Louisiana, and while we were never deprived of anything we needed, I cannot imagine him warming up to spending lots of hard-earned cash on trendy basketball shoes. The only thing that would have got warm was my behind if I had so much as got five notes of a whining song out of my mouth about what the other kids were wearing and then launched into a "Why can't I?" refrain.

I played with and against plenty of kids who looked the part with the most expensive shoes. My dad knew that it wasn't how good you looked out on the court but how well you played. Those shoes were one of the reminders that the old-school ways—mastering the funda-mentals, playing unselfishly, not drawing attention to yourself through playground flamboyance—were the real path to achievement. There were no shortcuts, and lacing up the latest pair of Nikes or whatever was not going to have me magically transported.

As I've said, my dad was a great believer in doing, and he seemed to think that when we kids weren't actively engaged in something, we should have been. That didn't just mean sports. I came of age when computers were just starting to be in schools. Learning how to use them meant learning how to type. My mom and dad took educa-tion seriously. They knew that to get anywhere in life, we were going to have to do well in school. As much as they supported me in my various sports activities, they made sure that I developed my off hand by involving me in lots of other activities—at school as well as outside of it.

I learned early on that I was supposed to be busy and productive—not just mindlessly or foolishly engaged in some activity, but doing something that could eventually benefit me. I had plenty of time to mess around and play, but an equal amount of time at home was devoted to developing my skills off the court. My parents understood that school meant using a computer, so they got one for the house. The school had these nice Apple II computers and monitors, but they were pretty pricey, so we ended up with some generic desktop PC clone. We were just glad to have it. The novelty of having a computer wore off quickly, especially when my dad got involved. To help us with our typing skills, we had software called Mavis Beacon Teaches Typing.

I remember that the box the disks came in featured a photograph of a nice-looking black woman—I assumed it was Mavis Beacon— and she was all smiles. Working on a computer at school was fun, and learning to type wasn't so bad. Being left-handed, I wanted to use my left thumb to hit the space bar, and the teacher at school kept admonishing me to use my right thumb. I didn't see why it mattered, but I worked at it as hard as I could. After school, my dad would make sure that in addition to doing all my homework, I also spent time working on my Mavis Beacon lessons. After a while, that smile on her face seemed to transform in my mind to an evil, sadistic grin as she watched me working away. I wanted to be outside with my friends, not pecking away at the keyboard. I wanted to be the quick brown fox out jumping around and not the lazy dog tied to his computer.

In time, I suspected that my father had his doubts about my ability to fully commit to things. I don't think he thought that I was lazy, but I was fairly reserved, not prone to showing the enthusiasm I felt for things. I loved basketball, but I wasn't going to jump around and act fired up about it all the time. I quietly went about my business without drawing much attention to myself. I figured that if I produced on the court and did the things my coaches asked of me, I should be rewarded with their praise and their attention. I didn't need to go out of my way to get it by either acting out negatively or being too much of a rah-rah, over-the-top kind of guy. Eventually, I was going to have to learn to develop that side of my personality and become more outgoing, but that would take a lot of years.

I got good grades, was mostly well-behaved, but definitely was not one of those butt-out-of-my-seat, hand-waving-in-the-air, please-call-on-me, please-call-on-me kind of kids. Being asked to read out loud didn't paralyze me with fear, but I wasn't going to be one of the first to volunteer. The same with going up to the board to solve a math problem. I figured that getting it right on my own was enough. No need to go up there and show everybody else what I had done. I think that part of my reluctance to call attention to myself reflected my parents' instilling in us kids respect for adults and others. They weren't overly into the idea that children should be seen and not heard, but we definitely knew our place.

Churchgoing also shaped me. I was not about to act out there. Church was not a place where you went to mess around with your friends. I'd occasionally take a look around the congregation and spot a buddy of mine, but though I was tempted to make a face at him to get him to crack up, I was there to worship the Lord. At mealtimes at home or when the family gathered for Sunday dinners or holidays, we kids behaved. We weren't little robots and we did our fair share of messing around, but it was usually outside the hearing and the sight of our parents. I developed some close and lasting relationships with several of my cousins, and being able to let loose a bit among one another helped forge those bonds.

Looking back, I think that maybe my being so quiet and polite made it seem as if I was indifferent. For most of my life I'd struggle with this idea that my being reserved meant I had little fire inside. Knowing that my dad suspected the same thing of me was hard to deal with, and I tried to show him that I was a passionate competitor, but I could only really be who I was. My dad tried to help me, and at times I thought he was trying to test me, by working out with me. This is an example of how he saw something inside me that maybe I didn't or he tried to develop a part of my personality that was lacking. When it became clear by the time I was ten or twelve that basketball was my game, my dad decided that he needed to teach me some lessons about hard work and giving my all. I guess he thought that if there was a pilot light inside me, he needed to bring it up to full burn.

Little Rock, Arkansas, is hillier than you might imagine. We lived on a rise that to me as a young boy seemed steep. Parts of our neighborhood dropped so severely that we had to walk our bikes uphill for long sections. I don't know if my father realized this, but the topography of that neighborhood helped to shape me as well.

One of the places we all liked to go to was a little corner grocery store called Mr. Worm's. At the time I didn't think much of the name, but now it seems odd. There was a Mr. Worm, though I can't say for sure that was his real name. He was the sole proprietor, and he lived upstairs from the store. If I had some money from my allowance or my mom had given me some spare change, I wanted to go to Mr. Worm's. I don't know that I had an especially strong sweet tooth, but as with most kids, a bit of spending money meant one thing—a sweet treat.

Getting to Mr. Worm's was anything but a treat. If we walked or rode our bikes, we had to travel a few streets over from my house, down one steep hill and up a second, even steeper hill to get there. So as much as we were treating ourselves to a sugary snack, we earned it. We also earned the money we spent there.

My parents weren't fanatical about having us do household chores—I think my mother ran interference for us and kept my dad from assigning us more. I had to take the trash out and do some lawn-care tasks. As much as I liked being outside, I didn't like having to mow the lawn. We lived on the corner, so our lot was bigger than our neighbors', and it sloped down to the street level on one side. When I was really young, I wasn't allowed to use the push lawn mower since that slope was dangerous, but I had to clean up after the lawn mower that my dad used. I'm sure that other people back then had lawn mowers with bags attached to catch the clippings, but I didn't know that. Everybody I knew had a bagless mower. That was what children were for, I guess. I had to go out after my dad had mowed to rake up the grass.

Worse was the fall. Raking leaves was fun the first time I had to do it for the season. I kind of liked the sounds they made when I kicked my way through them, and the smell of decaying leaves meant that basketball season was coming up. Messing around and throwing leaves at my friends or jumping in a big pile of them was fun also, but having to rake them up and stuff them in trash bags or in a big plastic garbage can was no fun at all. We also had a huge pine tree on our property, and while that didn't shed leaves, it did send down a regular shower of pinecones and needles. As hard as it was to get all the grass and the leaves, having to rake up the debris from the pine tree was truly, truly painful. I would gladly have accepted a scholarship to Stanford University, as one of my Parkview teammates eventually did, but I know that having to look at that big old pine tree in the middle of the school's logo would have been a considerable burden. But the yard work had to be done, and no matter what else was going on in my world, I was expected to be out in that patch of green and brown getting things done.

I don't know if my father knew how we all felt about the hills that led to Mr. Worm's, but he devised his own use for them. When I was about twelve years old, he decided that I needed to get a bit more serious about my preparation for basketball. He knew that during the season I was a good player and seemed serious about the games and, just as important, the practices. But as I said, I think he suspected that the fire in my belly was lacking. In today's game, when we talk about a player either lacking in intensity or one who is unwilling to go inside and bang hard on rebounds or when driving to the hoop, we say that they are "soft." That's a polite way of expressing it. In locker rooms or out on the court or in private discussions about opposing players (and sometimes teammates), we might use more cutting expressions, but they are all related to questioning someone's manhood. No one likes to have those terms applied to him or to have his willingness to endure physical contact (and the resulting pain of that contact) questioned.

My father, perhaps thinking I needed to be mentally or physically tougher, put me through some workouts that helped me to grow stronger in both areas. Like me, my father was a somewhat reserved man, and I never knew exactly what his life was like growing up in Louisiana. He didn't share many stories of his experiences with his family—from what he did say, I think that his relationship with his own father was either brief or distant (and possibly both). I got the impression that he had to grow up hard and fast and saw the comparative luxury of my life as something that he was glad he could provide for me, but also something he worried might make it more difficult for me to succeed in the world. He knew that the strong survived, and the stronger thrived. He wanted to make sure that I didn't just get by but really made the most of the opportunities I had.

I guess an incident I had in fourth grade on the basketball court wasn't enough to convince him of my toughness. Andrew Parker and I knew each other from the neighborhood and from Boys Club basketball. One day we were outside playing against each other during lunch. Andrew was much bigger than me. He wasn't as thickly built as I was; he was much more rangy but still strong. He was one of the team's better players, so he was guarding me. I would try to back him down, but he was putting his chest on me and bumping me and always trying to use his body to lever me out of the way. Some of it was good defensive positioning, but mostly he was just beating on me and thugging it up. I didn't like that at all. I wasn't intimidated by him, and his banging on me like that would have earned him a foul if this had been a real game.

Finally, after one flagrant push in the back, I'd had enough. I raised my left hand up and spun around, punching Andrew flush on the cheek and temple. He staggered back, and a teacher rushed in to separate the two of us. No more game for either of us that day. The incident did not go unpunished or unnoticed. My parents were called into school, and they were upset. The right thing to do was for me to go to Andrew's parents' house and explain to them what I'd done. Andrew turned out to be pretty cool about it, as were his parents. Andrew admitted that he was pushing me pretty good and I wasn't just going after him for no reason. We shook hands, a weak clasping that lasted about a millisecond, and that seemed to settle things.

My mom and dad were naturally upset with me, but I think my dad liked that I didn't let someone bully me on the court. Of course, I got a pretty good talking to, and I was on punishment for a week or two after that, but I believe I saw a bit of a gleam in my dad's eye. I think it was a few weeks after that when I began some of my workouts with my dad.

One morning, I was lying in bed on Saturday. Weak light was filtering through the thin fabric of my bedroom curtains. The wind was rattling the panes of the windows. I was half-asleep and drowsing in my warm bed. I sensed a presence in the room. I opened one eye, and there was my dad silhouetted in the doorway. He was standing in profile, and his head was partially tilted up as if he were looking at something far away.

"C'mon. Let's go." He inclined his head away from me, indicating the front door. "Got some work to do. Get your sweats and your shoes."

I shut my eyes and thought of asking for a few more minutes. I felt warm and comfortable, and based on what I'd heard and seen, this early-fall day was stormy and uninviting. Something told me not to wait too long before getting a move on, so I rolled out of bed and put on a pair of sweatpants, an old T-shirt, and a hoodie. I tugged on a pair of athletic socks, ignoring the slight tear in the toe seam, then worked my way into a pair of basketball shoes. My dad was standing in the driveway, dressed much as I was. His hands were thrust deep in the pockets of his sweatshirt. He raised his hand and formed a mound with the loose fabric. "This way."

Only when we started walking toward Parkwood Drive did I see that he had something slung over one shoulder, an old military flak jacket. Heavily padded, it had multiple pockets. It reminded me of a heavy-duty vest I'd seen photographers or hunters on television wear. It began to slip from his shoulder and he shrugged it back into place. We headed down Dorchester toward Twenty-fourth Street, and I knew both what was up and what I'd soon be going up—Boyle Park Road and the hills. When we got to Twenty-fourth Street and Dorchester, we turned onto Boyle Park. I looked up and saw the winding incline I knew that I would soon be climbing. The wind was whipping the bare trees that lined the road that encircled the park. I don't know how long that loop was, but I said a silent prayer that we'd only be doing that loop, a kind of loose knot, in the longer length of Boyle Park Road.

"Loosen up a bit," my dad said.

I did a couple of stretches, jogged in place for a bit.

"You ready for this?"

I nodded.

I was wrong. I was prepared for a long, loping jog around the park. Instead, my dad had me sprint up the entry road to the park. It was probably only four hundred yards or so, but it seemed to be pitched at a forty-five-degree angle. I'd sprint up, then jog back down. First, he had me run frontward up the incline, later he mixed in some backward running as well.

"I'm taking it a bit easier on you today. Weather's cool."

He may have been right about the temperature, but I was still sweating artillery shells. My chest heaved and my thighs and calves felt as if taut piano wires were running through them. On the last of the sprints, my dad went up with me. He gave me a second to catch my breath, then we walked into the park and onto one of the courts. That's when the flak jacket came into play. When he helped me into it, I felt as if someone had put a suit of armor on me. We hadn't brought a ball, but my dad put me through a set of drills that had my tongue wagging and my head spinning. We did variations of the line drill—running from the end line to the near free throw line and back, then immediately out to half-court and back, then the far free throw line and back, end line, etc. We did defensive shuttle drills with his constantly reminding me to move my feet as I went from one sideline to the other over and over.

I was glad we'd started out before eight in the morning, but that early-morning chill had been replaced by sunshine and humidity. As the temperature rose, I felt every degree of it. Every break when I got to go to the water fountain was an enormous relief. I greedily gulped down the water and stuck my face into the stream. We'd started out in isolation, but by the time we were heavily into the drills, a group of kids were shooting around at one end, laughing and messing with one another. A lazy game of horse developed, and I watched as one kid went off the court behind the basket to fire up a shot over the backboard. When it swished through, his buddies all yelled and screamed, gave him high fives. I looked at my dad and felt this connection with him. He'd seen the kid pull off the trick shot, just as he'd seen another player bounce in a free throw, and I saw on his face a reflection of my own sour expression.

When would you ever need that shot in a real basketball game? How much time and effort had those guys put into developing a shot that would win them a game of horse but they would never use in a real game of basketball? I was hot and sweaty, I hadn't eaten a thing yet and my stomach was pleading with me, but I finished my drink and walked over to where my father was standing. I got in a good spread-legged defensive position, put my palms to the asphalt. I looked up at him and asked, "Again?" He nodded, and off I went, backpedaling and turning from side to side, keeping my feet moving as quickly as I could, ignoring the pain of the flak jacket's collar digging into my neck each time I moved my chest to keep square to my father as he advanced down the court.

I wonder now if my dad knew that those other kids were going to be there on that first day he put me through my paces with his workout. I never suspected that my father was trying to be mean by working me out that way. He didn't say a whole lot about why he was doing that, but later when I saw the movie *Hoop Dreams,* I understood that what he wasn't saying was probably even more important. My dad never talked about my getting a college scholarship or playing in the NBA when I was doing those workouts with him. He wasn't looking at me as a meal ticket or filling my head with dreams of a life in basketball. He never talked about what opportunities he might have missed out on by leaving school and ending his ball career early. I didn't think much about it back then, but I'm grateful to him today for teaching me that the hard work I was doing was good for its own sake. It was a means to an end other than an NBA career.

Hard work and discipline applied to every aspect of my life and not just athletics. So, whether it was in the classroom, in the music room (I participated in the school choir and in the school band), or out on the court, knowing that it took practice and dedication to achieve any goal was an important lesson. And developing my other hand by being involved in other activities such as music made me realize that a whole other world existed outside the gym that I could participate in and enjoy. Those other activities could take me places that I might not have been able to go and expose me to ideas and people that I might not ever have encountered. Basketball eventually proved to be the key to my leaving Little Rock and experiencing things that I couldn't even have dreamed of back then, but developing my other hand—trying to improve myself and explore avenues outside of sports—is something that I'm extremely grateful my parents insisted on and aided me in.

I enjoyed playing music a lot. Again, I can see a pattern here. Most kids like listening to music, but that wasn't enough for my family and me. Why not *make* music instead of just passively listening to what someone else had produced? I began playing the trumpet in seventh grade and continued to be in bands until my junior year in high school. My forays into playing music and singing in the choir were a part of my learning to let my guard down a bit. I was anxious about performing in front of people initially, but I liked that slightly jittery butterflies-in-my-stomach feeling. I eventually earned my share of solos or featured sections in the choir and the band, and I enjoyed being out in front of a group of people and bringing pleasure to them and receiving pleasure in the form of applause. Standing up and taking a bow after a concert band or choir performance was almost as gratifying as hearing a crowd cheering at a basketball game.

Eventually those early lessons about the need to develop all sides of my personality and also to develop skills that could help off the court took root. I majored in communications in college, and all the study of and practice of various kinds of social interactions and speaking paid off for me. When I finally really blossomed on the court at the University of Arkansas, Little Rock, and later with the Lakers, a part of my job was being interviewed by newspaper and television reporters as well as doing public appearances. I always felt comfortable in front of the cameras or with microphones being placed in front of me.

I knew that if I was going to fit into Los Angeles and take advantage of all the opportunities that come with working in a major media market, and one as intensely media-centered as Los Angeles, my reserved nature wasn't going to get me far. I didn't know back in college that I'd play in the NBA or be living in Los Angeles, but I knew that no matter what career path I followed, many of my basketball lessons and skills would translate to success anywhere. Quiet confidence is a good thing, but being able to show that other side of yourself—that you can come out of your protective shell, that you can do things that people don't really expect of you—is important. For me, developing my off hand meant trying things and testing myself off the court in some ways people back home were really surprised to see.

In 1998, an agent contacted me. She knew that some of the urban television shows presented possible opportunities for me to explore. One of those was an appearance on L. L. Cool J's television show *In the House.* Kobe Bryant and I did cameo appearances along with our coach, Del Harris. According to the script, I was dating the character played by Kim Wayans. I had a lot of fun, prepared myself well for the taping, and took pride in being able to do my scenes in one take. The show's producers were so happy with how I did, they invited me back to wrap up the bit about my dating Kim—the script stated that I was getting too distracted so Coach Harris had to intervene. Later on, I did some acting on Jamie Foxx's show and then on *Moesha,* with the singer Brandy. I was serious enough about it that I took some acting classes as well. Unfortunately, I learned that as an NBA player, time is precious, and trying to do too much can mean that you don't do anything as well as you'd like. I had to stop taking those classes when it became clear just how much time I had to devote to training and rehab in the summer.

Those acting gigs gave me a chance to step out of my usual reality, to be silly, and to have some fun. Don't get me wrong, basketball was fun, but the longer I played and the higher up I advanced, the more intense the pressure became, and eventually I would come to think of it as my career, and my playing the game as the work I did. I still needed creative outlets, and I still needed to prove to other people and myself that I didn't live and breathe basketball 24-7. When I first started dating Candace, I would invite her onto the set so that she could see these other sides of me. I wanted to reassure her that I wasn't what she might have believed a stereotypical professional athlete was like. As you'll learn more later on, I was a pretty low-key, unassuming guy when it came to dating and romance, and I wanted to impress her with all of my skills. I didn't show off my typing ability, but she was convinced that there was far more to me than a strong left-hand dribble drive or a pull-up jumper.

Eventually I could confidently walk onto the set of a TV show and perform, and I have Parkview's programs and its emphasis on sports, academics, and the arts to thank for that. I know that some people perceive that high school athletes, particularly those who excel and go on to pro careers, are "too cool for school," as the expression goes. That wasn't the case with me. The school I attended had a well-rounded focus. Parkview has a longer name, Parkview Arts Science Magnet High School, and the school was one of Little Rock's finest. As a magnet school, it drew students from around the city, allowing high-achieving and motivated students to cross elementary- and middle-school boundary lines to attend. It remains the state's first and only full magnet school and has a statewide reputation for excellence in all areas from academics to athletics to the arts. The faculty and staff there made certain that we developed both hands, so to speak.

I was enrolled in the arts program, which was why I was in the choir and the band, but that didn't mean that I focused exclusively on those things. I also had to take the usual required academic courses. I was a hardworking student, earning a B average or just above. I took a couple of advanced-placement classes, but I wasn't on the fast track with the really smart kids. I felt comfortable at school and could be myself there. I think sometimes that my being left-handed played a part in that. Being a part of a small group and standing out gave me a sense of identity apart from what everyone else, the majority, was doing. Sports were a huge part of the life of the school and the community at large. I can't say that I made a conscious decision to be different, but I do know that I pursued my interests regardless of what it may have looked like to other people.

In high school cliques develop, and in lots of places if you belong to one group or another, you're not supposed to socialize with the others. I kind of cut through that and did my own thing. I like music, so I chose to be part of the concert band. No one ever gave me any grief for it. I think that people respected me because I didn't always go with the flow. I might have been expected, or people might have assumed I was going to go one way, but I could just as easily go the other. Just as I had to develop shooting and dribbling skills with my right hand, I felt it was important not to be one-dimensional in other areas of my life. I think being in a magnet school helped. For winning state championships in debate, other kids got nearly as much attention as the basketball players. This wasn't a typical jock-dominated place. Sure, basketball games were a big deal, but you were still expected to do your work in the classroom and participate in other activities.

With concert band, we got to perform at football games— marching band wasn't a big thing the way it was in some other parts of the state and country. We also traveled to various parts of the state to perform in concerts and competitions. I got to combine my favorite interests in 1991 when I was a sophomore and in my first year at Parkview High School (in Arkansas, junior high was seventh through ninth grades, and senior high school was tenth through twelfth). We went to Fayetteville and the University of Arkansas for a band competition just after the Christmas holidays. That meant that Coach Nolan Richardson and his team were in full swing. I was a huge college-basketball fan. Even though I idolized Magic Johnson and loved the Lakers, college ball was really my thing. I grew up idolizing guys from our local area who were great basketball players, and also guys in the NCAA whom I'd get a chance to see on Saturdays with the game(s) of the week on CBS television. If I wasn't out doing yard work on a Saturday (fortunately basketball season usually started after the last leaf had been raked), I would come home from my practice or game and sit down in front of the TV to watch Georgetown and Villanova go at it. If I was lucky, I'd be able to watch a second or a third game. It was like the sun moving from east to west across the country. After a Big East or Southeastern Conference game, it was on to the Big 10 or the Big 12—Kansas versus Oklahoma State—and then out west to the Pacific-10 and UCLA against Stanford.

Naturally, when I got onto the campus of the University of Arkansas that January weekend in 1991, I had to see if the U of A was playing. I was a huge Arkansas fan and by that age was dreaming of being able to play there. Nolan Richardson's bunch were known for their fanatical devotion to a pressing man-to-man defense and an up-and-down-the-floor game called Forty Minutes of Hell. Somehow, a U of A student who somebody in the band knew got a student ID I could borrow to get into the game. I was almost out of breath from anticipation when I filed in along with thousands of other devoted Razorback fans. This was the last year that the team would be in the Southwest Conference. The following season they were going to join the more competitive Southeastern Conference.

Interest in the Razorbacks that year was at a fever pitch—and that's saying something because after Nolan Richardson's style of play took hold on that program, the results were amazing and almost enough to make everyone forget about football. The previous year, they'd gone 25–7 overall and 13–3 in the conference. They'd lost in the second round of the NCAA tournament, but they were on a roll in the 1990–91 season. They'd eventually make it to the Final Four, losing in the national semifinal to a powerful Duke Devils team. I had no way of knowing that I was seeing a Final Four team that day, but the crowd was totally into it, and those Forty Minutes of Hell were devilish on my ears. One reason I wanted to go to the game so badly was because one of my favorite players, Lee Mayberry, was a starting guard. I idolized him and felt that we had a lot in common in our games. He wasn't flashy and played with a quiet confidence, a humility I admired. He was also supertalented. After the game, I got a chance to meet him. He shook my hand, and I remember thinking, I'm never going to wash this hand again.

I don't remember how we did in that band competition. Eventually I gave up band to concentrate on basketball for my senior year. I wasn't exactly crushed to give it up. My mom had gone out of her way to provide me with every possible opportunity to succeed in music. To help me catch up to some of my bandmates who had been playing for years before I began, she hired a private teacher for me to supplement my work at school. This private teacher had an honest— and I think too honest—conversation with me. He was critical of my embouchure, the position and formation of my lips. He told me that I'd never be a good trumpet player as a result. That hurt me. It wasn't as if I thought I was the next incarnation of Miles Davis, but instead of offering me some corrective tips or drills, he just basically said, "You don't have it."

I kind of understand that maybe it was his way to motivate me, to get me into an "I'll show you you're wrong about me" mode. That didn't work. I knew even then that we all have to face harsh criticism in our lives. I knew that I'd only been playing the trumpet for a few years while some of my bandmates had been playing since they were young. Compared to my basketball skills, my musical ability was pretty low. I didn't get angry, and I didn't get resentful, but I did feel the sting of those remarks. I loved music and singing in the choir, and playing in the school band helped me to develop a more well-rounded version of myself. Maybe it was a good thing that he didn't apply different standards to me and my ability on account of my being a basketball player or being relatively new to music. Maybe absolute standards exist in the music world, but instead of spurring me on, his words discouraged me.

I didn't have many of those kinds of experiences in school. I had several teachers whom I admired, and who I thought did an outstanding job. One thing that I've found about developing skills, especially early on, is that a little positive reinforcement goes a long way. I had a teacher in junior high school, Mr. Baker, who was influential in my development. He radiated such a positive energy and such a love of his subject matter that math became one of my favorites. I can now see why it was. I was always a pretty realistic kind of guy. In math, there were clean-cut answers. You were either right or wrong. There were no "yes, but . . ." responses as there were when I was in English class and someone offered up an opinion or explanation about a story we had read. That was one of the things I liked about basketball. You kept score. You knew who won or lost. Now that I think about it, that was probably one of the other reasons I don't remember how we did in the band competition. I know that scores were given, but it wasn't as if some electronic device was measuring the airwaves and determining that Parkview High School's concert band hit 97 percent of its notes in tune / on key. That was better than the next school's band, which achieved a score of 94 percent. Music didn't work that way, and as much as I enjoyed playing it, and still enjoy listening to it, I'm not temperamentally suited for it.

None of us are one-dimensional. Frequently, people want to know a lot about us professional athletes, and they judge us for things we do off the court as well as on the court. I'll get into some of those issues later, but I hope that people know that I'm much more than a spin move and dribble drive to the basket.

My Spanish instructor in high school, Señora Smith, was the very opposite of my private music teacher. I wasn't the most brilliant student in her class. I was pretty good at studying vocabulary, but then we got into conjugating verbs beyond the present tense and the simple past tense into things like the past perfect and the perfect tenses. Even though I stumbled and got flustered when I couldn't come up with the correct form of the verb, she never said, "You'll never be any good at this." I think she liked that I was generally quiet and respectful.

Parkview was one of the better schools in Little Rock, but we had our share of knuckleheads—including me at times—who liked nothing better than to cut up in class. I sometimes felt bad for teachers like Señora Smith who had to deal with students acting out. No one was ever really seriously out of control or violent, and I sometimes think that because she was so nice, students thought that they could take advantage of her. Because I wasn't any trouble most of the time, she went out of her way to work with me so that I maintained a B average in her class. I wasn't immune from schoolboy crushes, and Señora Smith's being so nice to me turned my head a little bit. She wasn't a young teacher fresh out of college, but her willingness to reach out to me had me feeling secretly affectionate toward her.

She wasn't the first female who caught my eye. Back in third grade, I was head over heels for a girl named Sharona. She had long, flowing hair and a really cute smile. I remember one day deciding that instead of admiring her from afar, I would take some action. (Had I told my dad, he would have been proud of me for being so assertive and not sitting back waiting for things to happen.) It took me a while because I was confused since I also had a crush on my third-grade teacher, Miss Leslie. Do you go with the veteran or give the young kid a shot? One of the eternal questions that NBA executives and coaches all have to deal with, and there I was in the third grade faced with this dilemma. After a few weeks of wondering about how Sharona felt about me, I had to do something. I wrote a little note asking, *Do you like me? Please check one: yes no.*

I waited until Sharona went up to the pencil sharpener. Only two of us were allowed up there at any time, so I had to act quickly. I hopped out of my chair—all that basketball had given me a quick first step—and dashed up to the sharpener behind Sharona. I waited until she was done and was blowing the shavings off her pencil before I tapped her on the shoulder and handed her the note. She tucked it into her fist and went back to her seat. It took all the discipline I had to keep looking down at the pencil sharpener. I can still remember that engraved on the little dial that you turned depending upon the thickness of your pencil was the word *Boston.*

I went back to my seat, and I'm happy to report that eventually I got the note back from Sharona and she had checked the yes box. I sat back feeling really happy with myself. Of course, years later when the social mores and methods of girls had advanced beyond the stage when they had those folded paper clackers (which looked like Venus flytraps) with which they interrogated us with questions and asked us for numbers so that they could peel back the folds of their paper monstrosities to reveal our fate, I would long for those simpler days when a simple yes or no could fill or empty my heart. It was one of those small things, and just as I would have to sharpen my skills on the court, I needed to figure out what to do off the court to keep me in the game. But the foundation was there for success in life, in love, and on the court. Work hard, develop your fundamentals, attack your weaknesses, and always do the right thing. I was fortunate to have parents and coaches who helped me to recognize what I needed to do to develop other parts of my personality and explore other areas of interest besides basketball. And if you ever make it to the big time, don't buy a house with a lot of pine trees.

CHAPTER FOUR

Knocking Them Down:

Free Throws and Seizing Opportunities

In the old days, sportswriters and announcers sometimes referred to it as the charity stripe. While I'm a great believer in giving back and helping out those in need, in some ways I never liked the basketball free throw line being referred to that way. Charity can sometimes mean a handout, being given something that you haven't been able to attain for yourself, something that you didn't work for. I can understand why sportscasters or sportswriters came up with that name for the free throw line. It's a colorful bit of language, but inaccurate. I don't think you'll find a single guy in the NBA, NCAA, or even in high school who's used the term. When it comes to free throws—or even better, call them foul shots—the inaccuracy of the term *charity stripe* is about the last thing you want associated with them.

First, in almost all cases, except if the opposing team has been whistled for a technical foul and your team gets to choose who goes to the line, the player shooting free throws has been fouled. You've earned the right to get to the "charity stripe," and if you've ever watched an NBA game, you know that sportscasters have also come up with the term *hard foul*. That's a more accurate term than *charity stripe,* since many times, as a result of a hard foul, the fouled player falls to the hard court, is struck hard by an opponent, or runs into a hard body on the other team. I'm not alone in having gone to the free throw line after having been smacked across the bridge of the nose or the back of the head. I was not the first player, nor will I be the last, who went in among the so-called trees and crashed to the floor after having made contact with one of the stout limbs or immovable trunks of the largest members of that species.

It's hard to pull yourself together when you've had that kind of experience, but you have to. So, I don't hold with the idea that a free throw is all that "free." Most of the time you've earned your way to the line, and you have to use your shooting skills to make that free throw. Even though you get a "free" opportunity to shoot the ball, you still have to make that fifteen-foot shot (the distance from the free throw line to the plane of the backboard), and in the heat of the battle, especially in an up-and-down-the-court type of game, sinking that shot isn't as easy as it looks. Even in a relatively "slow" half-court-type game, you're still moving a lot, running through or around offensive screens, and your heart and respiration rates are climbing. In an up-tempo game, you're doing a whole series of two-hundred-foot sprints. Gathering yourself and bringing your breathing under control isn't all that easy.

The only thing free about a foul shot is that you don't have a defender guarding you, but that experience, standing alone with the ball in your hands and everyone watching you, is uniquely different, making it either a pleasure or a nightmare for some players. I've played with and against some of the greatest and some of the poorest free throw shooters in the game—John Stockton, Ray Allen, and Steve Nash are among the best in the history of the NBA. Shaquille O'Neal's struggles at the line are legendary as well, but he wasn't alone in clanging the ball off the rim or the backboard. Ben Wallace has the lowest free throw percentage (41.8%) among NBA players who have played at least five hundred games, and even greats such as Bill Russell (56%) and Wilt Chamberlain (51%) were well below what most people consider a good free throw percentage of 75 percent. Obviously, those last two guys made up for that deficiency in other ways and easily earned their way into the NBA's Hall of Fame. I'm sure that Shaq will follow them into the hall as soon as he is eligible, and people will remember him more for other parts of his game than his misadventures at the free throw line.

I think that part of the reason you see so many big men at the bottom of the all-time free throw percentage list is that these guys are so used to banging underneath and have had to develop a body suitable for that kind of pounding that a more fine-motor-skill activity such as shooting free throws is harder for them. Also, the taller you are, the longer your arms tend to be, and the lever you use to shoot with can be harder to control as a result. It doesn't take much of a mechanical flaw to throw off a shot and make that sweet sound of a swish turn into a thudding clank. Despite his height and build, Karl Malone was one of the NBA's greatest free throw shooters, leading the league in free throw percentage eight times in his career (five seasons in a row from 1988 to 1993) and sinking 9,787 of them. That leaves me about 8,134 shy of his mark as I write this.

I've attempted just a little more than two thousand free throws in my years in the league, and I've heard both the swish and the clang, and let me tell you, it still really gets to me when I miss a free throw. It's almost as if that sound of a miss, or someone shouting "Off!" at one of my errant attempts, is directly transmitted to my spinal column and I feel those vibrations coursing through my whole body. Other than the obvious—my competitive desire—the reason I feel that sensation so fully is that a free throw represents an opportunity—one that you either seize or let pass you by. In my life, I've tried to take advantage of every opportunity I've ever had, and I feel I've done a good job.

Shooting free throws well is a matter of both mental and physical discipline and is one of the fundamentals that every NBA player works on. When we're working our way up through the ranks from recreation leagues to school teams, to Amateur Athletic Union, to college ball, we probably put more of an emphasis on practicing foul shooting. I've seen and heard stories of guys who were really good free throw shooters working on them all the time and demanding as close to perfection from themselves as they could. Calvin Murphy was regarded as one of the greatest free throw shooters of all time. He set an NBA record by making 78 consecutive free throws in 1980 and 1981. That same year, he made an astounding 95.8 percent of his free throws (206 out of 215). He credited his years spent as a baton twirler with helping him become a Hall of Fame basketball player. His free throw record stood for twelve years, before Micheal Williams, guard for the Minnesota Timberwolves out of Baylor University, broke it. Williams's streak lasted until the 1993–94 season when he finally missed one, ending his streak of 97 consecutive conversions. That kind of precision is pretty amazing.

Williams practiced his free throws religiously, shooting hundreds at a time. He also played little mind games with himself to keep his focus on the task. If he missed one, he told himself that he had to make ten in a row to make up for his mistake. He made a science of free throw shooting and even studied professional golfers as they putted to see if he could learn something he could apply to his own game. Everybody knows that practice makes perfect, but few of us are really willing to put in the effort it takes to truly practice a skill and not just go through the motions. Today, I admire Jose Calderon and his amazing touch from the line. For the 2008–9 season he hit an astounding 151 out of 154 (98%) from the line.

While I didn't really think of it that way back in the day, I was really preparing myself to be successful when I played in those imaginary games. That's an important part of being successful at anything.

Obviously, the more times you do something, even doing it mentally through visualization, the more you become comfortable at doing it, and the greater your chances to succeed. I can still remember a game from my junior year at the University of Arkansas, Little Rock. We were playing Sam Houston State in Huntsville, Texas, at the Johnson Coliseum. The Bearkats weren't in our conference, but any win was important, and as the clock wound down under ten seconds, the ball was in my hands. I figured that with good dribble penetration, I could either get up a shot, get fouled, or kick out. The defense converged on me, and I had no way to get the ball to anyone on the wing, so with just a few seconds left in the game, I pulled up for a short jumper. As soon as I left the floor, I knew I was going to get hammered, and sure enough, someone swatted my forearm. I could barely get the shot off, but it didn't matter. The referee blew the whistle and I got sent to the line with just a fraction over a second left. We were down 69 to 67, and if I made the two shots, chances were really good that we'd go to overtime.

I was always a decent free throw shooter, hovering around the low seventies as a percentage, and stepping up to the line, I was confident. Shooting in those situations, it is impossible to tell yourself and to believe that these are just any old free throws. As a player, you're always aware of the score and any other circumstances. Instead of that being a burden, I looked at it as an opportunity. I knew my team needed me to make those two foul shots, and I was glad to be in the position where everyone relied on me to do my job. But even though I knew that in a lot of ways these free throws were different, I couldn't do anything out of the ordinary in my approach.

For years, I had been following the same pre-shot and shot-taking routine. After the foul is called, I'll hang back from the line, at the top of the key, and wait for everyone to get set on either side of the lane or for any substitutions to be made and players to enter or exit. Once the referee has the ball in his hands and indicates by raising his hand that the game is going to resume, I step up to the line. Back then, most courts we played on were more or less permanent—they weren't periodically taken up for concerts, ice hockey games, or other uses as in the major venues I play in today. On nearly every wood court I've ever played on, there's something we refer to as the nail. In some cases, that nail is literally a metal fastener in the wood that fixes the court to the subflooring underneath it—whether that's cement, another layer of wood, or some composite material. The nail is the head of that fastener or sometimes a painted mark on the floor that is lined up with the exact center of the basket. In other words, it is the center point of the court from sideline to sideline and exactly fifteen feet from the baseline. I always looked down to find the nail so that I could put my feet, shoulder width apart, equidistant from that center mark.

Once the official handed me the ball, I would take it, and after eyeing the rim, I would dribble the ball three times while looking down at the floor. While doing that, I would visualize the ball as it dropped through the hoop—not a movie of its flight through the air, but a snapshot of the final result. I would bend my knees slightly while rotating the ball in my hands until the tip of my index finger came in contact with the ball's air hole. I like it so that the ball's seams are perpendicular to the rim. With the fingers of my shooting hand comfortably fanned out, I would rise and flex my knees again with my guide hand on the side of the ball approximately in the center. After I'd exhale, I'd flex my knees and hips, trying to limit the amount of side-to-side motion, and raise my arms up into the shot. As much as possible, I'd try to limit the amount of motion in other parts of my arms except from the elbow down to my hand.

Of course, when I was shooting, I couldn't think of all those fine points. Instead, I would let muscle memory take over completely, or I'd remind myself of one or at most two key points. After my having shot thousands and thousands of free throws, muscle memory has developed, but the key is that my muscles need to remember to do the proper things. I don't know of too many NBA-caliber players who have had to have their stroke completely rebuilt once they got into high school or college, let alone the pros. I take a more or less textbook approach to foul shooting, but guys such as Reggie Miller and Peja Stojakovic have little quirks in their style that you won't find in the textbook method. Despite those quirks, those two are great shooters, and the old cliché "If it ain't broke, don't fix it" applies here. Guys develop habits, and it's impossible for players to be mirror images of one another.

The key to any shot routine is that you repeat it as a way to eliminate thought. You want your body to take over to do what it knows best. By relying on the familiar and on past success, you eliminate negative thinking or distracting thoughts. You enter a weird mental state where you're not really thinking but reacting. In that game against Sam Houston State, I was aware that my uncle, who lived relatively nearby in Waco, was at the game, but I was not consciously thinking about him. I was grateful that all the practice I'd been doing paid off and I made both shots to get the game into overtime. I was thrilled that my uncle had been there to see me come through in the clutch. I was gratified that I had come through when it really mattered. We went on to win the game, and that was the most special part of the whole experience.

Since then, I've drawn on those clutch free throw attempts over and over. Having that past success to recall and to rely on is enormously helpful. Not only have I sunk thousands of free throws in practice, but I've come through when it was really needed in game situations. In college, I made between 75 and 76 percent of my free throws. In my first year in the NBA, that fell to 66 percent, but it has climbed steadily since then, until in 2007–8 I shot the best I ever have from the line, making 88 percent of my shots. Seizing 22 percent more of the opportunities to score a point isn't going to earn me headlines; free throw shooting is more noticeable when it's done poorly than when it's done well. Free throws aren't nearly as exciting as a thunderous jam or a rainbow three from the corner being buried, but I still take some gratification at having improved that much over time.

One reason I became a better foul shooter was a change in my technique. I'd gotten better and better at foul shooting, but in my second season with the Golden State Warriors in 2005–6 I began shooting fouls in games using an adjustment I'd practiced during the off-season. During the 2004–5 season I'd made 86 percent of my foul shots. That was the highest in my career to then. That off-season, I began to experiment with moving just off center of the nail. For my whole basketball career, I'd centered my feet on either side of the nail, but something told me that I could get even better results with this change in my placement. I realized that if I moved a few inches to the right of the nail, so that my left foot was to the right of it, I would place my left elbow (my shooting hand) in line with the center of the basket. That made sense to me logically—aligning myself that way would put me in a position to shoot even straighter at the basket.

When I first started shooting that way, it felt a little awkward, but the results were good. I continued to work on it all that off-season, until even after having shot one way for my first ten years in the league, I was ready to switch. A lot of factors were responsible for my shooting three percentage points lower from the line that first year with my new method, but in the two seasons since then, my percentage has increased over the previous personal best.

Why didn't I adapt the "If it ain't broke, don't fix it" mentality? I felt as if I'd done as much as I could to improve the other way, and as someone who is constantly trying to improve, I saw this as a viable opportunity to do so. I don't think you should ever be content with how things are going, just as I don't believe in change for the sake of change. I figured that if it wasn't working for me as well as I wanted it to, I could always go back to shooting as I had before. I'm sure that the change was as much mental as it was physical. I had assessed my strengths and weaknesses as a foul shooter and come up with what I saw as a solution. I believed that it would make a difference, and it did. How much of that had to do with the change in the flight path of the ball, and how much of that had to do with my belief that I had found a better way, is not something that can be measured. That's how it is in this game, in most games, and in many ways in all other aspects of life.

The important thing to remember is that I wasn't satisfied even though I'd achieved the best results of my career. I still wanted to get better. I guess that's just part of my nature to not be satisfied, but I think that most athletes and most successful people are that way.

I can remember that first year of the change facing the Detroit Pistons. I went to the line and made the first of two free throws. Rasheed Wallace, one of the more animated players in the game, looked at me with a startled expression on his face and said, "Fish, you always shoot your free throws that way?"

"No." I gave him a quick explanation.

I missed the second shot, and as I headed back up court, Rasheed needled me, saying, "Back to the drawing board, professor."

I framed this chapter around the idea of free throws and opportunity because I have to say, in looking back, if I can point to one thing as a reason for my success and longevity in the game, it's that nearly every time when an opportunity presented itself, I maximized it. And if I didn't, I looked back over the situation to learn why I had fallen short of my goal. To me, that's the definition of success—maximizing opportunity. I think that it's the rare person who doesn't get opportunities in life. A lot of people complain about not getting them, but I think that most often the person does not recognize the opportunities that are presented. I'm more than sympathetic to people who are truly downtrodden and denied opportunity, but for the vast majority of us that isn't the case. I'm sometimes troubled when I hear people say things like "It isn't what you know, it's who you know" or "The only way to get X [a job, a promotion, some tangible asset such as a house] is by being connected." Being connected helps, but the reason that most people are connected somehow is because they took the opportunity to seek out other people. Those connections are rarely just handed out.

I sensed from the very beginning when I succeeded because of my physical attributes (size and handedness) that I could turn those advantages into something else. Quickly, once I advanced to higher levels, those physical gifts I had (and I realize that they aren't the ones we typically associate with an NBA player) were no longer great advantages. As I progressed in the game, being left-handed wasn't any real advantage for me, and other players were just as, if not more, physically strong as I was. But that early success gave me a quiet confidence. That I wasn't the most skilled or physically gifted player on any of my teams made me hungry to prove to people that I was capa-

ble of playing the game and playing it well. I could also, briefly, oper-
ate in stealth mode. When I played with more physically imposing
players or with guys whose reputations exceeded mine, I'd take advantage of having someone or even a whole team focusing on stopping those other guys. I could have looked at my reputation as not
being as strong as a disadvantage and whined about lack of press or
lack of respect, but I turned that into an advantage. Life is all in how
you look at things, and developing that perspective of looking for opportunities to succeed and to make yourself more well-known is an
important trait.

While it was important for me to have had early success and
earned the praise of some of my coaches, having a father who didn't
lavish praise on me, and having parents who made certain that my hat
size never got too big, were also advantages. I may not have known,
but I had a fire in me that wanted to prove to people that even though
it didn't look as if I would grow to be six feet six or that I'd have 4.4
forty-yard dash or that I'd be able to grab a quarter off the top of the
backboard, I did have something. Sportswriters and sports people in
general sometimes refer to those things as "the intangibles," and we
have all kinds of clichés such as "It's not the size of the dog in the
fight, it's the size of the fight in the dog that matters." Call it good
fortune, call it intuition, call it a knack, a talent, or whatever, but I
have been able to turn opportunity into success.

Even when I made the transition from high school to college ball,
I had my doubters. Including my first college coach, Jim Platt. Even
though he'd recruited me, he still seemed to think that maybe I
wasn't cut out to lead his team. With all of the AAU ball and high
school ball I'd been playing throughout my teens, I'd competed
against the best players in the nation in my age group. I felt I could
compete against any of them. Everyone said that when you went to
the next level (from high school to the NCAA), everyone was going
to be faster, stronger, and more skilled. I wasn't intimidated by that
possibility. I thought I'd done what I could to prepare myself to win
the job as starting point guard. I also knew that I couldn't rest on
my accomplishments in high school. I'd been an Honorable Mention

McDonald's High School American, an AAU All-American, my high school team had won the state championship, my AAU team had won the national championship. Those team triumphs were most important. But I quickly realized none of that mattered. When I arrived in the summer to work out at the University of Arkansas, Little Rock, Coach Platt told me immediately, "I can't guarantee you any playing time. None at all. I just expect you to work hard and do the things you need to do."

I had no idea if he gave that speech to every incoming freshman, but it sure made an impact on me. I didn't expect to be handed anything, but I also didn't expect to be told that I might not play at all. What the coach said wasn't nearly as bad as the attitude with which he delivered those words. He seemed almost angry and a little bit dismissive, as if he couldn't wait to get out of the room and move on to something else. I felt that I was just one more piece of paper on his desk that was linked to a lengthy to-do list. Now that he'd done what he needed to do, it was off to the shredder for me. I felt as if I should go to a nearby washroom and check my forehead for a giant check mark.

I wasn't expecting him to roll out the red carpet for me. I was smart enough to know that coaches made all kinds of statements to high school kids that might not be true. During recruiting (more on that later) he'd never made it seem that he really wanted me to sign a letter of intent, that I figured in his plans for improving the team the next year. His assistants, Coach Finley and Coach White, were the ones who really pushed for him to offer me a scholarship. Every one of the starting five on my high school team earned a Division I scholarship—with guys going to such places as Florida State, Stanford, Oklahoma State, and Auburn. I knew that among us I'd gone to the smallest of the schools, but I didn't think that meant I'd get the smallest amount of playing time. I'd had other schools interested in me, but I'd considered things carefully and decided UALR was the place to be. Had the coach changed his mind?

I had all summer to think about that. I enrolled in school early so that I could work out with the school's strength-and-conditioning coach. One thing proved to be true about Division I ball—strength and conditioning workouts were a lot harder than what I'd experienced in high school. Parkview had one of the best strength training and conditioning programs of any high school, but that Arkansas, Little Rock, coach Ken Coggins put me through the workout of my life that first day—and all he was really doing was showing me each of the lifts I was going to have to do with free weights and what I would do on the various machines. All I can remember is feeling that I wanted to crawl out of that gym and drag my sorry butt to my car. I knew better than to let it show that I was hurting, so I casually strolled out. When I got to the car, I sat there for what seemed like twenty minutes. It felt as if someone had put a tourniquet around my triceps and biceps. Reaching for the steering wheel was sheer agony. The next few days were worse, but I persevered and actually looked forward to the workouts after a while.

I was also eager for the season to begin so that we could start practices in earnest. I found a group of guys to play with informally, but that was only making me hungrier to get out in front of the coaches and other players to really prove what I could do. Finally, in late November of 1992 we had a couple of exhibition games in anticipation of the season opener—a tournament at South West Missouri State University in Springfield. The Basketball Traveler's Tip-off Tournament was our first real test of the season, and as predicted, Coach Platt had me sitting on the bench when the game began. During that tournament, in the first two games, our starting guard got into early foul trouble. The rotation had not been completely set, but coach waved me into the game.

I can't say that I remember feeling any extra sense of pressure, but I must have known somewhere inside me that something was on the line other than just the game. When the whistle blew to stop play and I went into the game, I simply took a deep breath, said a quick prayer of thanks to God for this opportunity, then went into tunnel-vision mode. It's hard to describe what that mode looks and sounds like. Basically I was aware of my environment but only fully aware of a small part of it—the ninety-four-by-fifty-foot court. I also operated within a limited mental space—I couldn't consciously think, "Oh, this is an opportunity that I've worked so hard for. The coach hasn't demonstrated a lot of faith in me. This is a make-or-break moment for me." After having played the game for so many years, it was almost as if every cell in my body had that message encoded in it. I didn't need to think through all those thoughts and their associated feelings. Instead, I just let the instrument that I'd worked so hard to refine—my body—take over and do its thing.

I did have one conscious thought, one that I always had when I went into the game as a substitute or even as a starter. I wanted to make an impact right away. I don't mean that I went out there and took a huge risk—overplayed my man defensively so that I could get a steal (or alternatively give up an easy basket if my steal attempt failed) or fired up a shot at the first sign of being even remotely open. Instead, I took in all the data I'd collected while sitting on the bench observing, and looked for a chance to exploit the South West Missouri State's point guard's tendency to leave his feet prematurely on a pump fake. The first time he came out to guard me at the top of the circle, I rose up as if to shoot, got him in the air, and drove around him before dishing off when our center's man left him to help guard me. A nice easy layup and an assist for me. I went on to score 12 points, handed out a fistful of assists, and even managed a steal or two.

At every time-out, I came back to the bench and could see in the eyes of my teammates and the coaches a glimmer of respect. I think my guys understood that I could play the game, and I didn't think that I had anything to prove to them, but having evidence to back up my confidence and their belief in me made a big difference. After that game I never looked back, and started every game in each of my four years at Arkansas. It's impossible to say that my career hinged on my success in that game, but people always say that first impressions are important. Just as I always felt that it was important to make a difference right away when entering a game, it's equally important to start off a season, a career, or a comeback from injury on the right foot. More on comebacks and my foot in a bit.

The other major opportunity that I knew I had to seize came at the end of my senior year at UALR. Sometimes opportunities come at the most surprising times. When we lost our last game our senior year in our conference tournament, I was devastated. A buzzer beater knocked us out, and I just wanted to sink into the floor. That loss meant no conference tourney championship, no bid to the NCAA tournament (I've had a great career, but I would have loved to have played even a single game in March Madness), and the likely end of my basketball career. We had some consolation in being selected for the National Invitational Tournament, but that was like going to the big dance with the fifth or sixth girl you'd asked—even after your cousin said she couldn't because she had other plans. Losing in the first round of the NIT to Vanderbilt was equally tough. I was nursing a slight injury as well, and sitting in that locker room in Nashville contemplating the dying of my dream was incredibly difficult. Every now and then I'd look around the room and see some of the under-classmen, and I was a bit envious of them. When Coach Sanderson started talking about next year, I couldn't control my tears. For me, the odds were that there would be no next year.

Because of my half brother, I knew that there were other options besides the NBA. The Continental Basketball Association was a kind of feeder system/minor league to the NBA. I wasn't sure if I was ready to go through all that. The same with playing in Europe. At that point, in 1996, there hadn't been the huge influx of foreign players into the NBA that there is today. I was only twenty-one years old, had only traveled in the United States to play basketball, and the prospect of going to a foreign country and experiencing a vastly different culture with what seemed to me to be little in the way of reward for all that risk wasn't appealing. (Ask me today, and knowing what I know now, I would give you a different answer about overseas basketball as an opportunity.) I've never been much of a risk taker, and I was ready to finish out the school year and see what the world of work had waiting for me.

As I've said before, I think that God has a plan for each of us. The role He played in presenting opportunities and reminders to me of my ability is in my mind obvious and clear. Most college players who realistically assess their prospects of playing in the NBA know deep in their heart if not in their head whether they have a shot at the league. For most, that means being drafted. There are those other routes—the CBA, foreign leagues, otherwise being picked up as a free agent—but the vast majority of players in the NBA entered the league through the draft. When I was a senior, there was no NBA Development League, the D-League as we call it today. It began operations in 2001, my sixth year in the NBA. It has its own draft, and a number of players have made the jump from the D-League to the NBA. In fact, sixty players on NBA rosters in 2008–9 had once played in the D-League. That route didn't exist for me, so if I wanted to make it in the NBA, in my mind there was really only one path— getting drafted.

I didn't know if that was realistic. My heart told me that I was good enough and had the desire to succeed at that level. I remember Nike ran a series of print ads that said that the heart is the strongest muscle but also the stupidest. They meant that in a positive way— without our hearts refusing to surrender, without them continuing to pulse in our chests when our brains are screaming at us to just stop, no hill would be climbed, no race finished. The head/heart equation is always tough to balance, and I tend to rely as much on my head to tell me the truth as my instincts. I had been named the Sun Belt Conferences Player of the Year, but I wasn't among the NCAA leaders in any statistical category. At my position, point guard, all the talk that year had been about Georgetown University's sensation, Allen Iverson. Only a sophomore, he'd averaged 25 points per game playing in the Big East, one of the NCAA's premier conferences. He'd had the chance to showcase his talent in front of the nation and the NBA's top scouts while leading his team into the Elite Eight. Stephon Marbury was a freshman out of Georgia Tech who was a cinch to go in the draft, as was a little-known player out of tiny Santa Clara named Steve Nash. True hoops fans knew a high school kid out of Philadelphia by the name of Kobe Bryant who was projected to go high in the first round as a guard. If I looked at things realistically, I was definitely not a sure thing to go in the draft.

What I did have was the heart-sense belief in myself. I wasn't without other evidence. Again, as a sign that all things happen for a reason, during the summer between my freshmen and sophomore years in college, I got a chance to go to Houston to work out with my half brother, Duane Washington. His battles with substance abuse are well documented, and he, and many others who suffered from the same disease, were fortunate to have someone like John Lucas in their lives. Lucas was himself a former drug addict and recovering alcoholic. He was able to conquer his personal demons, and he also worked with other athletes/addicts/alcoholics to help them. Duane entered his program and kept in touch with Mr. Lucas over the years. Duane's been clean and sober for a very long time. Mr. Lucas had played in the NBA for fourteen seasons and coached three NBA teams as well. At one point during the summer, he approached me after a scrimmage. He introduced himself and asked, "How many more years of school?"

"Three," I told him.

He smiled, "Keep playing like you are, that might only be for two years."

I'd carried that bit of validation with me for the next three years. If John Lucas, a veteran player and coach thought that I had what it took to make it in the league—and could possibly leave college early to do so—then maybe my optimistic heart wasn't talking smack with me. I had no intention of not sticking around for four years, however.

While it took me some time to get over the disappointment of having my NCAA career come to a screeching halt, I did get some good news. At the conclusion of the season, I was invited to participate in the Portsmouth Invitational Tournament. Held in Portsmouth, Virginia, for the last fifty-six years, the tournament is a showcase for college basketball players. At the time I wasn't completely sold on the idea that this tournament was a stepping-stone to the NBA. I'd heard of it, and I knew that Scottie Pippen, John Stockton, and a few other players had gone on to stellar NBA careers after playing in it and catching the attention of the NBA scouts. Things had changed over the years in college basketball, and one major change was that underclassmen could make themselves available for the NBA draft. As a result, in my mind, some of the shine was taken off the honor of being selected to participate in the PIT. I mean no disrespect to the organizers of the event, and I'm glad that it exists and contributes not just to the chances of basketball players fulfilling their dream but as a charity for the local community. But since it was open only to seniors, a lot of the best players in the country, and those most likely to be picked in the upcoming NBA draft, weren't in attendance. It was a showcase, but also a kind of reward for those borderline-to-obviously-not-NBA-caliber college seniors who stuck around for four years.

I don't want to leave the impression that I was upset about being asked to participate. I did see it as an opportunity that I had to take advantage of, but I was also smart enough to understand that this opportunity meant nothing unless I really proved myself in those games. My game was going to have to be nasty because I was NASTY—Not A Sure Thing . . . Yet. In the back of my mind, I did hold out some hope that the PIT could lead to some good things. When I found out that the Chicago Bulls' Scottie Pippen had played there and improved his stock enough to be drafted by the Bulls and then go on to be a key component in the Michael Jordan–led Bulls championship streak, I was encouraged. I did a little more investigating about Pippen. Though I was a huge fan of NCAA basketball growing up and through high school (and even today), if Pippen weren't also from the state of Arkansas, I doubt if I would ever have heard about him.

Pippen is sure to be in the NBA Hall of Fame and was named one of the Fifty Greatest NBA Players when the league celebrated its fiftieth anniversary in 1996. Pippen was born in Hamburg, Arkansas, a small town of about three thousand in the southeastern part of the state. It's about 120 miles south of Little Rock, on the route we took to get to my dad's folks in Louisiana. This unremarkable little place produced a fairly remarkable player. Like me, Scottie Pippen was six feet one inch tall when he started college. Unlike me, he grew to six feet seven while in school and eventually topped out at six feet eight. Though so talented, he was considered too small and wasn't heavily recruited by any of the major college-basketball powerhouses. Instead, he enrolled at a non-NCAA school, the University of Central Arkansas, which is a part of the National Association of Intercollegiate Athletics. The NAIA is made up of mostly smaller private and state institutions like the University of Central Arkansas. At that level, the facilities aren't exactly top-notch, but some quality guys do come out of those schools. They don't get the same level of national press coverage, but that didn't stop Pippen. He was considered a legend at the PIT, one of the feel-good success stories of the tournament both because of what he did on the court and his underdog story. How a guy could go from being both the manager and a player on a tiny NAIA team, averaging 4 points a game his first year, to an NBA lottery pick is almost unimaginable.

I'd played at a small school, but not one as small and "obscure" (in terms of basketball) as he had. I tucked all those thoughts about the possibilities and the opportunities along with all my clothes and toiletries in my suitcase and headed to Portsmouth, Virginia. I'd also packed a few of my textbooks, but it was tough to do any studying on that plane. My mind was on the opportunity awaiting me, and it was hard to distract myself from thoughts of the future. I did hold out hopes of an NBA career, but of more immediate concern was doing well in Portsmouth and advancing to one of the other camps and hopefully getting invited to Chicago, where the major predraft camp was held.

First things first, I kept reminding myself. I couldn't be mentally booking a flight for Chicago if I didn't take care of business in Portsmouth. That's how I looked at the trip—as a kind of business excursion. A lot of the other guys knew that this was a kind of reward, a last hurrah, a chance to get away from school and the pressure of final exams and thoughts of what they were going to do with their lives after graduation. I roomed with Derrick Beattie, a center out of Temple University. He was a great guy, and though we were essentially competing against each other for draft position, we got along well. Among the campers was a guard from Mississippi State, Bubba Wilson, who played with Dontaé Jones and Erick Dampier. Jones would be drafted that year by the Knicks, with Dampier chosen by the Indiana Pacers. They wouldn't risk injury by playing in the tournament even if they had been invited.

Portsmouth, a quick ferry ride from Norfolk, had a quaint, small-town feeling, even though an enormous naval base is nearby. That quaint hometown feel extended to the tournament itself. Though the games were played according to NBA rules, they were played at one of the city's high schools, and the teams were sponsored by local businesses. Admission today for a single day is $10, so I can't imagine that back then they were any more than $3 or $4 for the two games held each day. While I can't remember who sponsored our team, some of last year's sponsors were Cherry, Beakart, and Holland Accountants, Tidewater Sealants, and the Norfolk Shipyards. Those sponsors past and present were great, and in addition to showcasing possible NBA talent, the tournament raises money for a scholarship fund that helps out local high school students. I'm proud to say that I participated, and the warm reception we received from the tournament organizers, local volunteers, and members of the community was outstanding. Even though I don't remember the scores of the games I played in, I do remember performing really well, averaging about 16 points a game, passing out a half dozen assists, and generally impressing others with my all-around game. I also remember signing autographs for the local kids who watched the games. I was happy to oblige them, and I could see a lot of myself in those kids and was reminded of my days hanging out in a gym at every opportunity.

I felt good about my performance during the three days of competition. I got on the flight back to Little Rock satisfied that I'd done what I'd gone there to do. I settled into my seat, pulled my Walkman out of my carry-on, and let Toni Braxton, Bone Thugs-N-Harmony, and R. Kelly sing me home courtesy of the mix tape my girlfriend had made for me. I was glad to be back among friends and family in Little Rock, and everyone wanted to know how things had gone. I kept it cool and said, "Fine. Fine." I didn't really know what else to say. How could I honestly evaluate my performance? I'd done as well as I could, gave it everything I could, and the rest was out of my hands. I hated that my fate was being decided by someone else. How objective could I really be? My teammates and the other players praised how I'd done, but did that mean my NBA dream was viable?

I waited a long time to find out. A month or so after Portsmouth ended, I was leaving for class when the phone rang. I wasn't going to answer it, but something told me I should. I picked up and heard the familiar voice of Coach Sanderson on the line. "Derek, congratulations." I hoped I knew what he was going to say next. "I just heard from Marty Blake. You've been invited to Chicago."

I let the pleasure at hearing those words sink in for a minute. Marty Blake was the director of scouting for the NBA. Blake has been associated with the NBA for more than fifty years. He was the long-time general manager of the NBA's St. Louis/Atlanta Hawks. In the seventeen years he guided the team as the GM, the club had the second-best record to the legendary Red Auerbach's Boston Celtics. Marty is renowned around the world for his basketball knowledge, and he was primarily responsible for establishing the system of scouting that enabled the NBA to find, draft, or sign the most talented players in the United States and later in the world. As with the PIT, the NBA predraft camp didn't draw the surefire lottery picks, but it did have the cream of the crop of the rest of the guys expected to go in the first or the second round. Coach explained some of the arrangements that we'd have to make to get me there in early June. All I heard was June, and all I could think of was the six weeks or so I'd have to prepare for that opportunity.

I thanked coach for letting me know the good news. While being drafted wasn't a certainty, I was getting all that I could have asked for—a shot. That's what most of us want in life—not a guarantee but a chance. I would have to figure out how to make the most of it, but that could wait. I had a class to get to, and my head was still spinning at the news. It felt strange walking through campus. It wasn't just as if I'd got a haircut or was wearing a new set of clothes or something, I felt different. I knew that the odds were still not fully in my favor, but they were considerably better than they had been just a few minutes earlier. I imagined that what I was experiencing was a lot like what some of my fellow seniors had experienced earlier in the semester when they'd gotten a job offer or been accepted to graduate school or some other professional school. I felt as if I were in two places simultaneously—physically there on campus, and mentally someplace far away, such as Chicago, and then after that who knew where I might be or what I might be doing there?

That feeling was frightening but far more exhilarating. For a while, I wanted to keep the news to myself, but that didn't last long. The first person I thought to call was my mother. I knew that she was at work, and I knew my girlfriend was in class. My dad would likely have been home; he was no longer working and no longer living with my mom at our place, and that made it difficult to pull the trigger on any phone call. I'd just let the good vibes continue to work their way through me. I'd figure it all out soon enough. I'd always been wary of thumping my chest and drawing too much attention to myself, and that wasn't going to change because of this news. Wrapped up in all this confusion about whom to call, what to say, and how to feel were some practical realities as well. Playing a sport at an NCAA Division I institution had been like having a full-time job. I was constantly having to juggle the priorities of my family, my sport, my classwork, and a social life. I'd been doing that for years, but suddenly the stakes felt a lot higher.

I'd been living in a kind of heightened state of anticipation and preparation. I don't mean that my every moment was freighted with importance and I was a stressed-out wreck who worried about every little thing possibly ruining my prospects in the NBA. I do mean that I had to live my life consciously and deliberately, which was probably different from how most teenagers and young twentysomethings did. I was cool with that. I was so used to living my life that way that I no longer gave it much thought. That phone call was a reward and a thrill, but also a wake-up call, alerting me that all those things that I had been doing for so long had put me on the brink of achieving something pretty amazing. In some ways, it was like stepping up to the free throw line with the game on the line. I was more comfortable when shooting than in the moments before I toed the line and put the ball into the air. I was used to blocking out distractions, but this was different. I just couldn't push some thoughts out of my mind no matter what. Then and now, I think that was a good thing. I could have tried to act all nonchalant, but I would have been doing exactly that—acting.

Being drafted and making it into the NBA mattered to me. I'm not ashamed to say that. As each year of my college career had gone on, that goal that I had visualized had come into sharper focus. The feeling is something like what you experience when you plan a vacation. You pick a spot, research all the accommodations, linger over descriptions of the things to do, restaurants to dine at, museums to visit, and you think about it and think about it and then you look at your calendar and it's two weeks away. Then a week away. You have all kinds of things at work and at home to finish up so that you can have a clear mind when you go, then some other assignment lands on your desk or some problem comes up that needs your attention. You finally get things squared away, then you are on your way to the airport, sitting on a jet, taking a cab into Paris or wherever, and you're on your way to the Louvre to see the *Mona Lisa,* a painting you'd always seen in books or on TV, and it all seems unreal to you.

That's where I was at. In the unreality-of-it-all zone, but I knew that I had to get out of there as soon as I could. I didn't want to have things hanging over my head or have my attention pulled in different directions. That's when one of those distractions popped up and I knew that I couldn't figure this one out all on my own. Coach Sanderson called me again to let me know that I'd been invited to another predraft camp, this one in Phoenix. The Phoenix camp was already under way, and I'd missed a day of practice and the first two games. A couple of the players had been injured, and one of the teams was out of point guards. The organizers were hoping that I could fill in. I didn't know what to say. My initial reaction was that I'd done what I'd needed to do—I'd got the invitation to Chicago, the one real shot I'd have at making a big-time impression on the scouts. What if I got hurt as those other guys had? I'd demonstrated in Portsmouth that I had what it took, but still the skill level in Phoenix was a step up. I wouldn't be competing against just the best seniors, but against the best of the draft-eligible nonlottery picks.

I talked to my dad about my mixed feelings, and he helped put things in perspective.

"Son," he said, "you've shown them what you can do on the court. What you have a chance to do now is to show them something about your character. They're asking for your help. Are you the kind of guy who's going to do the right thing or not? Pack your bag, son."

When I looked at things from my dad's perspective, I realized that I had to go back to the fundamentals—when called on, you respond. If there's a game, you play and put in your best effort. My dad was right. I'd be showing the scouts something else about me besides my outside shot. If I had enough confidence in myself and my abilities, then I didn't need to worry about damaging my chances or lowering the opinion that the scouts already had of me. I went to Phoenix. Four teams were there and the team I joined had lost its first two games. The guys seemed a bit disarrayed, but I was comfortable running the team even without practicing with the fellas. Over the next two days, we won three of our four games, and I was playing as well as I ever had, hitting my shots, dishing the ball off, and helping to control the game's tempo. I'd done nothing to diminish the value of my stock and had probably raised it a bit. My dad was right. Teams would be likely to draft and keep around someone they knew they could count on to do what was asked over an equally talented player with a bit of an attitude.

Once again, I found myself on a flight to Little Rock thinking about what was to come, but this time I hadn't even bothered to pack my books. I definitely felt that I'd arrived at a crossroads. With all the travel I'd been doing, I'd missed more classes than I was used to even at the height of basketball season. I was feeling overwhelmed. I knew how important my getting a degree was to my mom and dad. It was important to me, but with the Chicago camp coming up in just another week, it was hard to serve two masters. With so much on the line, I felt I had to make a choice—disappointing my parents or not give my dream every possible chance of success. I don't think I'd ever felt so much trepidation in approaching my mom and dad to talk with them about something. I'd spent a few hours organizing my thoughts, and as I drove to the house to meet with them, I put the finishing touches on my arguments.

I started out by telling them, "Mom, Dad, I think I should withdraw from school for this semester." I looked at my mom and saw a bit of confusion and hurt in her expression. "I promise you this. If you let me focus on just basketball and the upcoming camp, I honestly feel that I can make it. I will get drafted. If I do, that could change things for all of us." I saw my dad flinch at that last statement just a bit. I didn't think he liked the idea of my feeling I could step in somehow to help out. I plunged ahead. "If I don't make it, then I'll go back to school."

My parents looked at each other, and my mother managed to smile. My dad's stern expression didn't change, but he said, "Thanks for thinking of your mother and me. We both trust you and your judgment. You know we have your best interests in mind."

The rest of what he had to say went in one ear and out the other. Certain moments in a child's life mark the passage from one phase to the next. Hearing my dad say, "We both trust you and your judgment," was one of those milestones, such as getting my driver's license, falling in love for the first time, graduating from high school, and heading off to college. This was far more meaningful than those.

My mom had a few tears in her eyes, and I could hear her breath catch when I went to hug her. "I want you to live your dream, Derek. But you have to promise me you will get that degree."

"I promise, Mom, and I will."

I'm still eighteen credits short of my degree, but I will keep that promise to my mother.

The Chicago camp was held in early June while the Bulls were squaring off against Seattle in the NBA Finals. The town was going nuts, and I could feel the buzz in the air when I stepped off the plane at O'Hare. I had more of a rooting interest than I would otherwise have had during the finals because a former UALR player, Pete Myers, played for the Bulls, as did Scottie Pippen. I wished that I could have gone to a game, but we were kept busy with two-a-day sessions. Unlike the other two camps, where we did nothing but play games, we were put through a series of skill drills in Chicago. We also played some games, but we'd clearly arrived at another level entirely. A few times during the other camps, I'd see some of the scouts sitting around in a cluster, half paying attention to what was going on out on the floor. Not in Chicago. Each scout seemed to have come with a specific mission and didn't want to let any of the others know what that mission was. The same kind of ratcheted-up vibe moved through the players. If the atmosphere at PIT and Phoenix had been competitive but friendly, the Chicago camp was intense. We all knew that we were competing for just a few spots. The goal was to get into the first round. A few second-round picks might make a team's roster, but the odds on that weren't good.

It's hard to describe my performance there. The scouts weren't looking at the usual statistics and were more analytical. They looked at such minute things that we all felt we were under a microscope. My only gauge of my success at the Chicago camp was to count the number of teams that contacted my agents—I'd gone with the guys who had represented Corliss Williamson, my friend and former AAU teammate and standout at the University of Arkansas—to get me to fly into their city for a workout. I went to ten or twelve cities between the end of the camp in early June and the draft on June 26. Normally, a team would bring in about four different guys at a time, and the routine was somewhat similar. We had to do ball-handling drills, shooting drills, and even an old, reliable fundamental—make layups with each hand. We also did a lot of strength and fitness work. Fortunately I'd been put through all that at UALR by my strength-and-fitness coach, and his football background really helped. We maxed out on the bench press, squats, and in some cases the overhead press. We also met individually with assistant coaches and definitely got the feeling that our every move was being assessed. Generally, I was in and out of each city the same day, then it was on to the next. A lot of the time, I was with some of the same guys going from city to city. I can't say it was exciting because I didn't get to do much except go from the airport to the workout facility and then back. There were a few overnighters, but I was too exhausted and too preoccupied to see anything of the cities I was in. Lying in bed flipping the channels endlessly, occasionally stopping on ESPN's *SportsCenter,* was about the extent of my exploration.

I was excited and sometimes stopped to try to take it all in, but there was always another plane to catch, another set of questions to respond to, another look of skepticism to face from one team official or coach or another. No one gave you any sense of what he was think-ing. This wasn't like being recruited by a college. No one was trying to impress you—you were the commodity, the item up for bid, and the buyers didn't feel the need to behave as if they were your buddy. People weren't rude or indifferent, but clearly this was a serious busi-ness, and the people in it were professionals.

By the time June 26 rolled around, I was more than ready for it all to be over, good or bad. My agent was confident that I would go in the first round, and I was too. In my mind, the Knicks were the likely choice. They had three first-round picks as a result of some trading—the eighteenth, nineteenth, and twenty-first.

The athletic department at UALR had graciously provided us with a room in the athletic complex where family and friends could gather. We had people from our church, all kinds of cousins and aunts and uncles and family friends, all crowded into a single room to watch the draft on television. I was in the locker room with my mom and dad, Coach Sanderson, Corliss, and my agents, Elbert Crawford and Bill Ingram. Coach Sanderson knew several big-time agents, but I kept in the Arkansas family and went with two local guys. I wanted my being drafted to be about me and my skills and not about whom I had in my corner. Following a work stoppage in 1995, the new collective-bargaining agreement took a lot of the negotiating out of rookie contracts. I was satisfied with my guys and liked keeping it all low-key.

I was pretty cool during the first part of the draft. I knew that I wasn't likely to go in the top ten, so I was more curious than really involved as the draft unfolded. I was happy for the players who got to attend the draft in New York City, and seeing them react when their names were called, seeing them hug their family members and stride onto the stage to greet Commissioner Stern and put on the team hat was cool. Allen Iverson went number one, and the names that followed are all familiar to NBA fans—Marcus Camby, Shareef Abdur-Rahim, Stephon Marbury, Ray Allen, Antoine Walker, Lorenzen Wright, Kerry Kittles, Samaki Walker, Erick Dampier, Todd Fuller, Vitaly Potapenko, Kobe Bryant, and Peja Stojakovic.

By the time the fifteenth-round selection was announced, I started to get nervous. The Phoenix Suns selected Steve Nash out of Santa Clara. I'd played against Nash in Chicago and thought I'd matched up well against him. I knew that he had a bad hamstring, and I thought that might have worked against him, but it didn't seem to. With the first round halfway over, I was getting a bit worried about how far down the pole I might slip. The difference between a first-round selection and a second-round one was huge. No disrespect to these guys, but how many NBA fans remember the names Shawn Harvey, Joseph Blair, Steve Hamer, Joe Vogel, or Jamie Feick? It's tough to make it into the league from that position, with a huge difference financially also between first- and second-round picks.

When it got to the Knicks in the eighteenth round, the locker room got real quiet. When my name wasn't announced, we all exhaled and shook our heads. What was going on? Looking back on it now, I can understand why I had to wait so long to hear my name called. Many experts consider the 1996 draft one of the strongest ever, right up there with the 1984 draft that produced Hakeem Olajuwon, Michael Jordan, Charles Barkley, and John Stockton—all likely Hall of Famers. Eventually, one-third of those of us selected in the first round in 1996 would become NBA All-Stars (not to mention Ben Wallace, who went undrafted). Three of our crew have won the Most Valuable Player Award (Bryant, Iverson, and Nash) and seven guys out of that twenty-nine have been named to at least one All-NBA team—more than from any other draft.

I've stated before that I think our lives have a pattern designed for us. As agonizing as it was to sit there through all those announcements and not hear my name, when it came to round twenty-four and the L.A. Lakers selection, I was holding my breath. It was almost too much to wish for that my favorite team, now led in the front office by my favorite player of all time, Magic Johnson, might pick me. When Commissioner Stern began, "With the twenty-fourth pick, the Los Angeles Lakers select Derek—," my heart literally skipped a beat. For a second I thought that he said Beattie, my roommate from PIT. But when both rooms exploded in sound and motion, I knew that he'd said Fisher. After that, my mind went blank. I could barely register the sight and sound of everyone in the locker room jumping up and down and screaming and yelling and crying. A surge of adrenaline shot through me, and it felt as if every hair on my body was tingling. I don't remember this, but a newspaper photo shows me just after the announcement. I must have jumped out of my chair because the picture shows me leaning against one of the chalkboards, staggered by the news.

I do remember the big group hug we all joined in, and a warm feeling of deep satisfaction welling up inside me. I know that basketball is a team game, and I've been on teams that won some big championships, but nothing could compare with the moment I got drafted. I'd never been a selfish player, but that moment was all about earning something and taking advantage of opportunities. Yes, other people had contributed enormously to my success, but I was the one who had been drafted. It was the validation of all validations. A stunning recognition that the work I had put in was worth it, that my skills placed me among a rare few, that a dream that so many have had came true for me. As were their drafts moments for so many of the guys I've talked to around the league, the moment I heard my name called as a draft choice was the best day of my life to that point. The championships I'd later win as a part of the Lakers were phenomenal. Still June 26, 1996, holds a special place in my heart and in my career. Without it, none of what followed would have taken place. I stepped up to the line and knocked it down. Six months earlier, only the most die-hard fan outside Arkansas would have even recognized my name; now I was going to be a part of one of the most storied franchises in all of sports. In the middle of all that jubilation, we bowed our heads and said a prayer, with much of the eighth Street Baptist Church in attendance. God is indeed good, and the little guy with nothing to lose had stood up and done what it takes to seize the opportunities he'd been fortunate enough to have God put in front of him.

CHAPTER FIVE

Defending:

Protecting What's Important to You

The winner of any basketball game is the team that scores the most points. You can look at that from a slightly different perspective. The loser of the game is the one that scores fewer points. That gives you two options: concentrate on how to score, or concentrate on how to prevent the other team from scoring. That's pretty fundamental, but as you know, that's what we've been concentrating on. Just as some of the other basic elements of the game that we've talked about—developing your off hand, foul shooting, and boxing out—defense is not the headline-grabbing, glamorous task that offensive scoring is. I haven't seen many headlines on game stories shouting out, "Fisher's Steals Seal the Deal" or "Odom's Blocks Rocks Sonics." The headline and the lead in most stories about games is about which player led his team to victory with X number of points. I'm not arguing with the priority placed on offensive production. I'm as aware of my contributions on the offensive end as anyone. I know that one of my jobs is to put points on the board.

In basketball, or in nearly any sport I can think of, points aren't taken off the board for defensive plays. For example, a blocked shot doesn't result in two points being taken off the offensive team's score. In baseball, a diving catch doesn't reduce the number of runs a team has. In football, a goal-line stand or a fourth-down stop doesn't result in points being deducted. Instead, those things contribute to the ball being awarded to your team so that you can go on offense to try to score. The emphasis in almost all sports is always going to be on offensive play. The great thing about basketball is that every player has to be skilled at both offense and defense. Football is the obvious comparison. In that game, two or even three different teams exist within the whole team. With few exceptions (the defensive back/wide receiver, the defensive lineman inserted as a tight end) today's football players don't play on both sides of the ball the way they did back in the day. Football has become so specialized that some defensive players only come into the game in certain situations—on obvious running or passing downs, etc.

I have huge respect for football players at any level. It is a violent and fast-paced game with incredibly skilled guys demonstrating amazing athleticism and sometimes grace. But what I really love about basketball is that you have to make the transition from offense to defense so quickly and so continuously throughout the game. We all know that some players are better on one end of the floor than others. Some notably good offensive players were notoriously weak on defense, and some (far fewer) players who were strong defenders were comparatively weak on offense. But when you look at the list of the game's greats, you'll see guys who were outstanding on both ends of the court. High scorers frequently get a bad rap for being too offense-minded, but you won't last long in the league unless you can at least hold your own on the defensive end.

Just about every coach I've ever played for has emphasized one thing about defense: playing good defense generally comes down to desire. If you want to be a good defender, you can be a good defender by simply (for the most part) expending the necessary energy at that end of the floor. Phil Jackson has repeatedly said that you can have an off night shooting—some quirk in your mechanics shows up or something else goes wrong—but you should never have an off night on defense because good defense isn't so much about technique as it is about desire and energy. Coach Jackson isn't the only coach I've played for who feels that way. Coach Sloan of the Utah Jazz was a legendarily hard-nosed, take-no-prisoners defender as well as a good offensive player. He brought that same mentality with him to the bench as a coach.

I've always believed in bringing a distinct energy to the floor every night, particularly when coming off the bench or at the start of a game or a quarter. Setting the tempo early with a hustle play is something I pride myself on being able to do. I've heard hockey players talk about that same thing—how a hard check into the boards or a hip check at center ice can send a signal to an opposing team that they're not going to get an easy path to the goal. Some teams are known for their defensive intensity. The Detroit Pistons of the late 1980s cultivated an image and became known as the Motor City Bad Boys for their rough play and emphasis on defense. Part of that was a manipulated image—they wore black jerseys with skull-and-crossbones logos while practicing. Those were given to them by the owner of my dad's favorite football team—Al Davis of the Oakland Raiders. The Raiders also developed and in a sense marketed a bad-boy image in their silver and black, appropriate for a kind of blue-collar mentality. Detroit fans ate it up as well, and the regular rough-and-tumble bad boys against the more cultured, softer Los Angeles types got hyped a great deal in the media.

That reached a climax in the 1988–89 NBA Finals, when the two teams faced each other in a showdown of Showtime versus the Bad Boys. The Lakers were going for a three-peat (a term the savvy Pat

Riley had tried to trademark) after having won the previous two seasons. I remember watching the series with my dad, and he was hoping for the three-peat primarily because Kareem Abdul-Jabbar, at the age of forty-two, had announced his retirement. Talk about longevity and production at both ends of the court. Kareem was also an amazingly gracious and graceful player, an extremely intelligent guy, and someone my dad pointed to as a role model for how to conduct your life. Sentiment was on his side in our household, and though there were a lot of Lakers haters elsewhere, we felt confident that the royal colors of purple and gold would be crowned again.

Obviously, things didn't go as planned. Things unraveled pretty quickly for the Lakers, mostly due to injuries. Byron Scott tore up his hamstring in practice before the first game of the series, and Detroit's guards took advantage of his absence with Joe Dumars, Isiah Thomas, and Vinnie Johnson combing for 65 of the team's 109 points. For a defense-oriented team that 109 points was a lot of production, and the Pistons showed that they could perform at a high level on both ends of the court. I remember my dad muttering in frustration at the Lakers' guards inability to shut down the Pistons' guards. He knew that with a key element missing from the Lakers' lineup, a high-scoring game wasn't to the Lakers' advantage.

Game two was a heartbreaker. James Worthy went to the line with six seconds left. The Lakers were down 106–104. If he made both shots, the game would likely go into overtime. He missed the first but made the second. That was it. Isiah Thomas hit two free throws to seal it, and the Lakers lost 108–105. Don't believe for a second that my dad didn't reinforce what I already knew. If Worthy had hit those foul shots, the outcome could have been different. If Thomas didn't hit both of his, the Lakers would have had one last shot at winning. My dad wasn't too down on James Worthy for his miss because the man had done everything he could to bring his shorthanded team to victory. In the third quarter, Detroit was on a fast break. Magic was hustling back on defense; he turned to back-pedal and started hopping up and down and punching at the air. He had injured his hamstring and couldn't return for the rest of the game. He tried in game three, but had to sit down after the first few minutes in the first quarter. That game was painful but instructive to watch. With Byron Scott out, the Lakers had to rely on a backcourt of Michael Cooper and the rookie David Rivers at the point.

The Pistons tore up those guards with screens, and my dad kept pointing out to me how the Lakers were having so much trouble switching on defense, leaving Dumars and Vinnie Johnson wide open. Of course, the headlines the next day were about Joe Dumars's 31 points (and his making an incredible 17 consecutive points and a total of 21 in the third quarter) and Thomas's 26 and Johnson's 17. They needed every one of those 74 points from the backcourt to squeak by 114–110.

As we sat in our living room shaking our heads in disbelief that the defending champs had lost at home to fall behind three games to none, my dad kept saying, "Too many open shots. Bad. Bad. Bad. Bad defense." He went on to say that even at his age, he could at least have put a body on those guys or challenged those jump shots and not let them have such a clean look. Lesson learned. Not to take anything anyway from the remarkable MVP-earning efforts of Joe Dumars, but a little bit of defense would have gone a long way to alter the course of that series for the Lakers. In fact, a little bit of defense did alter the series—except it was a play by Joe Dumars on the defensive end that really capped the win. He blocked a last-second jumper by David Rivers. Not only did he block it, he kept the ball from going out of bounds so that the Pistons retained possession. Many people believe that play convinced writers to vote him the Most Valuable Player of the series.

What I also remember most is Kareem coming out of the last game. The series was essentially over, and the sweep completed. With just a few seconds left, Pat Riley, a class individual, took Kareem out of the game so that the fans at the Forum could thank "The Big Guy" for all he'd done for the team and the community over the years. Magic hobbled out to center court to greet him, and the rest of the Lakers joined the two, hugging and clapping. As much as the Bad Boys liked their thug image, they revealed themselves for who they really were. They all rose to their feet along their bench and joined in the applause. I sat there thinking about how cool it would be to play in a game like that and wondered how it would feel when everyone was standing and cheering for you, thanking you for all that you'd given.

"That's sportsmanship," my dad said. "Lay it all on the line and then be a man and show the other men the respect they deserve. I hate to see the Pistons win, but I've got to respect them for that. Just wish the Lakers could have played a little bit of defense."

He got up, snapped off the television, and said to me, "You've got some homework to get done, don't you?"

I knew that he knew that I'd done all my schoolwork, but I also knew he was giving me a hint that I had a lot of different things to think about. My dad was right about the Lakers and their inability to contain the Pistons' guards. Every time one of them got loose as a result of a failed attempt to go under or over a screener or when someone failed to help, we talked about what the defender should have done. The Pistons weren't doing anything but playing basic good offense, so it was surprising that the Lakers failed to react properly. I also thought about my dad and how he watched the game. Sure, he was a big fan of the Lakers and did emotionally root for his team, but he was also able to take a step back and analyze what was happening on the court. When the Lakers failed to do something he knew they should have, he called them on it. When the Lakers lost, he didn't whine and lament about bad calls by the referees or blame sunspot activity or curse the basketball gods for the injuries that had played a crucial role in the Lakers' falling short. Instead, he talked about the X's and O's and the game's strategic elements.

Without realizing it, I was sitting in a kind of classroom. This wasn't Basketball 101, but a slightly more advanced class. In 1989, I was fourteen years old, a freshman in high school just finishing up that year when the NBA Finals were being played. I'd competed in a number of tournaments on the state and national level by then, so I was pretty far advanced in my understanding of the game. I have to give credit to my dad and to my mom for the basketball schooling they provided me at home. Generally, when coaches were introducing new concepts, talking about the finer points of a defensive scheme or an offensive approach, I was able to pick up pretty quick what they were telling me. As a result of all those tutorial sessions with my dad (I hate to make it sound as if they weren't fun because they really were a good time), I could recognize what was happening on the court and draw on the bank of the knowledge I had to make adjustments. You always hear on NCAA telecasts the announcers talking about some point guard or another whose father coached him in high school, and *coach's kid* is a kind of shorthand for a smart, heads-up type of player. Though my dad didn't formally coach me in school, he was often an assistant coach on my youth-league teams and helped out the head coaches I had in AAU ball.

The fundamental skills of defense aren't all that complicated, but implementing them and learning your responsibilities when you play man-to-man, or one of the many variations on a zone defense, are more complex. They can be reduced to about a half dozen key points. The first is posture. Most coaches don't use that term, but it's probably the best one to describe how you hold your body. Coaches are always talking about getting down on defense. They seem to want players to get their butts down closer to the floor than we do. You can't play defense well by standing straight up—particularly if you're a guard. A good rule of thumb for how low to go is to make sure that your head is at least lower than that of the man you're guarding. You also want your weight back—not on your heels but centered over your feet. One frequent mistake I see young players making is waiting back a few feet from their man until he has the ball. They then come up on him with their weight going forward. In the time it takes to shift your weight back so that you can move laterally more easily, your opponent can slip past you, taking advantage of your moving in the wrong direction. You have to keep in mind that your back is to the basket. That's the goal you're defending, so keep your weight back.

One of the toughest things for most young players to master is dribbling the basketball. That takes a lot of concentration initially and good fine-motor skills. Because of that, as a defender you want to be up on your man the majority of the time. From that close position, you can bother his ballhandling. One of the first things we all learn on offense is to keep the ball in the triple-threat position—so that you can shoot, pass, or dribble left or right. As a defender your job is to interfere with your man's ability to do any of those three things and to also dictate which of the three your man does. Ideally, if nothing else, you should be the one forcing the offensive player to go in the direction you want him to with your defensive positioning. That's being offensive on defense. Going back to what I said earlier about my skills as a left-handed player, always figure out which is your opponent's weak hand and try to get him to use that hand—you have a better chance of making a steal or forcing a dribble turnover or even a bad shot if you have him moving in the direction he'd prefer not to go.

Hand position is also important. It's too easy to say that you should play defense with your hands up. I hear youth-league coaches yelling all the time, "Hands up! Hands up!" I feel that's robbing kids of a better understanding of some of the fundamentals. Instead of hands up all the time, developing players should know that it's hands down (but palms facing up) at waist or knee level when guarding a player dribbling the ball—so that you can make swipes at it; it's one hand up and one hand down when a player is within shooting range (both to block his vision and to make an attempt at blocking the shot). One of the last key points is to deny, deny, deny! A lot of players, especially poor defenders, forget this. Your man can only score when he has the ball in his possession. It makes sense then to limit the opportunities he has to possess the ball. Denying a pass is a great way to defend. Remembering to move without the ball is important on both offense and defense. If your man doesn't have it, make sure he doesn't get it by strategically positioning yourself on the court.

Defense is all about protecting your goal. Basketball evolved a great deal when the goaltending rules were adopted—in the early days and even more recently in international basketball, shots could be interfered with while in the so-called cylinder—and that led to players developing even more skills to keep the other team from scoring. A player has to have a certain mentality and personality to really excel as a defender. Sure, some physical attributes can help—long arms and quick feet come immediately to mind—but it is a question of mind-set as much as mechanics or genetics. I take a lot of pride in my defense, and even though we usually think of great defenders as openly defiant, demonstrative kinds of guys (Dikembe Mutombo and his finger-wagging at anyone whose shot he has blocked after that player dared come in his house), you don't have to be that kind of player to succeed defensively. Shot blocks are great, but the majority of them come from a shot put up in the lane rather than from a jump shot from the perimeter. They thus generally resulted from a defensive lapse. The highest-percentage shots are dunks and layups and other close-in shots. If the ball got inside that close to the basket, something broke down in the defense that required a shot blocker to come in and save the day. A lot of blocks come after an offensive rebound has been gathered—another defensive lapse—when you see players pogo-sticking up and down and the ball ping-ponging off hands, the backboard, the rim, etc. Again, ideally the ball should have been wrapped up as a result of good defensive position on the floor. The block is kind of a last resort, and the guys on the perimeter, the ones guarding the house from the outside, are responsible for not even letting those intruders into the house.

Off the court, playing defense makes a lot of sense as well. Now that I'm a parent, I'm even more conscious of protecting what's valuable to me and what's in my literal and figurative houses. Obviously, all parents want to protect their kids from harm and then do what they can to limit the damage when the seemingly inevitable happens. I don't mean the inevitable like Tatum's cancer, though Candace and I felt a fair amount of guilt and anxiety about somehow being responsible for that, but all the other kinds of bumps, bruises, and scrapes that can happen to the ones we love. That's true whether those hurts are physical, emotional, or spiritual. My parents weren't the kind to say to us, "You'll understand when you're a parent," in the face of something bad we did or that happened to us. They may have thought it, I don't know for sure, but at least they didn't say it much that I remember.

I feel my own kids' pain acutely myself. That was one of the things that was so hard about dealing with Tatum's cancer. She couldn't express any of the anxiety she felt about all the changes in her routine that were a part of her treatment. I know that we winced every time she got any kind of shot or was stuck with a needle for an IV or anything else. It's always harder I think to be the one watching or caring for the person who is sick or injured than it is to be that person.

Fortunately for me, I didn't put my parents through too many of those "I wish I could trade places with you" moments. However, back in 1981 when I was seven years old, we had a 1976 Mercury Montego sedan that my mom drove to work. We had picked it up used, and it must have been in a wreck of some kind because even though it was only five years old, it had some issues. For one, the passenger-side door latch would intermittently malfunction. We always had trouble getting it to close properly. My dad tried to fix it, but he couldn't, so we adapted to it. We knew that once that door got properly closed, none of us would use it. Whoever was in the passenger seat just slid over to the driver's side, and when we all went somewhere and had to use the backseat, we piled in and out from that side as well. It wasn't efficient, but it was cost-effective. Dad didn't need to remind us all the time about not using that door, but he did.

One afternoon, our neighbor Larry was over. A nice enough kid, he was at least five or six years older than me and the rest of my buddies including Clarence Finley, my best friend. Larry didn't seem to mind playing sports with younger kids, and we didn't think that much about it either. The only thing that irritated us about Larry was that his parents were strict about his being home in time for dinner, and they ate earlier than the rest of us. That meant that if we were in the middle of a football game or a baseball game or whatever, when Larry's mother's voice carried over the housetops calling him to dinner, that meant that the sides would be uneven. Larry's mother was Hispanic, I think from the Dominican Republic, and I can still hear her lilting voice calling, "Lar-eeeee! Lar-eeee!" Larry also told us that his mom was fanatical about his getting home in time to wash his hands, change his clothes, then get down to the dinner table.

I can't remember why Larry was at our house, but because he was with me, and my mom had to do some grocery shopping at the Kroger nearby, Larry came along with us. I slid into the front seat, and Larry got in the back from the driver's side also. But when we got to the store, Larry opened the passenger door to climb out. My mom hadn't explained to him about the door, and he did what you'd normally do—get out on the side closest to where you're sitting. When my mom saw Larry standing there trying to close that door and it was not quite catching properly, I saw a look of "Oh my God!" on my mother's face. She'd done something wrong by not following my dad's rules about not using that door. He seemed to be the only one who could shut it properly, and the rest of us had no business messing with it. My mom stepped around the car and Larry bucked the door shut with his hip and then my mom checked it. Satisfied that it was fully shut, we went into the store and my mom did her shopping.

My mom explained to Larry about the door and apologized for being so flustered earlier. Larry said he was sorry and that if he'd known, he wouldn't have opened the door. I don't know if it was because my mom was feeling bad about things or not, but she bought Larry and me each a can of Dr Pepper from the machine just inside the door before we exited. I was pretty excited. Dr Pepper was a sweet treat and I loved it. We helped my mom put the bags in the trunk, then got in the car, avoiding the passenger-side door. I was still small enough that I couldn't really see over the dashboard, but I was happily guzzling my soda. I heard my mother say something about all the traffic, then I felt myself lurching forward and bouncing a bit as we exited the store's parking lot, crossed a lane of oncoming traffic, and made a left turn. I could hear the tires squeal just a bit as we made that turn and I jolted to my right.

The next thing I remember I was tumbling along on the pavement. The first thing I did was look for my can of Dr Pepper, but then I felt something warm and wet and sharply painful on my knee. I looked down and saw that my pants were torn open, and I imagined I saw blood and bone. I started howling, then when I looked up, I thought I was in a Road Runner cartoon. I could see a semitrailer tractor truck bearing down on me. I looked at the wheels and then turned my head to see that my mom had completed the turn to get out of the way of traffic in that lane, and I could hear her screaming out my name, panicked and tearful.

I had the good sense to get out of the road, and I sat on the shoulder crying and crying. I was upset about being hurt, but I was even more upset about seeing my mother borderline hysterical and sobbing. A bunch of cars had stopped, and all these people were looking at us as my mom hugged me and rocked me and looked over my leg. After a minute or so, she scooped me up and put me back in the car, making me sit as close to her as I could. I was probably more scared than hurt, but I could not stop crying. I was practically screaming at the top of my lungs. The whole time, Larry was just staring at us wide-eyed as if we were the craziest family he'd ever been around. As we drove home, I kept staring at that passenger door. It wasn't fully closed so it was rattling, and I could see just a bit of daylight between the edge of the door and the car's rear quarter panel.

We dropped off Larry, and my mother carried me in the house and straight to the bathroom. She found some gauze pads and a washcloth and dabbed at my wound, and that set me to howling again. Blood was still oozing, and my mother didn't have what she needed to properly clean and dress the wound, so she loaded me back in the car and we went back to the Kroger, which also had a pharmacy. It may have been my being back at the scene of the accident, but I was still crying hysterically. Later on I thought that maybe it was as much over the loss of my Dr Pepper as it was over my leg—after all, my body could replace the blood I lost but not that treat. My mom initially wanted me to go in with her, thinking that maybe the pharmacist would recommend what to do for the wound. I was still chest-heaving crying, and either she didn't want to aggravate my injury by moving me again or she didn't want to haul a crying child through the store, so she left me in the car. I can still picture the wide-eyed stares of people as they passed by the car and saw me in there with my leg propped up, a bloody bit of cloth pressed against my leg, and me bawling like a newborn baby.

Eventually my mom got me back home and poured some hydrogen peroxide on the wound, which had finally stopped bleeding, then put a bit of Neosporin on it and a gauze pad and wrapped it with tape. Though no longer crying, I was still breathing hard and whimpering, hoping I guess to earn some sympathy points that I could use to my advantage. The worst part was the anticipation of the searing sting from that hydrogen peroxide. I didn't know what it was, but it sounded nasty, and the only thing I'd ever had put on my cuts and scrapes before was a bit of Bactine or some Mercurochrome. When that hydrogen peroxide bubbled, I was scared, thinking that it was going to eat away at my skin, but strangely it didn't hurt.

My mom told me to keep my leg elevated and propped some pillows behind me and one behind my knee so that I could be comfortable and rest. I was exhausted from all my crying, not from the trauma of having fallen out of the car. I wanted to get outside and play, and I spent most of my time "resting" scheming about how I could manage that. I also thought about how I didn't like seeing the lines of worry etched across my mother's forehead. Normally she was happy and upbeat, and seeing her downcast made me sad. She had given me all kinds of hugs and kisses on the head and face while she was tending to me, and I liked all that attention.

Later that afternoon my dad came back with my sister, and I could hear some murmuring from the kitchen. The sound reminded me of the wasps that had taken up residence in the eaves of our roof—an agitated kind of buzzing. I never knew if my mom told my dad what happened. As an adult, I can see her being upset about our having an unsafe car and him being upset that we'd violated one of the rules he'd laid down about not opening that door. We were the type of family who kept things to ourselves, so it doesn't surprise me that I have no recollection of my dad coming in to check on me. I also realize today that things could have turned out far worse than they did. My mother didn't lecture me on being careful or talk about what might have happened. The incident was quietly filed away. In my family we didn't speculate much, at least out loud, on what might have been or expend much energy on what-ifs. The here and now and what to do about it took precedence over pondering unproductively.

The next day I was back up and around, and I didn't really give the incident much thought. The car door continued to be a problem, but none of us needed to be reminded that we had to be careful. Sometimes, you have to take one for the team, and that may have been my role that day. While I still have a scar on my knee, it's barely noticeable. I wasn't scarred psychologically either. Within the next week or so, I was back to doing daredevil tricks on my bike. I can't say that I'm an overprotective or worrywart parent as a result of my experiences and knowing what could happen to my kids. Tatum's cancer put a scare in us, but at least it happened at an age when she won't have any memory of it. I know from psychology classes that the brain is a pretty amazing tool and that a lot of people who have gone through bad things have no conscious recollection of them. The brain knows what to protect us from without our telling ourselves to forget unpleasant or painful experiences.

Larry and I got along after that as if nothing had happened and he hadn't played any part in what could have been a serious accident. The next time I saw him he did ask how my knee was, and I said I was okay, and that was that. No grudges held. No banishment of Larry from the house. I can see a lot of positives from that incident and our response to it. We kept things in perspective, and despite my hysterical crying, I think my mother knew that nothing was seriously wrong with me, that I had only a nasty bit of what I've learned cyclists call road rash. While we didn't just rub some dirt on it and send me back in the game, we did keep moving forward. My mother did say that she offered up some prayers of thanks at Sunday services and also asked God to keep His eye out for me.

The only time I can recall testing that protection, but not realizing it at the time, was when a few years later during winter I was out with my cousin Byron and my friend Todd. My grandmother lived in an area of Little Rock that we all called Granny Mountain. We didn't know its official name was Granite Mountain, because of a granite quarry that bordered the area. We loved to play there because of all its mounds and hills of dirt that had been scooped out and piled up. It was a little bit of kid heaven on earth, a great place for hide-and-seek and war games, with a steady supply of rocks and pebbles as ammunition. Part of the quarry had flooded, forming a lake. After we had been out messing around for a few hours, we decided to head back inside. None of us felt like taking the long way around, so we walked across the ice on the quarry's lake. Didn't give it a thought. We made it safely home, but having been back there as an adult and seen that lake, I get the shivers.

We'd get a bit of snow each winter in Little Rock, but it never stays very, very cold for long—not long enough for a solid sheet of ice to have formed on that quarry lake. I also realize now how deep that lake was. If any of us had fallen through what had to have been thin ice, we wouldn't have survived. There's the old statement about ignorance being bliss, and I guess that someone was watching out for us that day since we made it across safely. But I was thinking about that walk across that lake the other day in light of this idea of protection. Obviously we all want to keep our loved ones free from harm. One of the things that I wonder about with my stepson Marshall and with Tatum and Drew and Chloe is how much to warn them about the dangers in the world. As I sit here writing, a gunman in Alabama opened fire and killed ten people—some family members and others—before ending his own life. The headlines in the papers also told of a school in Germany where a former student opened fire in several classrooms and later in town. He killed fifteen others before he was shot and killed by police.

I wonder how you balance keeping your kids safe, letting them be kids, and making them alert to the possible dangers lurking out there. I grew up in Little Rock at a time when we could play outside and our parents didn't worry about our being kidnapped, wounded, or killed in a drive-by gang-related shooting. We were pretty free to just roam around, and just as I crossed that quarry lake without thinking that something bad could happen, I went about my business every day kind of carefree. Only now when I look back do I realize that some of those dangers were lurking in the Little Rock of my era, and probably in every other community. The media have made us more aware of those dangers, and you can't turn on any news program without being warned about the potential dangers of something, whether it's the lead in toys, some cancer-causing agent in plastic, or some food. We as parents can make all kinds of rules and guidelines, but just as with that car door, something unexpected can come along when you think you've got things in control and it can all still go wrong.

I know that my parents did their best to protect us from some of the harsher realities of life. As I got older, I sometimes wondered if maybe we were too sheltered. As I said, we weren't the most openly emotional and communicative of families, but we had one another's back.

Neither of my parents grew up in Little Rock, which may explain why they never talked to me or my siblings about race and the history of Little Rock and desegregation and the civil rights struggle. I don't know if my parents struggled against any kind of discrimination as they grew up. Not until I was in school and we studied the civil rights movement and later at the University of Arkansas, Little Rock, when I took some African-American studies classes did I really learn about the role my hometown played. One of the first things we all learned about was the 1954 Supreme Court decision *Brown v. Board of Education,* which ruled that separate but equal facilities and in particular segregation in public schools was illegal. We lived in a fairly racially mixed area, my high school had about the same number of black students as white students, and even at UALR the students were almost one-third black, so the idea that at one time schools were legally all-white and all-black seemed almost unthinkable and definitely outside my experience.

I can't say that I was outraged to learn that Little Rock Central High's decision to desegregate voluntarily (as if they really had a choice) was so contentious and divisive in the community, but it definitely made me think. That it took three years after *Brown v. Board of Education* for this to happen surprised me. I also wondered why the Little Rock Nine wasn't a group that I had heard of and been told about in great detail somewhere along the line. Thanks to the efforts of the Little Rock Nine Foundation, the contributions of those nine individuals who braved angry mobs in September of 1957, who were turned back by Arkansas National Guardsmen under the order of Governor Orval Faubus (under the guise of protecting them), and who ultimately entered the school escorted by members of the U.S. Army's 101st Airborne Division on September 25 won't be forgotten.

It took until 2005, but a memorial statue was finally dedicated to the Little Rock Nine, who withstood ongoing harassment, with the governor ordering all Little Rock schools shut down in 1958 (only to be reopened following a U.S. Supreme Court ruling in 1959). The Little Rock Nine Civil Rights Memorial stands on the grounds of the state capitol. Nine life-size figures are accompanied by inscriptions of inspirational words they provided. Only when I read some of their statements did I realize that without coming out and stating it, my parents had been telling me about the Little Rock Nine and what they represented. Carlotta Walls was very much speaking for me when she wrote, "Hard work, determination, persistence, and faith in God were lessons learned from my parents, Cartelyou and Juanita Walls. I was only doing what was right."

The words Melba Patillo provided pretty much sum up my parents', and in particular my mother's, message regarding race: "The task that remains is to embrace our interdependence—to see ourselves reflected in every other human being, and to respect & honor differences." That was communicated to me loud and clear, but at times static interfered and the message was lost.

I inherited one other thing from my parents along with my penchant for basketball—a tendency to internalize things too much. I wish that I knew more about my parents' experiences, particularly my dad's experiences, because I think that they had a direct effect on me and my family. When I was in high school, my father stopped going to work at the post office. I never knew exactly why, but my mother did tell me that he hadn't been fired. He quit. Every now and then after that, I'd hear my dad make some passing and vague reference to being passed over. He had worked there for twelve or thirteen years, and from what I could piece together, he hadn't been promoted and, with the exception of a cost-of-living increase, hadn't even received a raise. I guess he just got fed up with that and quit.

Being out of work did not agree with my dad—he was the driving force in our have-to-be-occupied, have-to-be-productive lives. So, when he left his job with the post office, we all figured that he'd get on somewhere else as soon as possible. That didn't happen. In some ways fortunately and in other ways unfortunately, I was getting older and more involved in school activities, so I was able to distance myself from the home front a bit more. But it was sad to see my dad just hanging out at home, looking defeated. I didn't want to think about it, but on those rare occasions when I did, I wondered what had happened to the guy who'd preached to me and who'd demonstrated to me all the value of hard work and who had once embodied the idea that you don't give up. I think that was the hardest thing for me to deal with, but even in seeming to give up, my dad was teaching me a lesson.

My mom stepped up and did the best she could. We had gone from being a two-income family doing fairly well financially to a family with two incomes but only one person employed. My mom shouldered the burden and got another job part-time in the evenings to supplement her bank income. Through it all, she never complained, at least not to me, and though some of the extras we'd once enjoyed became a little more scarce, we definitely never went hungry, and my parents definitely never stopped supporting my siblings and me. If my parents didn't always sit right next to each other during my games, they were both very much a presence in my life, and continue to be, and for that I'm grateful.

My dad stuck around for my sister and me—Duane was long since gone and on his own—until she graduated from high school. My parents split up officially and divorced many years down the line. They clearly weren't in a productive relationship while I was in high school and college, but I still believe that I wouldn't be where I am today without them both. My dad has always been a presence in my life. On more than one occasion, as I was walking to class while at UALR, I heard footsteps coming up behind me. There was my dad. What I didn't know was that he had talked to the coaches at UALR and told them, "Anything going on with Derek, you call me." So if I had a semester when my grades weren't as good as they should have been, or if I was spending too much time socializing or chasing girls or whatever, he'd show up. His "Look here, man, you need to straighten this out" talks always had the desired effect on me.

Like any man, I want to have my father's respect, and I believe I do and that I've earned it. Still, neither of us seems all that willing or capable of ending that bit of disconnect between us. Candace encourages me to reach out to him, and my dad and I do talk, but something is still between us, this unspoken lack of understanding, because we haven't talked about the breakup of my parents' marriage and what went on with his job. I don't mean to trivialize this, but sometimes I wish that this whole thing were as easy as going to a zone defense and forcing the other team to beat us from the outside. I think my dad and I are wired that way—see a problem, fix it. Focus on a solution. Unfortunately the kinds of defenses we put up as humans when it comes to relationships and emotions aren't that easy to master.

I only hope that I'm able to provide my kids with more and better access to me and the truth about who I am and how I got to be this way. My stepson is at the age now that I was when my parents became estranged. I've become very conscious of my interactions with him. Again, I give my dad a lot of credit for helping me become the man I am today, but he did a lot of things to help me without really explaining what he was doing or why. I told you the flak jacket story earlier, and working out with it certainly helped me, but my father basically said, "Here. Put this on. Run up and down this hill." I felt that I couldn't really ask questions, and as irritating as it can be as a parent to hear "Why?" all the time, understanding life requires asking questions.

I sometimes wonder if my dad had some master plan for me, if he saw in me the potential to be an NBA player and worked out a blueprint for my success. If he had, it would have been great to know that he had that kind of belief in me. Eventually he showed me that he did, but that was after the fact. A flak jacket's purpose is to provide the wearer with protection. Problem is, as much as it can keep things from getting in, it can prevent things from getting out. I need to keep working at this, but with my kids, my wife, and in my other relationships, I want to let my guard down, let them know that they are welcome to score in my house, and that I'm not going to block their shot and not isolate so much of my life from them.

I also want them to know that I really do have my parents to thank in so many ways for my achievements. I know that they struggled with some issues and that they didn't always let me in on what was going on or why, but if they didn't talk about these things, it was because they were trying to protect us. In other cases, I'm grateful for what they did to keep us safe from all kinds of harm—emotional and physical.

I don't know if it was a result of their plan to keep us busy, but I avoided many of the pitfalls that plague young people whether they live in the city, the suburbs, or the country. As much as I thought growing up that Little Rock was a tight-knit, little community, it wasn't immune to some of the troubles that affect bigger cities. Candace, who grew up in Los Angeles, lived in a very different world from mine, in some ways because I wasn't aware of what was going on. As an athlete and a kid with involved parents, I lived in a kind of protective bubble. Sometimes that bubble got burst—one time in the most violent of ways.

In eighth grade I was attending Henderson Junior High, which was pretty calm and peaceful. A few guys got into fights on the playground when a game got a little out of control or when rumor had it that somebody had disrespected someone else. I got into a few of those little fights myself in elementary school, but they were generally broken up by the time any of the faculty came along, and no one got in any serious trouble. Something started to change while I was at Henderson, though I was too busy with basketball and my studies to pay that much attention to it. One signal was that we were locked out of the building until ten minutes before the first class at eight o'clock. Prior to that, we'd been able to congregate inside the building. None of us really minded having to wait outside, except on cold or rainy days, and we'd get a game going.

No one ever told us the reason for the new policy, but rumors were that every morning our lockers were being searched. That meant one thing—drugs. My mother and father had laid down the law early on about drugs. With my half brother's problems with substance abuse taking a toll on all of us at home, I knew better than to mess with that stuff. I'd seen how sad Duane's problems had made my mother and father, and I didn't want to do anything that would add to their pain. I'd heard enough antidrug slogans and seen enough ads and gone through enough classroom education that I felt pretty confident that I was not ever going to be tempted by them. I knew some kids were doing drugs, but I never saw anyone doing them, and I can't think of a time when someone showed or offered them to me. I was kept so busy and was under either my parents' direct care or the care of a respected coach or teacher that I didn't have the opportunity to be around those kinds of kids.

Even if I had been directly exposed to them, I don't think that I would have tried anything. Back then, and even for a long time after, no matter where I went, I felt that my father was in the room with me. I could feel his presence and hear his voice. So if I was ever anywhere kids were doing drugs, smoking cigarettes, or drinking, I'm pretty sure I would have got out of there as fast as I could. I knew that there was a line, and if I crossed it, I would have to pay for it dearly. I couldn't imagine any feeling a drug or a drink could produce that would be worth putting up with what my dad would do to me if he ever found out. And I had no doubt that he would.

I didn't need any reminders of the consequences of getting involved in things illegal, dangerous, or both. Unfortunately, I got a big-time reminder in eighth grade. One morning we were all out on the playground/parking lot. We were hooping it when I saw something out of the corner of my eye. Someone was moving fast toward a kid who was standing in a big cluster of my classmates. This guy raised his hand, I heard a pop, then I saw someone fall to the ground. At first it didn't register with me or with the rest of my schoolmates that someone had been shot. The gunshot wasn't a loud blast, and with all of us out there talking and laughing, it was pretty muffled. We were all so slow to react that before anyone started yelling or screaming, the kid who'd done it had moved off campus. We all learned later that he was arrested somewhere else in Little Rock.

A bunch of kids were around the victim, but when the faculty and security staff came out, they pushed them away and I could see that he was a kid from my math class. I didn't know him well, but he was not someone I would think would end up getting shot. I couldn't think of anyone I knew or had a class with who seemed like someone somebody else would want dead. Eventually, we were all herded into the school and told to get to our first period classes. My teacher made a halfhearted attempt to get us to quiet down so she could conduct class, but she eventually realized that it was not going to happen. We could see the flash of lights and hear all kinds of sirens and the squawk of police radios. By second period things had quieted down outside, so we went through the motions. I sat in class thinking about what I had kind of but not really seen. Everything was just a rush and a blur, then that little firecracker sound.

No one had asked us what we had seen, and the police hadn't come in to take any kind of statements, and I knew that I couldn't identify who did the shooting. A lot of other kids were closer to the action, and I wondered if they had been taken away to make a statement. What had gone on was so far from my experience that it was almost impossible to think logically about any of it. It was truly the definition of surreal. Bells rang, teachers talked, we shuffled to the next class. Just before noon, the principal got on the intercom to announce that the shooting victim had died en route to the hospital. That's when things got really weird. I could hear shouts and screams and a whole chorus of "Oh my God" and "No" echoing down the hallways. The principal told us that school was dismissed for the day. Once the buses arrived, we'd leave.

I wandered out to the parking lot. It felt so strange standing there, knowing that the last time I'd been outside the school some kid I knew had lost his life. To add to the bizarre mass, a television news crew was on school grounds. Of all the kids milling around out there, they came up to me to get my reaction and ask if I knew the victim. I remember thinking how sad it was that he went from being a kid with a name, a boy in my math class, a guy like me with a locker combination, to a victim, a dead person. I told the reporter that he was in my math class but I didn't know him well. I also said that it didn't make sense, that I couldn't understand why someone would do that to him and that the person shouldn't have.

Of course, my parents heard about the shooting and my school being let out. My mother came home from the bank and picked up my sister and me from school. She was as shaken as we were, if not more. She told us how glad she was that we were okay and asked that we all say a prayer for the boy who'd died. I was kind of numb. None of it made any sense to me. We all watched the local evening news, and when the newscaster and on-scene reporter mentioned that gang activity was suspected as part of the motive, that didn't make any sense either. My interview came on after that and jolted me out of my numbed state. There I was on television being critical of whoever had done this. I had said what any normal person would have, but if this was a gang thing, would they come after me because of what I'd said? I kept my mouth shut and didn't tell either of my parents how I felt. I didn't want to worry them, but I was concerned that I'd accidentally broken some kind of gang rule by saying what I had.

That night I lay in bed, and the reality of what had taken place really started to sink in. This was my first real encounter with death, and even though I was already thirteen, the thought that death could come so quickly, that one minute you could be talking with your friends and the next minute bleeding out on the ground, scared me. Added to that, I couldn't escape the thought that whoever were in that gang were going to come after me, so I had nightmares for weeks. I was also troubled that this kid, who I thought was as normal as me and my friends, was in a gang and had done something to make someone want to shoot him. Who knew what else was going on around me that I didn't know about? I was grateful that my parents were so active in my life and kept me from those kinds of things.

Not until I went to college and later moved to L.A. to play for the Lakers did I really find out what was going on in parts of Little Rock and even in my own backyard and at other schools. I saw an HBO documentary called *Gang War: Bangin' in Little Rock* about how gang violence had erupted in my hometown. I had thought of my neighborhood and really all of Little Rock as this nice, safe community, but here was all this stuff going on that I just hadn't seen. The documentary opened with an introduction to North Little Rock coroner Steve Nawojczyk as the narrator. After seeing hundreds of dead bodies over ten years, he is fed up with the killings and decides to do something about it. Each day Steve visits the most dangerous neighborhoods in Little Rock and attempts to calm tensions between gangs such as the Crips, Bloods, Hoover Folks, OGC, Vice Lords, and many more. A lot of these gangs originated in the inner-city ghettos of Los Angeles, New York, and Chicago, but they have migrated to Arkansas and elsewhere and expanded with the easy access to guns.

I was disturbed to see guys I'd gone to school with on-screen talking about the gang lifestyle. I couldn't believe it. Sitting in the place I'd rented in a high-rise in Marina Del Rey, California, I see a little dude who was gangbanging and I'd been in the choir with him! How could that kid have gone in one direction and me in another? I guess that while I was at basketball practice, other guys were out in the streets being exposed to things that I hadn't been exposed to. Besides being sad that these guys felt that they had no alternative to crime and drugs, I was even more grateful for what my parents had done for me.

Though this is kind of a cliché and not necessarily a cool way to think, sports really does teach you a lot about teamwork and dedication. At the time when I thought of the Penick Boys Club and Coach Ripley at Parkview and how he kept the gym open, I assumed that was just the way it was everywhere. I now realize that programs like that and people like that who work in their communities and offer after-school programs or who run midnight basketball leagues are really the best defenders. They're offering kids refuge and hope. I've always felt comfortable out on the basketball court, but I can't imagine what it must be like for some kids who feel that the only place they can go and be safe is in a gym.

I'm fortunate to be in a position, and to work in an industry that has the desire and the ability, to give back to the communities that support us. I know that I've been able to help, both directly and indirectly, in some of the efforts to better the lives of kids who are far less fortunate than I was back then. The mission statement of the Lakers Youth Foundation sums up our goal nicely:

"The Los Angeles Lakers Youth Foundation's goal is to assist nonprofit community organizations based on need. With the Foundation's focus on the use of sports to promote education, teamwork and self-esteem among Los Angeles area youth, our fundraising directly supports these initiatives by providing financial assistance to children and local youth programs."

Among the many things that we do, one simple one produces great results. Because of the pounding that our feet take in practice and in games, we go through dozens of pairs of shoes each season. I generally have a game pair—one for home games and one for away games. I also have practice pairs that I rotate. Generally, I only wear my game shoes for three or four games before they break down and I have to start a new pair. If I wear a practice shoe for more than a week, that's pushing it to its limit. That may sound excessive and like a huge waste, but nearly every one of the pairs I discard I sign and turn over to our team's communications director. They then get donated to a variety of community organizations, who then auction or raffle them off to raise funds. We also use some of those items and jerseys and other memorabilia in our own team-sponsored auctions.

We have to thank the fans who generously bid on the stuff to help raise money for the Lakers Youth Foundation. Since 1999, we've raised more than $1.1 million through these auctions, which take place at every home game. Some of that money goes toward a favorite project of all of ours—the Lakers' basketball court refurbishments. In combination with the NBA Cares Live, Learn, or Play program, we've renovated courts throughout the city, recently at Hawthorne High School, at the Boys and Girls Club of Venice, and at the Boys and Girls clubs in Santa Monica and Hollywood. You read those names and you might think, why there? No matter how glamorous you might think the address, some kids in those communities are still underserved and their clubs underfunded. We've done our fair share in all parts of the city.

I've attended many of these opening ceremonies, and it is always great to see the kids, parents, and local community leaders show up. We often conduct a clinic after the dedication ceremony, and it is incredibly gratifying to see the kids out on the court running around and having a great time. It took me a while to get used to seeing the kids looking at me all bug-eyed. I didn't know that a lot of them had a hard time believing that we players were real. They'd seen us on television, but seeing us in person boggled their minds. Getting down on the younger kids' level helps a lot—at these times I'm glad that I'm not a seven-footer—and shaking their hand or putting your hand on their shoulder makes it all the more real for them and they soon forget that they were in awe.

As much as I enjoy and find valuable the court-renovation program, I'm a huge fan of the NBA Cares Lakers Reading Centers. Last October, I attended the first opening of the season at the East L.A. Boys and Girls Club. Toyota partnered with us on the renovation project. We remodeled three rooms and a hallway at the sixty-year-old club. Fresh paint, new floor coverings, furniture, wall decorations, books, audio/visual equipment, framed photos—all went in thanks to the foundation and Toyota's Project Rebound. Along with me, Pau Gasol, Sasha Vujacic, Andrew Bynum, Luke Walton, and several Lakers Girls joined Clyde Drexler and other folks in attendance.

Asked to speak, I let the kids, about a hundred of them, know that their reading and learning center was a sign that adults do care about them, and their futures. I told them how important the Penick Boys and Girls Club was in my life. "I got into trouble there," I admitted to the students, "but a lot of my dreams started there too."

After that, I got to do one of my favorite things. I went into the Lakers Reading Room, a space where only elementary-school kids were allowed. Pau, Clyde, and I took turns reading aloud to the kids from *Curious George Visits the Library*. I loved seeing the kids sitting there getting into the story. Every night I'm home, I read a book to the twins, and it's my favorite part of the day. Later we joined the other guys in The Club, the room designed for teens, and laughed at one another as Sasha, who had an injured ankle, attempted to keep up with some of the teens playing the Dance Dance Revolution. While they used the floor pad, Sasha did his thing with the handheld controller. He was pretty impressive.

The great thing about the club and the additions and renovations we helped bring about is that they provide a safe and caring environment for kids. It isn't all about the basketball at those places. Kids can get into art, get help with homework, or just hang out and be free of some of the negative influences that are out there preying on them. With our schedules, it is sometimes hard to give up what little free time we players have to attend these events. I'm always glad that I do. As much as I might be grumbling after practice, after a late-night flight, or after a game the evening before, I walk out of those buildings energized after seeing those kids and how excited they are to see us and to have a great place to hang out. Frequently after attending those events, I get caught up in the rest of my life and those memories and feelings recede. But a few weeks later, a stack of letters will be sitting on the stool in front of my locker. Each of them will have the telltale handwriting of one of the little guys or girls from an event. Reading their thank-you notes and hearing how much it meant to them for us to be there makes it all real again. Their reaching out to us and communicating their feelings breaks down whatever defenses I might have built up. Once again, the message is clear: From those to whom much has been given, much is expected.

While we can't protect every kid in L.A. and defend them from all of the influences out there, a good offense is still the best defense. It would be easy for all of us to feel that the problems of this world are too large and too complex for any of us to make a difference in solving. We shouldn't ever underestimate the power of right action. Finding that balance between being overprotective and indifferent, just as you need to keep your body weight centered over your feet as a defender on the court, is crucial to our success as parents and adults.

CHAPTER SIX

Rebounding:

Bouncing Back from Disappointment

By now the story is legendary. Michael Jordan, considered by many to be the greatest basketball player in history, was cut from the basketball team his sophomore year in high school. As Jordan himself later said on his website, "I think that not making the Varsity team drove me to really work at my game, and also taught me that if you set goals, and work hard to achieve them—the hard work can pay off." I heard that story myself when I was in school, and while I didn't ever fail to make the team at any point in my career, I experienced my fair share of ups and downs then and even today. Though Michael Jordan wasn't known as, or expected to be, a great rebounder in the strictest sense, his career totals are still impressive. He averaged a little more than 6 rebounds a game during the regular season, and nearly a half rebound more than that in the play-offs. Even more impressive, when he needed to or wanted to, he could really go after them. His career one-game high was 18, which he accomplished twice. That's impressive, but pales in comparison to what the greatest rebounders could do. To put Jordan's number in perspective, Wilt Chamberlain had 55 rebounds in a game in 1960. That man had a nose for the ball and went after it with a ferocity that I can only imagine.

Rebounding, like playing defense, is almost all about hustle. You need to learn a couple techniques, and a few truly great rebounders either had an instinctive ability or developed a talent for reading shots that enabled them to put themselves in the right position to gather in the loose ball, but desire really makes the difference. Being in the right place is important in almost anything you do, and knowing such things as that nearly three-quarters of all misses from the corner or from the wing go long and end up on the weak side (the side opposite where the ball was shot from) definitely helps. Being able to time your leap correctly also helps a lot when it comes to rebounding, but you don't necessarily need big hops to be a good rebounder. I see that the vast majority of rebounds are made when the ball is below the rim. It's more of a question of how quickly and how often you go up rather than how high.

If you can get off your feet quickly, come back down, and go up again (and sometimes again and again), then you can develop into a great rebounder. When I'm watching a game and see a big man go up for a rebound, see it tapped back up, see that big guy go up after it again and maybe multiple times, I marvel at that desire combined with athleticism and skill. As a perimeter player, I'm often an outside observer of those duels and am fascinated. I don't know if anyone who hasn't played the game on a highly competitive level can appreciate how much energy gets expended then. Seeing guys as large as Karl Malone, Dikembe Mutombo, Yao Ming, and others get off the

ground and go after the ball is just one of the things that make basketball such an amazing sport to watch.

One of my coaches, I can't remember who, said to think of every
shot that goes up as a pass to you. That means that you have to develop an awareness of where the ball is going, figure out where it
might end up, and go after at it as if it were intended for you. Some
of that awareness is a physical thing you can do, but most of it is
mental. I think that coach said to think of a rebound as a pass because, when your team has possession of the ball and a pass comes
your way, it is an opportunity for your team (or you) to shoot and
score. We all want to contribute offensively, and thinking offensively
about rebounds is important, even if it is a defensive rebound—your
team gets the ball and a chance to score. The more possessions you
have, the more chances you have to score. Again, elementary, fundamental stuff.

I started off talking about Michael Jordan and his rebounding not
so much because of his literal ability to rebound the basketball, but
because of how he came back from injury, adversity, and even from
retirement. As I said, I faced a few ups and downs in my career, as has
nearly every other player who played the game, and I really think that
the test of any man is what he does after he's either been knocked
down or otherwise suffered a tough period in his career or his personal
life. I've been fortunate that, because of my upbringing, the coaches
and teachers I've worked under, and simply the grace of God, my
down times have been brief (though they didn't feel that way at the
time) and I've always experienced some upswing. This hasn't been
just a matter of perspective, finding that proverbial silver lining;
things have continued to get better and better for me on and off the
court.

In so many ways, my basketball career doesn't make any sense. I
don't have that dramatic comeback from being cut that Michael Jordan does, and I didn't make his side venture into professional baseball, nor did I suffer the devastating loss of my father like him. But I
think of myself as having faced and passed a lot of tests along the way.
I sometimes feel as if every season I've been in the NBA, I've faced

more than one moment when I had to prove that I belonged. I've accumulated enough experiences over the years and have proved myself enough times that I feel confident when those tests come. Even before I had accumulated all those experiences and could draw on them as evidence when faced with a jury of my peers and coaches and management, I've always felt inside that I could succeed. The trouble was, sometimes I kept those feelings so deep inside that my quiet confidence went unheard in the rush of noise that other people made. It wasn't only my father who urged me to be a little more vocal, a little more outgoing and willing to let myself shine. My basketball abilities have never held me back as much as who I am.

One factor that worked against me was that I 100 percent bought into the coaches' saying there was no *I* in *team*. From the time I began playing competitively to today, coaches have preached the team concept, with everyone to be on the same page, sacrificing individual achievement for team success. I believe that's necessary, but something is also to be said for selfishness. That's where competitiveness comes into play. Every guy in the NBA has to believe that he deserves to start or that he is good enough to start or to play significant minutes. If you didn't take that attitude, I don't see how you would have got into the league in the first place. Just because you don't vocalize that—and sometimes players do it in the most negative of ways by complaining to the media or to their teammates about playing time—doesn't mean that you don't feel that.

What has held me back, again from the time I was a ten-year-old making my first venture into the "elite" world of youth AAU basketball to national tournaments to the NBA, is that people have mistaken my being quiet with my not really caring. Because I didn't put on a big show of emotion whether I was on the court playing or accepting a coach's decision to bench me, people felt that I lacked intensity or faith in myself. I know a lot of people struggle with that same issue. In a kind of variation on the saying that the squeaky wheel gets the grease, the one who plays loudest, the one who hits the biggest notes, often gets the solo. He may not be the best player, but he gets the most attention. Obviously, I overcame the misperception about me to get where I am today, but it still crops up too frequently for me.

I believe that results should speak for themselves, but they don't always do that. When I was much younger, I took being passed over for playing time or recognition very, very personally. It bothered me that at every level I had to prove myself and my worth to the team again and again. What enabled me to do that is the deep confidence I have in my ability to play this game at a high level. A lot of my early success helped me, but at those earliest stages, I did need evidence to support my case even to myself. Belief in oneself isn't enough. You have to have some evidence, some success you can point to, no matter how small, and use that as a foundation on which to place your faith in your abilities. I played with enough guys at various levels who had complaints similar to mine—that they weren't getting enough playing time, that they were more skilled than the guy ahead of them in the rotation, etc. Not all of them could say as confidently as I could that not only could I show the coach if given the chance, but when I'd been given the chance, I had succeeded.

The difference is this: I never used lack of playing time, lack of a coach's faith in me, or his lack of praise as an excuse for those few times when I didn't perform up to expectations. That was a place I could not let myself go—to Excuseland. If I was given an opportunity and proved myself capable of starting or contributing significant minutes, then had that opportunity disappear or diminish, it was never because I got too comfortable or complacent. Thanks to my mother and father, I really lived the motto "What have you done today to make yourself better?" Maybe it was my generally shy and somewhat withdrawn nature, but I never had to worry about anyone thinking that my head had got too big.

Being consistently effective at what you do is a double-edged sword. When you can be counted on to deliver consistent results, it is easy to wind up overlooked or underestimated. I still battle against that too frequently. I know my opponents' tendencies after so long, but that doesn't mean that I don't suffer from battle fatigue, a kind of "not this again" frustration. I know that some of this can sound pretty out of context, and I'm grateful for the career that I've had and my opportunities, but the just-happy-to-be-here mentality is a surefire way to end up not being there for long. Everyone wants happy campers on their team, and you have to toe that fine line between easy to get along with and easy to forget. How you handle those times when you need to make your dissatisfaction known is a topic for another chapter, but at times I've made myself heard. Picking and choosing those spots is all a part of growing up.

A huge part of my growing up and learning lessons about the game and all that goes with it took place in those first few years in AAU ball. I feel that I was being prepared for an NBA career from early on, and the ups and downs of those AAU and scholastic years made my days in the NBA feel comfortable in some regards and a little bit too much like déjà vu in others.

In Little Rock, the schools didn't have organized teams until you reached junior high—seventh, eighth, and ninth grades. That's where Boys Club and AAU ball came in. Their seasons didn't overlap, so when I was ten and playing in my first AAU games, I went from being on the Kinko Sixers in the Penick Boys Club to playing for the Sixers in AAU under twelve tournaments. In the state championship game we faced off against another team of guys from the Penick Boys Club, the Arkansas Spirits. We were all from the local area, but the Spirits were made up of guys from Boys Clubs all around the state. Unfortunately we lost, but my buddy and teammate Corliss Williamson and I were asked to play for the Spirits in the national tournament to be held in Orlando, Florida. At the time, for the under-twelve-year-old tournament, only the state champion was eligible for the national title. AAU rules allowed a tournament-eligible team to adjust their roster between the state and the national tournament, so the Spirits weren't doing anything out of the ordinary. I didn't think at all about the kid whose spot I might have taken or whose minutes I would be taking. That didn't mean that I had no compassion or loyalty; instead, I was really torn over what to do. I knew that this was a great opportunity to play in a big-time tournament, but I was loyal to my coach and the guys on our team. Coach Barry of the Spirits and my dad had coached together, and that may have prompted some of what happened next.

I was already conflicted about whether to play with the Spirits and then the coach of the Sixers made my decision even tougher. He told Corliss and me that if we went to play with the Spirits, we could forget about ever playing for the Sixers again. Here I was a ten-year-old, and I'd developed close friendships with all these guys on the Sixers and I didn't know anybody on that other team, so it was hard for me to think of going with the Spirits, and then I received this threat. I was too young to understand everything that was going on, but my parents stepped in and said that I was going regardless of what the Sixers coach said or did.

All I wanted was to play ball and have my friends, and my "Why can't we all get along?" mentality seems pretty naive to me today. It took some time, but based on this and on some later experiences, I realized that not everyone in a position of authority had my best interests at heart. It saddens me to realize that all kinds of politics and personal relationships and possible jealousies and infighting affected things when I was only ten. Fortunately, I was only vaguely aware of what was going on, and I got a huge boost of confidence. Here was a state championship team who'd played together all that season choosing me to go with them to the national tournament.

My parents couldn't make it for the whole tournament, but Corliss's family did. In fact, we left a couple of days early so that they could enjoy some time in Florida before the tournament started. We stopped in Pensacola before Orlando. It's funny to think of it now, but even at ten, I was already acting like a little pro ballplayer. Instead of my remembering the two days in Pensacola and running around and frolicking in the ocean and eating ice cream or fried shrimp or even enjoying road-trip snacks in their car, that part is almost a complete blank. I was a serious little dude and all I could think about was the games coming up. I'm sure the trip was fun, but we had business to take care of. This was the first time I'd be playing against kids I truly didn't know. In the Boys Club league and in the

AAU games, I was always going up against familiar competition. Even if you didn't know the kids personally or go to school with them, the Little Rock and the Arkansas leagues were small enough that eventually you knew and played against just about everyone enough times so that you knew who they were.

I didn't really even think about making the adjustment to the Spirits. Though I'd never played with them before and only faced them a couple times, we didn't run such sophisticated offenses or defenses that we had to do a lot of chalk talk. We had a couple of practices in Arkansas before we left, but once the tourney got under way, it was play, play, play. We relied on everybody's having an understanding of the fundamentals, and that worked well for us. Even then I was what sometimes gets called a floor general, which sounds as much like a vacuum cleaner as it does a necessary role on a basketball team. I guess I don't like *floor general* because it implies a guy who gives orders but doesn't get involved in the hard work. I liked being in charge, but I also liked being involved in every aspect of the game.

I don't know if it was my floor leadership or just sheer talent, but we finished third in the nation that year. Losing in the semifinals was tough, but I'm proud that we came back in the third-place game and won. I kind of miss the "consolation final"—a nice euphemism for the third-place game—in the NCAA tournament. I figure if you make the Final Four, you ought to at least know if you finished third or fourth. If you're going to play, then keep score. I don't think any kid who when asked what place his team came in would say, "Consolation." There's no consolation in losing or not knowing if you were third or fourth. I'm also a believer that finishing second is the same as being first loser—though as I've got older and played more and had more experiences, I'm not quite as disconsolate of a loser as I was—just a little bit better, but not much.

Finishing third in the nation was a nice accomplishment, and I was pretty happy that my parents had been able to come down however briefly to see me play. I wasn't a star, but I contributed substantially to our success. I also was glad to get to know Corliss and his family better. I remember the first time we met when he joined the

Sixers. He lived in Russellville, thirty or forty miles outside Little Rock just off Interstate 40. A tall, lanky guy as a grade-schooler, he was like that proverbial young colt on spindly legs that hasn't quite developed the coordination he'd exhibit when he became a true thoroughbred. When he was thirteen, one of his cousins gave him the name Big Nasty, and it stuck. The NASTY (Not A Sure Thing Yet) nickname would only apply to him for a few more years. Later, his skills and power amazed me just as his awkwardness had before. He played for the University of Arkansas and entered the draft one year before me in 1995. He played in the NBA for twelve years and was a legend in Arkansas.

Many people consider him the finest high school player the state ever produced. He was a three-time all-conference and all-state selection. He was also named Gatorade National Player of the Year in 1991 and 1992. As a senior Corliss averaged 28 points and 9 rebounds per game. His sophomore year at Arkansas, in 1994, he helped the Razorbacks to a 31-3 record. I sat and watched the NCAA tournament that year feeling all kinds of pride and a little bit of envy as he was named its Most Outstanding Player. He led the Razorbacks to their only NCAA basketball championship under Coach Nolan Richardson by defeating the Duke Blue Devils. Corliss earned every bit of the recognition he received. I only wish, and I know that he does too, that they'd been able to repeat as national champions, but they fell just short, losing in the final in 1995.

Corliss is a great guy and a good friend, and the Big Nasty name is kind of funny when you consider that when his high school team won the King Cotton National Holiday Tournament, he blocked Jason Kidd's last-second shot to seal the win in the final. Corliss was voted the Most Valuable Player of the tournament, but when he was standing on the podium with the rest of the all-tournament team, he gave his medal to Jason in a show of sportsmanship.

It's too bad our Sixers coach couldn't have had the same attitude. Whether he was serious about his threat to not let us play on his team didn't matter. We stuck with the Spirits for the entire season and for every season after that. I wasn't bitter about it, but either because of our choice or just because we were immature and took the game so seriously, even when I was playing for our school teams with some of the other guys who were still on the Sixers, as soon as the season ended and it became AAU time, we stopped talking to one another. We were fine when we were teammates, but when we were on opposite sides, we just flat out didn't communicate with one another and barely acknowledged one another's presence.

It seems kind of silly to me now, but back then I wasn't about to break what seemed to me a tradition, an unspoken rule. The enemy was the enemy, and whether on the court or off, as long as at some point they wore a different uniform, you didn't have anything to do with them. As a professional, it's rare to play on the same team for your entire career, so you're frequently going up against former teammates and sometimes guys you consider close friends. I don't know too many guys at this level who aren't able to separate their two lives—personal and professional. We don't have to resort to what we did as kids and not speak to one another. That doesn't mean that we don't have the same competitive spirit, it just means that we're now better able to compartmentalize. People ask me all the time what it's like to face former teams or former teammates, and it really is true that we're able to just flip a switch and go. It's such a common part of our experience when you've been in the league awhile that you don't even give it much thought. That doesn't mean that you don't get special satisfaction from beating a team that traded you, it just means that you can better keep things in perspective.

That Corliss and I were welcomed on the Spirits (we'd eventually change our name to the Wings) was a good thing despite whatever hard feelings came before. The Wings were by far a better team than the Sixers. They had an aura about them that carried over onto the court. Success breeds success, and in our little world of AAU ball in Little Rock, being on the Wings was like being on the Lakers, Celtics, or any other team with a tradition of winning. Even though it seems like something that the media make up or that people wish were true, I think there is a lot to the notion of being on a team with a long tradition of success. I've heard New York Yankees talk about what it's like to put on Yankee pinstripes or to set foot on the field where Gehrig, Ruth, and some of the other greats played. There is something special about looking up into the rafters and seeing all those championship banners hanging there. There is such a thing as a winning environment, and as players we do feel those effects. Just as my individual success helped me immeasurably and gave me something to draw on throughout the rest of my career, the same is true for team success. Maybe you weren't there when Magic and Kareem won their championships, but you can still feel that success. It raises your level of play, and surrounding yourself with successful people is one of the crucial steps you need to take to achieve your own success. Just being around them and watching how they conduct themselves is an invaluable education. Seeing how they handle the up times and the down times is also important.

I still do that. I still feel I have a lot to learn, and I look at guys like Tiger Woods to see how they conduct themselves. Roger Federer is someone I admire for how he plays his game and conducts himself. I wish that I could just stop my life sometimes so that I could study the men and women who've attained success but who also seem comfortable with who they are and where they're at. They seem to be so in control, and I look at people like Oprah Winfrey or President Obama, and they exude this sense that they are exactly where they want to be in their life. I'd imagine that just by being around them some of what they do would have to rub off on you.

During the 1999–2000 season with the Lakers, the place where we all wanted to be and where everyone else expected us to be was on court celebrating an NBA championship. That season was all about rebounding from the previous years of disappointment in the play-offs. With Phil Jackson and his staff coming to coach and manage our team, there was going to be a new way of doing things. Phil's was the most successful coaching staff in basketball since the Lakers' eighties teams coached by Pat Riley. They'd led Michael Jordan, Scottie Pippen, and the Chicago Bulls to six NBA World Championships in the previous nine seasons.

I recall stating to the L.A. media immediately after the hiring that

Dr. Buss and the Lakers had just shifted the accountability for our success to the players. The whole world knew the pedigree of the coaching staff; they were the best in the business. Now we had no excuses. The players had to set up and get the job done and return the Lakers to NBA dominance. And that we did! It wasn't easy. We initially struggled as a group to get the principles of the infamous triangle offense down. In practice and early in the preseason, we were bumping into one another as we tried to execute. The triangle offense is a system of ball and player movement that requires all five players to think as one unit. If one person is in the wrong place or not moving the ball to the proper place, the entire system breaks down. The first ten to fifteen games of the regular season we weren't playing at a particularly high level, and since a 6-6 start to the season before had led to our coach's being fired, we didn't have much time before the media would start to give us a hard time.

I didn't know this coming in, but Phil likes to let his players think for themselves in a lot of situations out on the floor. Although we have an offensive and a defensive system that we're trained to follow, he recognizes that things don't always go according to plan, and you have to be able to read, adjust, and adapt to situations. That being said, Phil is the coach! I found that out the hard way in one of our early regular-season games in 1999–2000. We'd gotten off to a slow start against Portland and they'd jumped out to an early lead. Most coaches call time-outs if they don't like the way their team is playing, and that's what most players are accustomed to in the NBA, high school, and college. Our time-out wasn't coming from the sideline as we fell behind 12–2, so I decided I'd "think for myself" and call a time-out. As we walked toward the bench, Phil was trying to figure out who'd called the time-out because he knew he hadn't. Everyone else looked around, and I was the only person who knew the truth, so I said, "I called it." Before I could completely finish my sentence, Phil stepped right up beside me and said with calm irritation in his voice, "Fish, don't ever do that again." Including that season, I've played almost six full NBA seasons, including play-offs, for Phil, and guess what, I've never done that again.

As much as Lakers fans remember the thrill of that championship series, we almost didn't get to that point. Sacramento took us to five games in the first round. We won the deciding fifth game, and the sense of accomplishment and relief was palpable in our locker room. In a true win-or-go-home game, we thrashed the Kings 113–86. We'd struggled in situations like that in the past, and I think that every team needs to face a stern test before they can win it all. Unfortunately, or maybe I should fortunately (for NBA fans), we would have to face that test one more time.

Our Western Conference Finals against the Portland Trail Blazers is about the most dramatic experience I've had in a team rebounding from defeat and near-defeat. The previous two seasons, 1997–98 and 1998–99, we'd bounced Portland out of the play-offs in the first round. That season, they'd retooled a bit, just as we had, with some key players coming over—Scottie Pippen for them and Ron Harper for us. The way Shaquille O'Neal dominated in game one of the series, which we won 109–94, few would have believed that we'd end up in game seven fifteen days later. Shaq was a monster, scoring 41 points on 14-of-25 shooting and making 13 of 27 field goal attempts. That last number is important. It showed what Portland was going to do. Along with double- and sometimes triple-teaming Shaq, they were going to send him to the foul line with the "Hack-a-Shaq" strategy. One play that made all the highlight shows was Glen Rice passing the ball from the wing in to Kobe under the basket. With three Blazers surrounding him, he handed the ball off to Shaq, who nearly tore the backboard down with a dunk. If we could get the ball inside that easily, it looked as if the team some had said was the most talented in the league was going to be in big trouble. But we knew better than to write the Blazers off after only one game.

Whether it was the physical toll that first game took on Shaq or something else, the double and triple teams seemed much more effective in game two. We lost home-court advantage in a 106–77 defeat, and though my minutes increased in the blowout, I was anything but happy. By game three it became clear what the Blazers were trying to do. If they could take Shaq out of the game by double- and triple-teaming him, they were daring someone else to step up and beat them. In game two, none of us had. Shaq's 23 points still led the team, and Kobe Bryant's 12 was the next highest total. I don't know if I'd go so far as to say that we received a wake-up call in that game since we weren't taking the Blazers lightly at all, but neither game had been close.

We went up to Portland for game three. The three days in be-tween games gave both teams some time to rest and to strategize, and it paid off in a classic battle. The game didn't start out looking like a classic with Portland, energized by the home crowd, jumping out to a 15–2 lead. We were down only by 10 at halftime, thanks mostly to Kobe Bryant's shooting.

With Rasheed Wallace still hounding Shaq, and Pippen and oth-ers coming in to help on defending the big guy, Kobe stepped up and rebounded off his poor performance in game two to contribute 25 points and 7 assists. Kobe had only taken nine shots in each of the first two games, but he took charge in the first half of game three, scoring 18. At halftime, the coaches told Shaq to be more aggressive—he'd been passing out of the double team a lot—and he responded, scoring 13 in the third quarter. We couldn't shake the Trail Blazers, and as the game wound down to the final few seconds, the score was tied at 91. Shaq and Kobe had essentially carried the scoring load for us throughout that game and the series, and everyone in the arena *knew* that one of them was going to take the last shot. That's when veteran leadership took over.

Ron Harper had been telling the other guys that he had been open in the corner most of the game. With Steve Smith sagging off him to help on penetration or on Shaq in the post, Ron was left wide open. As the shot clock wound down and we neared half a minute to play, Kobe stood at the top of the key with the ball in what appeared to be a kind of clear-out. He drove to the basket, Smith came over to help, and Kobe fired a pass to Harp. He was eighteen feet from the basket, essentially wide open, and he rose up and fired that sweet, no-nonsense jumper of his. I remember standing on the sideline watching that thing rise, and it seemed to just hang up there for a moment before it completed its flight and put us up by two with just under thirty seconds to play.

Kobe proved that he was more than just an offensive force when he blocked Arvydas Sabonis's driving shot just before the buzzer. That shot and that block seemed to break Portland's back. We won games three and four to go up three games to one. Notable in game four was Shaq's being perfect from the free throw line (9 for 9), seeming to negate whatever ambitions Portland had of Hacking their way to the finals. All we had to do was win one of the three remaining games to move on to the NBA Finals. Game five proved to be my most effective game. I hit a pair of threes and scored 10 points, but we couldn't overcome Portland's back-against-the-wall intensity in a 96–88 loss in front of our home crowd. We returned to Portland confident that with two games remaining, all we had to do was win one to close out the Blazers and advance. We had that confidence despite our having a 2-4 record in trying to close a series.

Make that 2-5. Portland took advantage of some matchups and we had no answer for Bonzi Wells in the fourth quarter, and they beat us 103–93 to force a game seven back in L.A. We'd started the play-offs looking pretty invincible, but after our 2-0 start, we'd gone 8-6. We hadn't lost three games in a row all year, and that was what it would take for Portland to win the series. Momentum was clearly on their side, and it carried through most of game seven.

It's strange to think that an entire season came down to the last ten minutes of that Western Conference Final game seven. As we would be reminded again and again in the off-season, we were on the verge of the greatest collapse in NBA play-off history, being 15 points down with ten minutes to play. Having just recently been on the other end of one of those kinds of defeats, I can understand what happened from Portland's perspective. Missing 13 consecutive shots is nearly incomprehensible, but a lot of that had to do with the defensive intensity we brought to those final minutes. We played with an urgency that was never a panic. Like everyone in the arena that day, until Brian Shaw hit a three-pointer at the end of the third quarter, I was wondering if things were ever going to start to go our way. When he stepped up during that fourth-quarter rally and buried two more treys, I could almost see the Trail Blazers physically deflating. I sensed what they were thinking. They'd been doing a good job of holding Kobe and Shaq down to that point, and here comes this other guy putting it to us. Well, in my mind, that's the way it should always be. That's not to say that Kobe and Shaq didn't contribute. With a little more than a minute and a half remaining, Shaq stepped to the foul line with the score tied.

I'm sure you've seen it dozens of times. A team fights back to pull close or to tie, and they have expended so much energy that they just can't go to the next step. Well, if there was any thought that that was going to happen to us, Shaq squashed it by sinking both of those foul shots to finally put us ahead 81–79. I could feel the crowd's thunderous ovation rattling my rib cage after that, but less than a minute later, Kobe drove toward the basket and Portland's interior defense collapsed around him and he sent a pass lofting toward the rim. Shaq grabbed the lob and set off some thunder of his own with a powerful jam that put us up by 6. Shaq ran back downcourt with his mouth open in amazement and his index fingers wagging. His expression encapsulated everything we were all feeling—jubilation, relief, astonishment, and to borrow a phrase, shock and awe. We missed a few free throws in that final minute that kept the game close, but won 89–84. We'd managed to overcome Portland's 21–4 run, we'd managed to overcome the label of underachievers not capable of closing out a series, and we were back on track to being exactly where we wanted to be. We bounced back when it mattered most, and we did a lot of growing up. At various points throughout that series, it would have been easy for either team to give up, but that's not what professionals and competitors do. You continue to go after it hard, and if you keep working and don't let the negatives get in the way, ultimately you're bound to be in possession of the ball and the win.

Every year from the time I was ten to the time I was sixteen, I went to the AAU National Tournament. From Syracuse to San Antonio, we traveled the country, but we could never break through and win the championship until we finally did in San Antonio, earning the sixteen-and-under title. Playing at the national level was interesting and beneficial in a lot of ways. As the Wings earned a reputation as a strong team, we were able to pick up guys from other areas in the state who wanted to play with us. That was difficult to adjust to because that meant some of the guys you liked and had started out with were cut. The good thing was that we seemed to be getting better and better each year, particularly after my best friend Clarence Finley's dad took over as head coach. As fifteen-year-olds, we lost in the finals to a team from Baltimore. We seemed to have a lot of trouble with teams from the East Coast urban areas. They played a different brand of basketball from what we were used to. We were as physical and played as hard, but their trash-talking and cursing was something we would never do. It seemed that for years we couldn't get past one or another of those East Coast teams.

I was a little disappointed in my play as well. I seemed to have plateaued both physically and with my skills. I was still playing a lot and doing fairly well, but when I looked around at my teammates and my opponents each year, the guys seemed to be getting more aggressive. My dad was an assistant coach, and he and Coach Finley kept trying to figure out what it would take to get us over the hump. In San Antonio, things just seemed to click for us. We ran through all the preliminary games easily. When we got into the late rounds and the championship rounds, it was a lot more difficult, but we rose to the occasion. Before the championship game, we were sitting in our locker room and Coach Finley said, "We're going to make a change tonight. We think we match up better this way. Kenneth, you're in for Derek."

I felt sick to my stomach. What was going on here? I'd been a key part of our success the whole season, gotten us to the championship game, and now I wasn't starting? Coach Finley couldn't even look at me, and Dad wasn't in the room. Coach talked some more about our upcoming opponent, but all I could do was look at my hands. I did my best to just deal with it and told myself that I'd probably get in there at some point. I had to be ready. They'd see that they needed me, but as the game played out, I didn't even touch the floor for the first time in I couldn't even remember when. When the buzzer sounded and we were national champions at last, I had a mix of emotions. I was happy that we had won, and it was fun to run out on the court and be there for the trophy presentation and to receive our champions' jackets, but a part of me thought I didn't do anything to contribute. I'd been a starter all season, I'd been with the team for years, been a part of our gradual development, but I felt empty. Why, at the moment when we were all making that final push to get over the top, was I not asked to be a part of that effort?

When we got back to Little Rock, I had to do a lot of soul-searching to sort things out. I never went to my dad or Coach Finley to ask why they had decided to make that switch to Kenneth. We'd picked up Kenneth the year before. He was a flashier player than I was, a little more athletic, quicker, and could definitely outjump me. I didn't think that he ran the team as well as I did, didn't understand how to play the game to the same degree that I did. I'd heard people comment about other players and how effortless they made the game look, but I never heard anyone say that about me. I was the grinder, the intense guy who looked to be working hard, so even if I performed at the same level as, say, someone like Kenneth, most people would think he was the better player. He was also far more assertive than I was.

I can still remember sitting in our living room watching videos of my games with my dad. He'd point out my mistakes, and he seemed to always be saying, "You've got to be more aggressive. Don't worry so much about making mistakes." That last part was hard for me to hear, because the way my dad ran things around the house, if I did make a mistake, I got punished. It's true that you can't play the game looking back over your shoulder at the bench wondering what the coach's reaction is going to be or if you're going to be replaced. For a long time, even as a professional, I played it safe, hoping to avoid mistakes. Other guys seemed to have more of a "If I screw up, I screw up, so what?" kind of attitude. If the coach said something about what they'd done wrong, they'd listen, then let it go. I hated being told I'd made a mistake and it would drag me down, and I'm sure I let it show, and that made my coaches doubt my toughness.

In junior high, my coach was Charlie Johnson. He instilled a lot of confidence in me because he praised me, he encouraged me. He didn't tell me just about what I'd done wrong, but he'd say to me, "Shoot the ball. Do your thing." I flourished under that kind of treatment. He also had a funny way of critiquing us or correcting us. He could turn it into a kind of joke that took some of the sting out of his remark without losing the point. In some ways, having my dad there as a coach and as someone who had to be critical of me wasn't the best idea. I know now that when my dad corrected me, he wasn't making a comment about me as a person. But when I was a kid and he said, "That was a bad play," I heard, "You are a bad player." I personalized it too much.

There's a fine line between being able to take responsibility for the things you do and taking things too personally. If someone criticized what I did, it was like they were criticizing me as a person. It's taken me a long time to realize that you have to separate who you are from what you do—not completely, but enough that you don't beat yourself up over mistakes you make.

Along with all that soul-searching, I spent some serious time in the weight room and in the gym working on my physical conditioning. While not playing in that championship wasn't the same as Michael Jordan's being cut from the squad, it did do something similar for me. It rocked my world. I had never experienced anything like that before, and I didn't like how it felt. I'd always played regularly, and I had to consider whether I'd done the one thing my father said that I should never do—become complacent. I didn't think that I had, but I didn't want anyone to even remotely consider that I had. It's true that you don't know what you've got until it's gone, and I decided that I was going to have to really rededicate myself.

Though it wasn't my style, I could easily have gone into pity-party mode, gone into a shell, and shut everyone and everything out and just quit. I'd seen guys do that. It seemed as if every year of AAU ball and school ball some guys got cut or quit, and the squads just kept getting whittled down to fewer and fewer guys. If I felt as bad as I did about sitting out an entire game, then how bad would I feel if I had to sit out an entire season or had my career end? I was not going to let that happen. As angry and resentful as I was at Mr. Finley and possibly at my father for their decision, maybe I should have thanked them. Maybe they were just trying to light a fire under me and they took the opportunity to do it when I was most likely to notice the heat and the smell of my roasted flesh?

Regardless of their intentions, it obviously had the desired effect. I did make a stronger commitment to the game than I ever had. What's interesting to me is that it seemed as if everyone had a different vision of who I was. I think that while my dad saw me as a nonaggressive, too cautious player, he always saw that I had a lot of ability. If he didn't, I don't think he would have been so critical. Coach Finley shared that vision of my ability, but he took a different approach to getting me to be more aggressive. I saw myself as a talented player who really did have the drive and the desire that others thought I lacked, who were blinded by their preconceptions. Ultimately, whether I had it and they didn't see it, or I didn't have it (whatever that it might be), I had to get all the thems in the world to stop seeing what I lacked and focus on what I possessed. I think that for every young person, that struggle to merge your identity with the expectations and demands of peers, parents, and other adults is filled with ups and downs. Mine were taking place on the basketball court in a very public way. That's continued to be true. Having some of your issues made public adds a dimension that most people don't have to deal with.

As I look back, I see definite parallels between what was going on in basketball and in my family life. The two were so intertwined that it was almost impossible to separate them. If I had been able to see the pattern, maybe I could have dealt better with both sides of it. Just as the Sixers/Spirits controversy forced me to choose sides, shortly after that my parents were splitting up. To their credit, neither of them ever put me in the position the Sixers coach did. Neither of them tried to align me with him or her, or to turn me against the other. They always put their children's interests first. That didn't mean that it hurt any less. Every kid wants his or her parents to be together, and even though my mom and dad went to all my games and showed collective support—even today they will sometimes attend a Lakers game together—I knew that the division existed and I know that it does now. I appreciate having them both around and active in my life.

What I haven't said so far about all this is that my mom was and is a remarkable and steady influence in my life. If I was anxious about pleasing my father and not making mistakes, my mom was the unconditionally devoted mother that we all dream of. She was at every game cheering me on. After every game she praised me or offered her counsel or a shoulder to cry on or was a sounding board. She clipped stories out of newspapers and put together scrapbooks of my exploits. She worked two jobs so that we could eat well and be appropriately and comfortably clothed. She did all the little things necessary to keep the household functioning and her kids on track. I might figuratively have been looking over my shoulder worrying about what my dad thought—good and bad—about how I was doing, but I never did that with my mother. I knew that she was in my corner always and forever. Maybe I didn't express my appreciation and my love for her as openly as I might have, but beneath all my confusion and upset and worry, she was there as a calming influence, the steady heartbeat that underlay the frenetic pace of my adolescent uncertainty.

If not for my father and the lessons he'd taught me about hard work and digging deep, I could easily have given up on basketball after the San Antonio benching. The thought crossed my mind briefly, but was gone in the next instant. One of the reasons for that was simple: I *loved* the game. If anything frustrated me, it was all the people who seemed to think that I was too complacent or not fiery enough on the court, who couldn't see that I had a passion for basketball that transcended outward displays. To this day, I don't think I can adequately articulate how I feel about the game and the joy that it brings me. In those rough patches, basketball also became my solace and the court a refuge where I didn't have to think about my mom and dad, my hopes of playing in college, my worries about my half brother, Duane, or anything else. Sports teach you a lot about living in the moment. You have to be aware, almost subconsciously, of the score, the time on the clock, and your game strategy and how to execute it, but the rest is just existing in that flow and movement and the sheer pleasure that comes from having command over your body. Everything else in life can be swirling around you and feel as if it is totally out of your control, but on the court you can feel powerful and in command.

Bouncing back from the disappointment of San Antonio was going to take some time, but being denied the pleasure of being out on the court and contributing made me come back. As much as I loved the game, being a fan and watching it didn't feed my needs and desires in the same way that playing it did. Not even close. My mom and dad's belief that action and activity were important had made an indelible impression on me. I didn't make any grand announcements or hold a press conference in our kitchen to tell everybody how I felt about the state final. I didn't lay out a seven-point plan for how I was going to improve my game. I also decided that I wasn't going to become the person whom they all seemed to want me to become—the rah-rah, overtly emotional, devil-may-care, attention-grabbing guy. That just wasn't me, and it would have been wrong for me to fake it. I was going to do it on my terms and my way, based on the fundamentals that had been drilled into me from the time I was a young kid. I also realized that as much influence as my parents had on me, this was my life. I'd been the one who would stay at the gym until midnight shooting jumpers. My parents weren't signing me up to go to clinics or summer camps where I could improve my skills or be exposed to scouts.

If I was going to bounce back from disappointment, I was going to do it not to please anybody else but to do what I had always wanted to do.

My next chance at redeeming myself wouldn't come until the following season when I was a junior at Parkview. Coach Ripley had built a strong program at the school, and everyone pretty much knew where he stood. You paid your dues as a sophomore and as a junior, then when you were a senior, you got the bulk of your playing time. So, as a junior I played on the junior varsity and also on the varsity. We all respected Coach Johnson, and he did really nurture us. For example, when I was a sophomore, I had a great season, and when it came time for the state play-offs, he allowed me to dress with the varsity guys. Chances are I wouldn't play a minute, but he thought it was important for the younger guys to experience and learn from that level of play. I'd spent so many years wanting to be a Parkview Patriot that the first time I got to dress with the varsity and go out onto the court and do our pregame ritual—a defensive slide drill with a chant letting everyone know that Parkview was in the house—the adrenaline was pumping so hard I felt I could have jumped right out of that gym.

I've seen the movie *Hoosiers,* and even though Little Rock had a population of around 180,000, when it came to Parkview basketball games, it felt like the same small-town atmosphere of tiny Marion, Indiana. Even if you didn't have kids at the school or on the team, the place to be on a Friday night was Parkview. And unlike a lot of schools, we didn't have a tiny bandbox of a gymnasium. Our court had two levels of stands and seated about thirty-five hundred people. It could get loud in that joint and had a great atmosphere for high school basketball. With all that focus and attention on the game came high expectations. We seldom let anyone down.

My junior season, we had some strong seniors, but almost everyone agreed that the crop of juniors I was in was a stronger group overall. Nikki Carruthers (who went to play at MIT), Dion Cross (basketball scholarship at Stanford), and I just had to be patient. Finishing third in the state our junior year sounds like a big accomplishment, and I suppose it was, but we had our eyes on a bigger prize for the next season—winning state. Before we could do that, we had one more thing to do—go back and win another national championship in AAU ball.

It seems as if much of my life has gone in cycles, and as a teen I experienced some of the things I would later as a pro. After winning the national title the year before, we returned to the national championship tournament that year as the favorites to win it all. The only thing harder than winning that first championship is repeating. Coach Finley and my dad had guided us to the championship, but they were no longer the coaches. The sponsor of the team decided that he wanted to coach us. We didn't have much say in any of that, and neither did my dad or Mr. Finley. This guy controlled the team and paid the bills, so he could do whatever he wanted. However, he didn't have the same kind of relationship with us that Mr. Finley and my father did. I'd eaten dinner at the Finleys' house probably three times a week since I was in the third grade. I respected him a lot. I didn't like the decision he'd made the previous year, and coming from him, it hurt maybe more than it would have coming from somebody else, but I still respected and trusted him.

Unfortunately, our new coach seemed to be more into the spectacle of the tournament and what it might mean for him than he was for us. In my mind, his biggest contribution was getting us brand-new warm-ups and uniforms. Why would a guy invest a lot of his time and money in running an AAU team? Most people do it because they love the game and they want to help out kids, and our "owner" was motivated by that. However, once we won the national title, I think he also saw this as an opportunity to get himself some attention and headlines. AAU ball is a launching pad for a lot of kids. As much as college coaches and the scouting agencies pay attention to the high school season, they pay even more attention to AAU ball in the summer. That's when you see kids and their potential in a different light. We were playing the cream of the crop. Our AAU team was essentially an all-star team, a kind of All–Little Rock squad composed of some of the best players in the area and then the state. The competition was even more intense in AAU ball than it was in high school. And since we were playing against teams from all over the country, recruiters would naturally be all over the stands at these games.

Everybody likes to be a part of something successful, and I'm sure a bit of ego was involved in the sponsor's deciding to come down from the stands and be on the sidelines for that year. College coaches would have to go through him to gain access to us. I'm not accusing him of doing anything unethical, only noting it was good for his ego to have guys like Jim Boeheim of Syracuse, Bobby Knight of Indiana, John Chaney of Temple, or John Thompson of Georgetown talking to him.

Pressure does funny things to people, and in our case it made the game less fun. I can't say exactly why it happened, or how it happened, but we weren't a bunch of kids playing the game because we loved it and had fun doing it at that national tournament. Instead, we became about as businesslike and serious as a tax audit. We were heading into our senior year of high school, and a lot of us wanted to be early "committers"—that is, guys who accepted a scholarship at an NCAA school before our senior season even started. Having that taken care of and out of the way would be one less thing to worry about and really enable you to enjoy that last year. I don't know if it was the added pressure of the scouts/coaches in the crowd, wanting to impress them so that you could get that scholarship early—which also earned you some respect from your peers, because if you were good enough for a school to want you before you even played your senior season, you really were a sure thing—or if it was just other teams really gunning for us because we were the defending champs, but it was a struggle.

In the semifinals, we played a team from Memphis featuring Tony Delk. He would go on to win Most Outstanding Player in leading Kentucky to the 1996 NCAA championship title. He was a combination point guard/shooting guard, but in the first half I didn't guard him. He was relatively quiet while I scored 10 points, but in the second half he just exploded on us, scoring 30. Corliss was our best matchup against them, but he would have had to have played completely out of his mind to match Delk's output. Unfortunately for us, because of our "owner's" relative inexperience on the bench, we didn't make any of the adjustments we needed to slow them down. Our coach seemed to be flustered and incapable of coming up with a plan, and we reflected his demeanor on the court. Things unraveled pretty quickly, and our dream of repeating as champions died. What also didn't help was that we were seen as the favorites, so when the underdog Memphis team went on a roll, they had the crowd behind them. Even though it was a neutral-site game, you'd have thought we were playing right on Beale Street with Howlin' Wolf and Junior Wells playing during the time-outs. We were shell-shocked, and when the buzzer sounded and we lost, I could only feel relief that the game was over. Only the next day did it sink in that we weren't going to repeat as champions. I can say this: we weren't overconfident, just underprepared. They were the better team on that occasion, but if my dad and Mr. Finley had still been coaching us, I don't think that would have been the case—they knew how to prepare us for anything and frequently brought in adults to scrimmage against us. Not just guys off the street but former college players with real skills.

So far, my plan at redemption wasn't off to a great start. I did play significant minutes in all the games, not as many in the second half of the semifinal loss as I would have liked to, but with another season coming up in a few months—the tournament ended in mid-August and the basketball season officially began in November—I could concentrate on getting ready for what I expected to be a terrific senior year. I had played football up until I got into ninth grade, but then my dad said that he didn't think it would be a good idea for me to play. Basketball was where it was at for me, and that fall of my senior year in particular I didn't mind not being a part of the football program. Fall meant the homecoming game and the dance that went along with it. To me, the homecoming dance meant that the gym would be closed for a couple of days while it was decorated, the dance was held, and then the decorations came down.

In other words, I wasn't the most social of guys. During the season get-togethers were usually held after the games, supervised and unsupervised parties alike, but I never went. I decided though that since this was my senior year and I would be playing a lot, I would mend my ways and hang out a bit more. During preseason practice I noticed something that made me stop and think. When the first team was running plays, I was out there most but not all of the time. That was a departure from how coach usually did things. The guy who played behind me was the son of one of the assistant coaches, and he saw a lot more minutes with the starters than any of the other second-team players. I chalked it up to Coach Ripley's having faith in me after I'd been in the program so long. No one could deny that I knew my responsibilities as a point guard or could question my basketball intellect. Why make me do all the repetitions when I had already demonstrated that I knew what was up?

Our opening game of the season, I was in the starting lineup, but about halfway through the first quarter I was taken out. It was early in the season and none of us had our fitness level up to midseason form yet, so I figured I was just going to be on the bench long enough to catch my breath, then I'd head back on out. That didn't happen. Instead, my replacement played the rest of the quarter and well into the second. I went back in, and the two of us had just about shared the minutes. The same thing happened in the second half. I played well, took a few more shots than I might have the year before under similar circumstances, and was pleased that we won big. I tried not to think too much about it, and I noted the look of surprise on my mother's face when I said that I was going to the postgame party. Everyone was jacked up about the game and the blowout win. I hung out with a couple of teammates, drinking soda and eating chips. We were checking out all the girls, but I was way too shy to talk to any of them. Eventually that would change and I would have a girlfriend for most of that year, but that was going to have to wait until after the season. I was wondering about my playing time, but I tried to just let go of it and figured that it was just one game.

Unfortunately, that pattern continued in the first few weeks of the season. I had been taught to always respect a coach's decisions and not question them, so I didn't talk to Coach Ripley about what was going on. I wasn't the only one who noticed that his senior preference wasn't being applied to me. The starting five were all seniors and noticed what was going on and talked to me about it privately. My parents were at the games, and they saw what was up and didn't like it. I believe that even if it hadn't been happening to me, my parents would have spoken up. After all, what was fair was fair and what was right was right. I was producing and the team was on a tear, winning every game out of the gate. My dad had a talk with Coach Ripley to express his frustration that the senior policy was not being upheld in my case.

My dad had been involved in enough basketball in town and with me and Duane that he felt comfortable taking that step. He didn't ask me if I thought he should, he just went ahead and did it, and that was fine with me. Because of how I'd been raised and because of my shyness, I would probably have wound up sounding like a whiner instead of talking to coach logically and dispassionately. Today, I have no problems discussing concerns I have with the coaching staff. It's very different as an adult going to another adult to talk about something. No one ever teased me or otherwise gave me a hard time about my parents intervening on my behalf. I think that's because of the respect they had for my parents and also because they knew that what my father was saying was correct.

By the time we went to Las Vegas to play in a holiday tournament, things had settled down. I was still starting, and I began to play more and more minutes, especially after we lost to a team from L.A. in the championship game of that tournament. From that point forward it was smooth sailing for me and the Parkview Patriots. We went the rest of the season without a loss, finishing first in the state tournament and fourth overall in the nation according to *USA Today*. I'd weathered the storm. I'd hated the feeling that my senior season might slip away from me and felt that the right thing had finally been done. Any thoughts of why things always had to be so hard were forgotten in the joy of being able to say that we were the best high school team in Arkansas. One of our big men had been injured in that loss in Las Vegas, and another key player had fouled out. We lost in overtime, and that was all that separated us from a perfect season and likely the number one ranking in the country. That one blemish was, in a lot of ways, a good thing. It demonstrated the lesson that I had learned in San Antonio two summers before—you always have to keep improving. I was gratified that I had bounced back from that low point. It took a long time, but the wait was worth it.

Early in my basketball days, success had come fairly easily. This time, success for me individually had taken more time than I really wanted it to, but it had come. I'd been as persistent and focused as I'd ever been. My parents pitched in with their support, and I was rewarded. I could have been one of those problem players, undermining morale and team unity, but I had taken the right road and arrived at the right destination.

The next thing on my list was settling on a college. Most of my teammates had signed their letters of intent that November. I was still a man-child without a school to play for. With the state championship taken care of, it was time to focus on a personal goal—getting a full-ride scholarship to a NCAA Division I college.

If you haven't figured it out by now, I was never one of those blue-chip prospects, the kind of player who was spotted in junior high, recruited heavily by the who's who of Division I basketball power-houses, inundated with phone calls and enough mailings to fill a bedroom, and going to bed each night with the thoughts of eager coaches touting their respective programs. That isn't to say that I didn't hear from anyone. Mostly because of my performance in the summer before my junior year in high school (the year we won the AAU championship), I'd attracted some notice from the so-called midmajor schools such as Rice University, Baylor University, Texas A&M, other schools in that region. I even visited Liberty University, which was Jerry Falwell's school, as well as Samford University, outside Birmingham, Alabama. When I went on my recruiting visit there, it was the same weekend as the Auburn-Alabama college football game. They took me to a local mall, and when we first got there, it was crowded. Then, within thirty minutes, with the game coming on, the mall just cleared out. All of a sudden, we were the only ones in the mall. I was looking around thinking, "Where did everybody go? Oh, yeah, the game's starting." The whole place shut down for the Auburn-Alabama football game.

The Division I schools appealed to me the most. They were decent schools in terms of basketball, but outstanding schools academically. I also considered some of the historically black colleges and universities (HBCUs). I even wrote to the legendary Clarence "Big House" Gaines, who ran the program at Winston-Salem State University. I told him how much I admired him and his program, gave him the rundown on my accomplishments, and told him that I would love to hear from him. WSSU was the first HBCU to win an NCAA national championship in Division II, when its basketball team, led by the future first-round pick Earl "the Pearl" Monroe, won it all in 1967.

I'm sure that Coach Gaines (who passed away in 2005) got lots of calls and letters similar to mine, but I was still disappointed that I never received any kind of response. Small schools appealed to me; WSSU was a Division II school with an enrollment of less than five thousand students. That would have suited me academically and socially, but something told me that it would be better to hold out for those Division I schools. Unfortunately, they didn't want to wait for me to make up my mind. Once I told everybody that I would decide late in the signing period, some of the schools backed away. Rice, Baylor, and Texas A&M all said, "Look, if you don't want to commit to us during the signing period, we can't wait." They were worried that if they waited too long, they might lose out on someone else as well. That was okay with me. I didn't want to rush the decision, and I hoped that if I had a great senior year, someone might enter the picture at the last minute. I'd always wanted to play for the University of Arkansas, but I knew that was not going to happen.

The coaches at the University of Arkansas, Little Rock, had been in contact with me for almost a year. That they expressed interest even when I wasn't playing full-time mattered a lot to me. But the truth was, Coach Finley was also an assistant coach at UALR. He and assistant coach Dennis White were the ones who really recruited me. Coach Platt, the head coach at UALR, was on the fence about me, but his assistants convinced him that I had some talent and could really help the team. So, as excited as I was about the opportunity to get a scholarship to a Division I school, I wasn't walking into the best of situations. I wouldn't find that out until I showed up there for my first season. I got to enjoy what every one of our Parkview starting five did. Coach White came to the school on late signing day in March, and my mom and dad and Coach Ripley were all in the room watching as I signed my NCAA letter of intent. My mom still has a photo of that moment, which ran in the *Arkansas Democrat-Gazette.* It was official. I was going to college on a basketball scholarship. Signing that letter was one of the highlights of my life, if not the best thing that had ever happened to me until then. I couldn't know what was to follow, but even then I felt I'd made the right choice. My mom and dad were thrilled. They wanted me to go to college obviously, and knowing that I'd be playing so close to home made them even happier. I was glad that I wouldn't have to burden them with loans for tuition and housing or any of that. I liked the idea of being able to come home whenever I needed to and to be away whenever I wanted to.

Along with graduating from high school, one of the events that I was most looking forward to as that part of my life was drawing to a close was another chance to win an AAU national championship—this time with me really contributing all the way to the end. Unfortunately, I seemed to be the only one of the guys who felt that way. Our "owner" had decided one year of coaching us was enough. Coach Finley was busy at UALR, and my dad didn't want to get involved again after a year away. The sour taste of how things had gone down with the coaching change the year before hadn't gone away. This was the last summer my teammates and I were eligible to play AAU ball, but we'd all earned scholarships, and no one wanted to jeopardize his college career before it began by getting injured. I could understand that, but I hated that there was unfinished business and no one wanted to pitch in to get it done. I also think that I felt a little sentimental about it all. This would have been our last chance to all play together. We'd been through so much and for so long, and I hated that it was going to end, and that our last game together would be that loss to Memphis the year before.

Ultimately our owner left it up to us: "If you guys want to play nineteen and under this year, it's on you. I'll support whatever decision you make." He said that he could find us another coach, a lawyer in town who'd coached AAU teams. We ended up playing together, but after we won the state tournament, the same questions and objections came up about our continuing to play. Also, at the end of July our coach had a trial that was going to go on for some time. He couldn't just tell his client, "Sorry," so we were out a coach as well. To complicate things further, the Arkansas state high school all-star game was coming up, and guys wanted to play in that. It wasn't a direct conflict with the national tournament, but the dates were close enough that they'd have to do some hustling to get from the all-star game to the national tournament in Rochester, Minnesota. Things were not looking good. Normally, after we won the state tournament, we'd get airline tickets booked, hotel reservations made, and we'd be synchronizing our watches to make sure that we were all where we needed to be on time. I don't think I'd ever seen so many shoulders being shrugged in my life.

Finally, with just a few days to go before the national tournament, everybody made his decision. Three of our starting five, Dion Cross, Jabali Barrett, and I, would play. Our owner's disinterest was a bit frustrating, but he did have some cash for us. It took some of the parents, including my mom and dad, to get things organized. We didn't have enough cash to fly out there, so they rented a couple of vans and we loaded up and headed for Rochester. In some ways, going by van was cool. It was as if we were taking a step back into the past. I can say that because at six feet one inch, I could at least get semicomfortable in the vans. The taller guys had to struggle more with the cramped quarters—which they would have had to do just for a short period if we'd flown. Eight hundred and twenty-seven miles and nearly fourteen hours later, we arrived at our hotel. We had just a few hours to get some sleep before our first game. I remember waking up to the sound of Kurtis Blow's song "Basketball" blaring down the hallway. It had always been one of my favorite songs growing up, and hearing it again took me all the way back to 1984, when I first heard it. We all staggered out of our rooms bleary-eyed and had breakfast as a team before going to the gym. We won that day, but eventually our fatigue and lack of preparedness caught up to us. We lost one game in pool play but got into the championship round.

Once again a team out of Baltimore had been our nemesis, and losing to them wasn't anything to be embarrassed about. Dante Bright was on that team, and he eventually went to the University of Massachusetts and had a good career, and they had a couple of other Division I guys. Losing to them in pool play seemed to fire us all up. We adopted a kind of "if we're here, we might as well bust our tails" mentality. Unfortunately for us, Dion Cross, who was Stanford-bound, dislocated his shoulder in the last game of pool play. I'd been coming off the bench and doing well, but with Dion out, that meant that I'd be inserted in the starting lineup. I always seemed to be able to take advantage of opportunities, and I played extremely well and we advanced to the national semifinals to face Dante's crew again.

I suppose it might have been more dramatic if we'd played them in the final, but just getting a chance to go up against the kind of team that had dogged us so frequently in the past was fitting enough. We rose to the challenge and beat them, advancing to the finals after having fallen short of that the year before. I went on a tear in all three of those championship-round games, and we ended up winning it all and I was named an AAU All-American. I was as surprised as I was pleased by the recognition. I'd only started the last three games of the tournament, but I think I was being recognized for my overall contribution to AAU ball. I'd played for nine years and had been a good citizen the whole time. I think the other coaches understood and wanted to reward that and to set me up as an example of how persistence can pay off.

Most gratifying to me was winning the championship. It seemed as if every possible obstacle to our success had been placed in our way: losing our coach (his father agreed to take over, but we essentially coached ourselves), guys either not wanting to play or then getting hurt, making a last-minute decision to play. I'd also played a key role in our winning in our last shot at it all, and in way it was as if we'd presented a thank-you gift to our parents. They had saved the day for us by organizing the trip and making certain we had that opportunity to shine. During the awards presentation, I stood there looking into the half-darkness of the stands, and I could see my mom waving her arms and jumping up and down, still as enthusiastic and supportive as ever. Afterward, my dad took me aside and looked at the trophy and the medallion I'd got as national champion and as an All-American. He didn't say a lot; I remember him patting me on the heart and saying, "Hard-earned. Hard-earned." He didn't need to say a whole lot more; the look on his face spoke as eloquently as anyone could. All I could manage to say back was a quick thank-you. The vans were packed and we needed to get on the road. With the "We love that basketball" song lyric bouncing around in my head, I walked out of that arena feeling really satisfied.

Almost eight years to the day that we won that national championship, I was in a television studio in Hollywood. I'd just won my first NBA championship with the Lakers. I was doing a cameo on a FOX sitcom along with Kevin Garnett. During the setup for a new scene, Kevin asked me how it felt to be world champion and what was next. I told him the feeling was great, but the thing I most wanted was to be out there on the floor at the end—and not just because the game was at hand. I wanted to be one of the go-to guys, an essential component of the team's success. After Kevin walked away to get some water from the craft-services table, I thought back to that tournament in Rochester. It had felt different, immeasurably different, to own the floor and feel as if I'd really helped push us to the title. I wanted that feeling of accomplishment and satisfaction to wash over me like a tidal wave again. There would be still more work to do, but that was more than okay with me.

I was gratified that my decision to refocus and to refine my game had paid off. All the work I did in the weight room, all the extra time I spent in the gym post–San Antonio, paid off. It took a while, almost two years, but the results showed: a high school state championship, a college scholarship, and an AAU national championship. Even if I had visions of having arrived somewhere, the truth was that the "where" was just a waypoint—one more mark on the longer journey.

If I had any fantasy that college ball was going to be different since I had "made it" and wouldn't need to prove myself all over again, I checked back into the reality hotel immediately. The person who showed me to my room was my coach at UALR, Jim Platt.

I've already told you a bit about Coach Platt and his initial lack of faith in me and how I overcame that. What I didn't talk so much about was how he treated the rest of the guys too. Coach Platt was definitely a graduate of the Bobby Knight school of coaching and charm. He believed that a harsh word, a cutting word, a denigrating word, was the best tool to fashion a player into the image he had in mind for him. When I walked into practice the first week at UALR, he sized me up and said, "You're fat. How out of shape are you?" He then walked away. The man had my immediate respect because of the position that he was in. I'd respected every one of my coaches. Some had been critical of me and my game, but I was always fortunate that other people on the staff had reached out to me in a more positive way. Coach Platt's bad-cop/good-cop act wasn't an act. Based on the personal nature of his remarks, he seemed to genuinely not respect a lot of us. That was hard to deal with, but I took the man at his word and started to be a lot more conscious of what I ate. When we'd go to the student union for dinner, I'd see the other guys on the team grabbing plate after plate of food and I'd head to the salad bar.

Being new to the program and thrilled to be playing college ball and to be starting and contributing in a big way from the beginning, I was willing to put up with Coach Platt and his ways. I had been strong coming into his program, but I was what we called football strong. I had rounded, bulky muscles and not the long and lean "cut" muscles of a basketball player. I took my work in the weight room as seriously as I did the games. The summer after my freshmen year, when we finished with a respectable but certainly not great record overall and in the conference, I stayed on campus to take some classes and to work out in the gym and the weight room. By the time my sophomore season rolled around, my body was beginning a transformation. Coach Platt must have noticed because he didn't trot out all his tired lines about how fat I was. But he found plenty of other things to nitpick about in his sarcastic, bitter tone. In some ways, I felt sorry for the guy. He seemed perpetually unhappy and unpleasant. The game can't be all happiness and light and unicorns and sugarplum fairies, but you shouldn't dread going to the gym. I don't think I felt as strongly about this as my teammates, but I'd only been there one year.

I'd been around complainers and whiners enough to know who had a legitimate gripe and who didn't. The statistical evidence was overwhelming. Given how we later decided to all take action, every one of us from the starting five to the last man off the bench felt that Coach Platt crossed the line between trying to motivate us to trying to beat us down as players and as men. That's a strong statement, but it was true. By roughly midseason of my sophomore year, we had all reached a breaking point. We'd had some minor flareups with our coach when we'd tried to get him to understand our point of view, but that had just made things worse. Finally, at an informal meeting, we unanimously decided that we had to do something. We could not let this go on. I had worked so hard and put up with so much to get to that point, then I had to deal with this.

The next day, instead of going to practice, we all went to the local mall together. By not showing up, we hoped that we'd send the message that we'd been trying to send in person. We didn't want to stay in our apartments because that was the first place someone from the team or the athletic department would check for us. We didn't want to just do our own thing in case one of us was discovered and had to take the heat or explain for all of us.

I can still remember feeling as if I were sneaking out of my parents' house at night and that when I came back home or even before that, I was going to get busted. I had that giddy kind-of-scared, kind-of-angry feeling. Of course, we're walking through the mall and who do we bump into? Mrs. Platt and her daughters out shopping. We all just tried to be cool and stroll on past them, but we saw that she saw us, and her face said it all: "Shouldn't you guys be at practice?"

Well, ma'am, we should, but because of your husband's behavior, we thought it necessary to take this step. Things went awry even further when the local news heard about our informal boycott of practice and broadcast the story that night. That's when things got really uncomfortable for everyone. Even though I was only a sophomore, as the point guard and the guy who ran the team out on the floor, the role of team spokesman fell on me. Even though I hadn't spearheaded this campaign, my teammates selected me to talk this out with the coaches. As uncomfortable as I was with being disrespectful to a coach, I believed wholeheartedly that we needed to do something. Today, I'm not sure I would have handled it that way, but I do have to admire some of our strategic thinking. We had a huge game with in-state rival Arkansas State in a few days, and we didn't think that anyone would want to see that game forfeited or attention taken away from it by our walkout.

We were right. That same night, Coach White came to my apartment to talk to me. We'd always had a good rapport, and he had actively recruited me and spoken on my behalf to Coach Platt, so we were able to be completely honest with each other. He heard me out, then excused himself to make a phone call. A little while later, I got a knock on the door and the athletic director was standing there with Coach White. I ushered them both in and repeated what I had told Coach White. The athletic director, Coach White, and I agreed that we would all hold a team meeting the next day with all the players and staff except Coach Platt. They wanted to hear from all the guys so that they could get a fuller picture of what our grievances were.

At that meeting when we were asked if anyone had anything to say, all eyes fell on me. I briefly reiterated what I had said the night before. I scanned the room looking for backup, and a couple of guys added a few things to what I'd said. I was no John Grisham hero lawyer, but I knew that we weren't presenting a strong case, so I picked up the loose ball and ran with it. I told them what we had all discussed. If Coach Platt wasn't immediately replaced, we weren't going to play that next game against Arkansas State. We weren't bluffing with that demand, but the athletic director said that they couldn't fire him like that. He explained some things about wrongful termination, etc. He did however agree to investigate our grievances. He said that he would attend our practices to see just how Coach Platt treated us. That didn't sit too well with me because Coach Platt would know what was going on and probably wouldn't unload on us in front of his boss the way he normally did. The athletic director did add that he would put Coach Platt on a kind of probation and promised to evaluate the situation at the end of the season.

We agreed to take that under advisement, and we met without any of the coaches or administration present. After talking it out, we decided to go back to playing. We'd been heard, and that was all we really wanted in the first place. Coach Platt didn't have a warm and welcoming open-door policy, but in retrospect we could have more formally approached him. Failing that, we could have gone to Coach Finley or Coach White or talked to someone else in the athletic department about our concerns. We'd all risked our scholarships or at least our standing on the team by doing what we did, and that, if nothing else, is proof of how bad the situation was. This wasn't just a bunch of unhappy guys saying if you don't stop picking on us, we're going to tell our mom on you. And it wasn't as if we were a terrible team. At that point we were around a .500 club.

When we reported back to practice, Coach Platt did clean up his act for a bit. Of course, it was hard to play with all that going on. I don't think he trusted us anymore, and we didn't trust him. We lost our next four games in a row, and at the end of that two-week stretch, Coach Platt was gone. The assistants ran the team the rest of the year, and we finished up about how we'd started, but it was as if a giant block of cement dangling from a chain around our neck was gone.

I sensed from that experience that my guys were looking at me as a leader. I didn't like what Coach Platt was doing, but I wouldn't have spoken so strongly except for the responsibility that I felt to my teammates. They were looking to me to speak for us all, and that's what I did. I felt bad for Coach Platt and his family. I didn't keep track of him after that. I believe that everybody deserves a second shot, a chance to rebound, and I hope that he took from the experience some lessons just as I did. For a guy who was as shy and reserved as I was to take a stand and speak out was huge. That was especially true because, on my own, I would probably have just kept putting up with that kind of verbal abuse. I believed that the boss was the boss and he set the rules and the tone. Of course, if he had crossed the line in other ways, I would immediately have responded.

I've heard people say that one of the things about college is that you learn as much outside the classroom as you do inside. Another benefit is that you get exposed to all different kinds of people, and you learn a lot about relationships and personal interactions. That was certainly true for me those first two years at UALR. I was also learning that you can't paint with too broad of a brush. Despite this painful experience, I didn't let it color my perceptions of everyone and everything at the school. I didn't regret the decision to accept the scholarship offer, and when that season and that semester were over, I went right back to work. I had to get strong because I was certain there'd be more obstacles and more challenges. I also decided that it was best to really enjoy those up times, to take in the view from there and to use that as a vision for what I wanted the rest of my time to be like.

I also realized that the old line "this too shall pass" is true. Going through all that drama, it felt as if this were the worst thing in the world. My values and beliefs were tested in that situation. What was most difficult was staying true to myself. I relied on the solid base of values and beliefs that I had. I wasn't going to disrespect myself, and most of the guys felt that way. Whether our approach was right or wrong, I firmly believed then and now that we brought about a change that was necessary and right. Our coach was supposed to be on our side, was supposed to help lift us up and not bring us down. By staying true to our belief in ourselves and by demanding that he respect us in return for how we'd respected him and tolerated his lack of respect, in the long run we came out ahead.

My parents taught me that it is best to do something, to take action, and when the time came and I had the team's best interests and intents behind me, I helped bring about a positive change for all of us. Believe me, I wish that the circumstances had been different, but in the end we wound up in a better place than where we started. That's the thing about rebounding and being resilient—the effort may not seem worth it at the time, but when the final score is on the board, you know that your efforts contributed to the victory.

CHAPTER SEVEN

Staying in Bounds:

Understanding the Rules of the Game and of Life

In mid-November of 2008, I came home from a Lakers practice on a Sunday afternoon to kids napping as usual. Feeling that I needed to wind down a bit, I did what millions of Americans do on fall weekends—I sat down to watch an NFL game. I flipped around the channels for a while, hoping to find a game of interest. Week eleven in the NFL had a few close games and its share of blowouts—a traditional-rivalry game between the Chicago Bears and the Green Bay Packers was one of the latter, with the Pack handing the Bears a spanking. With Green Bay up 24–3 at the end of the third quarter, I figured I'd move on. I tuned in to a game without the same kind of intense rivalry—the Philadelphia Eagles and the Cincinnati Bengals. Heading into the last few minutes of the fourth quarter, the teams were tied 13–13.

Figuring on overtime at the worst, and a last-second decision at best, I settled in to watch the conclusion of the game. I'm a fan of Donovan McNabb, the veteran Eagle's quarterback. I knew that he was a pretty fair basketball player as a high schooler in the Chicago area before he went to Syracuse University on a football scholarship. He's a stud athlete, and I admire his courage, especially as he was attempting to come back from a serious knee injury that wiped out his 2007 season. Unfortunately for the Bengals, most of what I knew about them was not good. Their players had had a series of run-ins with the law in the previous seasons, and you seldom read or heard anything positive about their program. Whatever the cause of the breakdown in discipline, I felt bad for the team and for the city and for the sport. I never like to hear about athletes in any sport discrediting the profession. I am not one to pass judgment, but the Bengals had either a stretch of bad luck or immaturity that led them to be regarded as representing everything that critics find wrong with pro sports generally and pro athletes specifically.

I figured that Cincinnati had to be the underdog, and their 1-8 record had me rooting for them. I like to see anyone overcome adversity and succeed, and from what I knew, the guys out of Cincy were dealing with adversity with a capital *A* on and off the field. What I saw in those last few minutes of the game made me think that something was up with both clubs. Neither of them could move the ball, and the game slipped into overtime. Deciding that my little rest was over, I shut down the television and joined my kids and my wife in the family room.

The next day, driving to practice, I had the radio on. I wanted to find the news to see if President-elect Barack Obama had made any announcements of cabinet nominations or about the economic bailout so many were counting on to revitalize the country's financial markets. I hit the scan button on the radio, waiting for it to pick up KABC 790 AM. Before that all-news station came in, I heard a mention of Donovan McNabb when the radio paused on a different channel. Remembering the previous day's overtime game, I hit the scan button again. After hearing the distinctive sound of ESPN radio's theme, one of their morning-show hosts started ripping into Donovan McNabb for something he'd said in a postgame interview. Normally I don't listen to sports/talk radio, but when they played a bit of his interview, I decided to stick with it. Apparently, neither the Eagles nor the Bengals had scored in that overtime and the game ended in a tie. Worse, McNabb had admitted that he didn't know that NFL rules allowed for a game to end in a tie. He stated that when their last possession in the overtime ended, he assumed that he was going to get another shot at a victory in the next overtime.

In the NFL, regular-season games can end in a tie when neither team scores in the single overtime they play. Wow. I felt bad for McNabb for the flak he was getting. He was doing the right thing by standing up and admitting his mistake. "I never even knew that was in the rule book," McNabb said. "It's part of the rules and we have to go with it. I was looking forward to the next opportunity to get out there and try to win the game."

He wasn't alone in his misunderstanding. His coach, Andy Reid, admitted that he didn't know how a tied game would count in the standings. Ties are rare in the NFL, the last one prior to this being in 2002, but I kept thinking, "Fellas, as professionals you need to know the rules of your own game." The same is true at every level of sports and in every walk of life.

I immediately remembered watching the 1993 NCAA men's basketball final between the University of Michigan's Fab Five and the University of North Carolina. Chris Webber rebounded a missed free throw with nineteen seconds left and his team down by 2. He dribbled past the center line and signaled for a time-out. Unfortunately for Webber and the Wolverines, they'd burned all their time-outs already. The ball went back to North Carolina and so did the game. Webber was a freshman that night, and it was an easy mistake to make, but it's almost impossible even today to think of Webber without thinking of that non-time-out. I'm sometimes amazed how people can forget about all that you've contributed and be unable to forget your "crimes." Breaking the rules or not knowing what they are can have long-term effects on your reputation—and sometimes in this world all people will have to judge you on is your reputation.

As the week went on, McNabb and his coach came under more fire for not fully understanding the rules of the game. Philly fans are among the most passionate out there; they are so tough that legend has it they booed Santa Claus when he made an appearance at an Eagles game. I could understand people being upset about the outcome, and I hoped that the lesson McNabb learned stuck with him. I followed the story for a while and heard other NFL players say that they didn't know the details of the NFL's policies on overtime games. I had a feeling that in team meeting rooms across the country, regardless of the sport and the level at which it was played, coaches were telling their players to study their rule books.

I have to admit that I don't know every nuance of the sixty-one pages of the NBA rule book, but I think I've got a pretty good grasp of things. I decided to check it out just to get a better sense of what it covers. Every year during the preseason, we go over any rule changes, but contrary to popular belief, I don't sleep with the rule book under my pillow at home or when on the road. I recently logged on to NBA .com, where you can easily view the rule book in its entirety.

I just happened to scroll down to page thirty-seven of the document. There, all the rules for a traveling violation were spelled out. Section XIII sets up two possible scenarios: receiving the ball while standing still or while moving. The first is relatively simple to explain, and it only takes two single-sentence subpoints to cover all the possible ways a player can travel when receiving the ball while standing still. The second scenario is far more complicated and the explanation goes on for paragraph after paragraph and subpoint after subpoint. I'll spare you all the details, but here's a small sample: "A player who jumps off one foot on the count of one may land with both feet simultaneously for count two. In this situation, the player may not pivot with either foot and if one or both feet leave the floor the ball must be released before either returns to the floor."

Got it? I doubt it. Taken out of context its difficult to figure out the one count and two count, but you'd know this violation when you saw it during the course of a game.

This is just one of the many nuances to traveling in the rule book, so you can imagine the details for all the fouls and all the rules of play. The truth is that the rule book wouldn't be under my pillow but right there alongside me because by the time I would get to subpoint *d* in the traveling section, I'd be out like a light.

When Dr. James Naismith set out the rules of the game in 1891, he could have handed them out on a single sheet of paper, unlike the sixty-one we have today. Here are his thirteen rules:

1. The ball may be thrown in any direction with one or both hands.
2. The ball may be batted in any direction with one or both hands, but never with the fist.
3. A player cannot run with the ball. The player must throw it from the spot on which he catches it, allowance to be made for a man running at good speed.
4. The ball must be held in or between the hands. The arms or body must not be used for holding it.
5. No shouldering, holding, pushing, striking or tripping in any way of an opponent. The first infringement of this rule by any person shall count as a foul; the second shall disqualify him until the next goal is made or, if there was evident intent to injure the person, for the whole of the game. No substitution shall be allowed.
6. A foul is striking at the ball with the fist, violations of Rules 3 and 4 and such as described in Rule 5.
7. If either side makes three consecutive fouls it shall count as a goal for the opponents (consecutive means without the opponents in the meantime making a foul).
8. Goal shall be made when the ball is thrown or batted from the ground

into the basket and stays there, providing those defending the goal do not touch or disturb the goal. If the ball rests on the edge and the opponents move the basket, it shall count as a goal.

9. When the ball goes out of bounds, it shall be thrown into the field and played by the first person touching it. In case of dispute the umpire shall throw it straight into the field. The thrower-in is allowed five seconds. If he holds it longer, it shall go to the opponent. If any side persists in delaying the game, the umpire shall call a foul on them.

10. The umpire shall be judge of the men and shall note the fouls and notify the referee when three consecutive fouls have been made. He shall have the power to disqualify men according to Rule 5.

11. The referee shall be the judge of the ball and decide when it is in play in bounds, to which side it belongs, and shall keep the time. He shall decide when a goal has been made and keep account of the goals with any other duties that are usually performed by a referee.

12. The time shall be two 15-minute halves with five minutes' rest between.

13. The side making the most goals in that time shall be declared the winners.

As the game progressed, it obviously became a lot more complicated, and the rule book had to expand and develop to accommodate the increasing size of the players and other factors.

There is, of course, a big difference between reading the rules and knowing them and obeying them. Certainly, any kid coming up ought to know what constitutes a traveling violation. My coaches at the Penick Boys Club in Little Rock didn't sit us all down as six-year-olds and go over the rule book with us, explaining all the ways you can commit a traveling violation. We didn't have quizzes where you had to know the court dimensions and such things as "Four hash marks shall be drawn (2" wide) perpendicular to the sideline on each side of the court and 28' from the baseline. These hash marks shall extend 3' onto the court." They put the emphasis on developing our skills as players and most of the time relied on us to have some basic knowledge of the rules. When we violated those rules, that was when we learned a lesson about what not to do.

I can still picture some of my peewee-league teammates staring bug-eyed and drop-jawed at a referee who'd called them for a violation when they didn't know that they'd done anything wrong. On the basketball court or off, it's not a good idea to make it a practice to wait for a violation to be called on you in order to learn the rules. Always better to avoid the pain with a gain in knowledge. Having an older brother who played the game, as well as parents who did, gave me an advantage over a lot of other kids. I never abused my knowledge of the rules though.

Every neighborhood has them—the debaters. Those are the kids who, when you are playing any sandlot or playground game—football, baseball, basketball, soccer, whatever—seem more interested in having an argument about the rules than they do in actually playing the game. If you're like me, you can remember standing out in the middle of the baseball diamond, the football field, or the basketball court with your head in your hands looking skyward hoping for some relief from the fools who've decided that it is more fun to argue about whether a runner was safe or out, whether the guy with the ball had been touched before reaching the goal line, or if the guy lying on the court with the gashed knees was just clumsy or had been hacked on a layup attempt. I'm all for intellectual stimulation, the appropriate exercise of the First Amendment, and the various philosophical approaches to the nature of reality and perception, but, man, let's just get on with the game.

One of the great innovations we came up with as kids—we didn't invent this Solomon-like solution to disputes, but we used it a lot—was the "shoot-for-it solution." I realize that it has limited applications in adult life and outside the realm of sports, but I sometimes wonder if maybe it exists in disguise and lurks in all corners of life. The shoot-for-it solution was, and is, exactly what its name implies. In any dispute about whether a player stepped out of bounds, traveled, was fouled, etc., if the two sides couldn't agree, each team would select a shooter to decide the issue. Depending on where you grew up, the rules of the shoot-for-it varied, but at least everyone should have walked away from the dispute feeling that it had been settled "fairly."

Whether it was from my parents, or from the Reverend Mr. Sawyer at the Eighth Street Baptist Church, or from my teachers at Wilson Elementary School, I learned early on that rules were rules and I needed to abide by them. But when I was six or seven and out playing with the guys in Boyle Park, I learned some valuable lessons about human nature. The first was that not everybody held the truth in the same high regard as my family did. I was no saint, but if I fouled somebody or committed some kind of turnover on the basketball court or didn't foul tip a third strike, I'd admit it straight up. My mother and father would not tolerate lying. If I did something wrong, I'd own up to it. At first, I did that because I feared the punishment for lying about something was going to be worse than the punishment for doing that something. Later on, as my sense of ethics and morality more fully developed, I understood more clearly that there were the right things and the wrong things to do because of certain absolutes.

With my mom and dad, especially when I was younger, there were no "Yes, but . . ." or fuzzy gray areas.

Rules were rules.

My dad, an ex-military guy, expected discipline and would only put up with so much nonsense. But like a lot of kids, I discovered early that rules were made to be broken—or at least bent. I was recently talking to a friend of mine I went to college with back in Little Rock. He lives in Southern California now too, though. He's married and has two kids as I do, so we were swapping stories about family life. We both have stepsons—mine was twelve and his was eleven—and our talked turned to the knucklehead stuff that kids do in sixth and seventh grade. You tell them something fifty thousand times, and they still don't remember.

Now we get what our parents tried to tell us and how we didn't listen. The difference was, though, we knew what the rules were. We sometimes ignored them—and suffered the consequences. "I didn't know" would not cut it with my mom and dad. "Ignorance is no excuse. Ignorance is ignorance, and I didn't raise an ignorant child," my mother used to say. And they did spell out the rules clearly for us. They didn't issue a sixty-one-page document with all kinds of subparagraphs, but we understood—but.

For example, my mom and dad told me that I wasn't allowed to go to somebody else's house to play with them unless their parents were home. That meant that if I wanted to hang out with Rodney, Crash, or Larry, I'd have to check to see if their folks were home. Picking up the phone and calling was a pain in the butt, so I'd often just go over there to check things out. My other buddy Clarence had a basketball hoop in his driveway, and I loved nothing better than shooting hoops—if I couldn't be inside playing video games. I would go down the block to Clarence's place and knock on his bedroom window—front doors were for adults and not kids—to see if he was home. If he wasn't there, I'd be a little disappointed, but I also figured, "Hey, Clarence isn't home. I'm not playing with anybody but myself, so even if Clarence's parents aren't home, I'm okay. The rule says, don't play with somebody else at their house if their parents aren't home." I was a little lawyer in the making back then, as most kids are. In my heart, I knew I was breaking the rule. In my head, I invented all kinds of rationalizations for my misbehavior. Somehow, someway, my parents always seemed to know when I had broken a rule.

We had a fairly tight-knit community, and parents looked out for one another's kids. I think that's a good thing, and it's one aspect of small-town life that I miss living in the Los Angeles area. We had a real sense of community back in my Little Rock neighborhood, and at times when I drive through the area I live in today and I scan the backyards looking for groups of kids playing a pickup game of touch or baseball, I see no one. I see driveway and playground basketball hoops standing like dinosaur skeletons in an empty museum. All that makes me wonder if kids are learning about different approaches to solving problems, settling disputes, and how people have different views about rules and regulations. Sometimes when I'm with friends who have kids, I see them acting as referee and commissioner as they settle squabbles. We were expected to figure things out for ourselves. My parents laid down the broad outline of what was expected of us, and my siblings and I resolved our differences without running to the big authorities.

Throughout my life, in addition to my parents, I've had coaches who've been influential in shaping my view of the game and life. I've been fortunate in my NBA career to work under two of the most talented and successful coaches in the history of the pro game. Jerry Sloan was a hard-nosed guard who spent most of his playing career with the Chicago Bulls. He was a tenacious defender, and in his eleven-year career he made the All-Star squad in two seasons, while being named All-Defensive First Team four times and All-Defensive Second Team an additional two seasons. As a coach, he brought a lot of the same attributes he had as a player, and the results speak for themselves. As of the end of the 2007–8 season, Jerry was the fourth-winningest coach in NBA history, with 1,086 victories. Born in McLeansboro, Illinois, Jerry would be the first to admit that the small-town values he learned in rural mid-America shaped who he is and how he approaches coaching.

Like Coach Sloan, Phil Jackson enjoyed a stellar NBA playing career. Spending his entire thirteen-year career in the New York and New Jersey area, Phil cultivated a reputation as a thinking man's player and as someone with interests far beyond the boundary lines of the basketball court. Though he didn't get to play in the 1970 Knicks' championship series due to an injury, he did publish a book called *Take It All!* that was a photo diary of that championship season. As a coach, he's led his teams to ten NBA championships. Until our 2009 championship, they were equally divided among three three-peats—two with the Bulls and one with the Lakers. His teams have won at an astounding .701 clip—70 percent. He's also earned a reputation for working well with so-called troubled players.

Like Jerry, his values were shaped by his upbringing in rural America—except Phil decided to pursue his own path. The son of two Assembly of God ministers who wouldn't permit their children to watch television, see movies, or dance, Phil grew up in a strict and austere environment in Deer Lodge, Montana. Yet he became influenced by Eastern philosophy (that's why he's known as the Zen Master) and Native American spirituality.

I feel privileged to have played under two living legends and to have seen how two different approaches to the game and how to treat players can both produce winning teams. The Jazz and the Lakers organizations each have a reputation among players in the league. Much of that sense is a reflection of the head coaches. In addition to understanding the rules of the game, as professionals we need to understand and respect the rules that our coaches lay down for us governing our conduct on and off the court. The NBA also has certain expectations regarding the use of drugs, but the teams also have guidelines covering everything from curfews when we are on the road to how we are expected to dress while traveling with the team. When I first played for the Jazz, I was introduced to the Sloan Way in a surprising manner. During training camp, we were issued a pamphlet that ran down the team's regulations. In one meeting, Jerry discussed the possibility of a curfew for road trips. We all knew that one was coming, but we didn't get all the details. Nothing really surprising there, the Jazz had one of the most extensively written codes of conduct.

On our first road trip of the season, we traveled to the East Coast. Traveling is one of the most difficult parts of our profession, and it's easy to believe that NBA players are pampered crybabies. I'm aware of that perception, but when we travel, we have to perform at a high level in front of thousands of fans at the game and potentially millions more on television. This is no knock on New Jersey, but when you compare staying at the Secaucus, New Jersey, Sheraton to the Four Seasons in Manhattan, Jersey doesn't quite cut it. For West Coast teams traveling east and vice versa, those trips are the toughest because of the time-zone changes. On this particular trip, we got into the Sheraton a little after 9 p.m. for a game the following evening. My body was still on West Coast time, so I was eating dinner late but not terribly late. Room-service food was the only real option since the Sheraton is stuck in the middle of the Meadowlands in a sea of pavement and outlet malls and such. You've got a great view of Manhattan's skyline, but that view is no substitute for being in Manhattan and having every type of food imaginable (and some I can't) available to you just outside your hotel.

I didn't eat a whole lot, and by eleven thirty that night I was tired of flipping channels and still had a bit of a gnawing sensation in my belly. Normally, I would just have got something from the minibar, but the Sheraton's rooms don't have them. So I pulled on a pair of shoes and went to the lobby to get a cab. The driver took me to a convenience store, where I picked up some snacks and a Gatorade before returning to my room—inside scoop on the glamorous NBA life, right? I didn't get back to the room until a little after midnight. I ate and turned in for the night.

The next morning at our shootaround at what was then known as the Brendan Byrne Arena, one of the assistant coaches told me that Coach Sloan wanted to see me after practice. After I'd showered, I went to the visiting coach's office and knocked on the door. Coach Sloan waved me in. He was doing paperwork of some kind and told me he'd be with me in a minute.

"Derek," he said as he looked up from his work, "I heard that you got in at twelve fifteen last night."

I nodded. "That's about right."

"Well, we have a curfew of midnight and you violated that curfew," he began, then said a couple of other things. I knew some of our younger guys had had a few off-court problems in the preseason. Coach Sloan was doing what he could to make sure that we didn't go completely off the rails. At age thirty-two, I could appreciate better why he was saying the things he was saying, but one thought kept nagging at me. When he was through, I said, "Coach Sloan, I appreciate what you're saying, but we were never given a clear directive about curfew. You said that you were thinking about a midnight road curfew, but you never specifically stated that it was in effect." There I was back again reading the fine print, but in this case I really wasn't. I didn't object that I was just going out to get snacks and complain that other players were doing worse things than eating pretzels. Instead, I simply stood up for myself and the essential truth of the situation: we didn't have a curfew, so how could I have violated it?

Coach Sloan leaned back in his chair and his angular face looked thoughtful. Normally he was a black-and-white, yes/no kind of guy. I could see that my comments didn't fit into an easy scheme like that. He thanked me and told me that he had to check on some things before deciding what course of action to take. I'd been raised to believe in fairness and justice, and I was sure that the outcome would reflect those. I was right. At our next team meeting, Coach Sloan stated that we were all going to be subject to a midnight curfew on road trips starting that day. He didn't mention me or my situation, and I thought that was good. Some coaches might have tried to make themselves look good by letting everyone on the team know that he'd cut a player some slack.

As a younger guy, and I've seen other younger players do this, I could have got all upset when Coach Sloan said I came in "late." I could have viewed all the rules as just another attempt by management to be on the backs and at the throats of the players. Instead, I simply relied on a strict interpretation of what had not been stated clearly. What I appreciated from Coach Sloan was his willingness to listen to my side and not to make a snap judgment—both attributes that I try to emulate in dealing with my family, friends, and colleagues.

In Coach Sloan's approach to team discipline on and off the court, he established clear boundaries. This is what I expect. He's old-school in that sense: clear boundaries and clear consequences. If we talk about working the clock and you fire up a jumper early and don't make it, you almost certainly will hear about it—while sitting on the bench. While I have great respect and appreciation for his approach to rules, I also realized that I couldn't take that same approach with my kids or as a coach. Setting up boundaries makes it easier for the person establishing the rules, but I'm not convinced that creating a strictly black/white, yes/no set of expectations works as well with adults as it does with kids. Nuance and allowing for individual differences seems more like the ideal approach to take.

In contrast to Coach Sloan, Phil has far fewer rules. Both of them have the same outcome in mind when it comes to the team's rules: to create an environment conducive to success on the court; to have players respect themselves, their opponents, and the league. They just take different routes to get there. Phil simply makes the objectives clear, then lets his players decide on how to behave to produce those results. He believes that you need to know the rules and it's up to you to figure out how to conduct yourself like a professional. He's less focused on the small details, and for that reason I always felt a bit freer on and off the court when playing for him. He understands the need to find a balance between a rigid system and too little discipline that meets everybody's needs.

In a lot of ways, we are all still like kids. We need structure, but we also need freedom. The two aren't contradictory, and gradually through trial and error, we all do or don't find that balance essential to success. I believe that the teams that are the most successful have a shared concept. In that sense, discipline is key. There is always some correlation between how you conduct yourself off the court and on, but I don't think it's a direct connection. The teams with the fewest curfew violations don't always win the NBA championship.

I guess that I'm a lot like Phil in that we both grew up in homes in which adherence to rules was important. We also both grew in a slightly different direction from our roots. Balance and flexibility are more important to us than structure and exactness. While we don't resort to the shoot-for-it solution to resolve conflicts, we do believe people can have different perspectives, yet put aside some of those differences to execute the shared vision of the team. One approach is somewhat simple and reduces complexity, while the other acknowledges that any human enterprise is complicated and that needs to be accounted for and acknowledged up front. Again, same destination, but different routes.

Because of my attitude and perceptions I have even more respect for NBA officials than I otherwise might. I've always been respectful of authority figures in our game and outside it. That's just how I was raised, but today in the NBA I see a little too much rigid adherence to rules going on. By that, I don't mean that officials shouldn't call a foul a foul, but they should also be allowed to find the balance and flexibility they need to perform at their best. I believe that our officials are among the best in sports. They are under such scrutiny by the director of officiating, and with the kinds of critiques and monitoring they are subject to in calling the game, I don't envy their position at all. It's as if they are to be computer-controlled robots assigned certain positions on the court, and that limits their ability to really "see" and call the game as they feel it. As players we're encouraged to let the game come to us, but if the officials are controlling the flow of the game because of some edict handed down from the league office, then we could be waiting a long time for the game to arrive.

Consequently, the game doesn't unfold as naturally as it possibly could. What troubles me from a player's perspective is that we each have individual strengths and weakness, and because of the way the game is called today, we end up being forced to play the game as if we all had the same skill set. Big physical players such as Shaq and others need to be subjected to a different set of parameters than smaller, quicker players. That makes sense to me, but it doesn't fit with the kind of strict-interpretation guidelines that seem to dominate the game. As with the Sloan method, the NBA's policies do make clear what the expectations are, and I suppose it is up to us to adjust to them, but that feels a little like putting the horse before the cart.

A zero-tolerance, black-and-white assessment is a good thing in the NBA when it comes to illegal conduct by anyone associated with the game. The NBA, and the sports world in general, were rocked by the revelations that NBA game official, Tim Donaghy, had bet on games. When he plead guilty in August 2007 to charges of wirefraud and transmitting betting information, that didn't put the issue to rest. Just as baseball's steroids scandal called into question the integrity of the game, Donaghy's actions made people question the legitimacy of the outcome of some of the NBA's games.

I'm not about to pass judgment on someone like Donaghy. I can't put myself into his shoes, but his claims that he was under pressure to comply with the wishes of gamblers because of alleged threats against his family members certainly complicate my feelings about his violating league rules and federal law. I've spent more time thinking about the enormous impact one person's misdeeds can have on so many other people. Donaghy's decision must have been motivated by self-interest at first, and I can empathize with him as one bad decision spiraled into others and others, but he could still have come forward and notified the authorities and got himself out of the jam and limited the damage to himself and to the league.

Clearly, he crossed a line with his misconduct, and I was deeply troubled by the revelations of his violations and the subsequent aftermath. There is a real difference between knowingly entering into that kind of illegal activity and doing so out of ignorance. In no way do I equate what Donovan McNabb did with Donaghy's misdeeds, but they do illustrate my point about knowledge and ignorance and understanding the rules. I almost fell into a similar trap to Donovan McNabb's when I was at the University of Arkansas, Little Rock. One day at the start of my freshmen year, Coach Platt called me into his office and said, "Derek, I need to speak with you about some possible NCAA violations."

I felt as if I'd been punched in the gut. I hadn't even played a game yet, and I was being accused of some kind of infraction?

Coach Platt said someone reported that while I was a senior in high school and playing AAU ball, I had been using a gasoline charge card for personal use. I was shocked and angry. I'd heard of the kinds of recruiting violations that went on at major universities with some athletes receiving cars or their families getting low-interest loans and a whole host of other big-money perks. I explained to coach that I was using a gas credit card that belonged to my AAU team's owner. He had asked me to pick up various players who couldn't yet drive or who were coming in on buses from other parts of the state for practices. Sometimes I used his car or my family's car, and he wanted to make sure that I didn't incur any out-of-pocket expenses. I didn't realize it at the time, but that was a possible violation of NCCA regulations involving illegal inducements. Fortunately, after I explained the situation and Coach Platt worked things out with the NCAA, neither the team nor I were subject to any sanctions. Lesson learned about not knowing all the rules.

Life outside basketball is as filled with as many rules and possible stumbling blocks that can put you out of bounds as is the game. Mark Cuban, the owner of the Dallas Mavericks, is one of the most successful men I've ever met. I like Mark, and his passionate devotion to his team is admirable. He sometimes runs afoul of NBA management (the commissioner) and other owners because he sometimes allows his emotions to get the better of him, and in the past he's made comments critical of the league's officiating and other policies. Mark is his own man, and I would never tell him what to do or how to conduct himself. I offer him up as an example to help illustrate that toeing the line and keeping your emotions in check can pay big dividends. (I've not been as successful in business as Mark Cuban has, and he's someone I would like to emulate in that regard.)

Among the reasons that I am so respectful of rules and those who enforce them in the NBA is that I truly believe in karma. I'm certain that you get in return what you put out into the universe. That's not a truly 100 percent idealistic statement as it pertains to basketball. I believe that if I conduct myself respectfully and treat others, in particular referees, with the respect they deserve, I might benefit from that down the line. If there's a borderline call, it may go my way if I don't have a reputation for giving out hard fouls needlessly. If I don't have a history of getting T'ed up by the referees, then I may be able to get in a few words with a referee to possibly influence how the game is called. Earning my team a strategic advantage is a good thing. That my teammates, coaches, fans, the opposition, and the league office know that I'm not a troublemaker puts currency in my bank account that I can earn interest on and withdraw later.

I'm honest enough with myself to know that I've stayed in the league because of my talent +. What is that +? Being a guy who knows the game and also respects the game and his teammates and the league. Being a guy who is a good teammate and a reliable, steady presence. There is a big difference between a butt kisser and someone who conducts himself professionally as much as possible all the time. We're known as *players,* but I think of myself as a *professional.* Just as a doctor, lawyer, teacher, investment banker, etc., has to conduct himself or herself in a specified manner, I believe it's my responsibility to behave in way that enhances my standing in the eyes of management, fans, and my colleagues on the court.

My mother used to tell me that it was a good idea to treat people kindly, even strangers, because you never knew. Not that you never knew who was watching and judging you, but that you never knew under what circumstances you might meet that person again. In the business world you have to be careful what you say and whom you say it to because as big as this world is, it is also small. That lesson was driven home when I watched the reaction to Mark Cuban's possible purchase of the Chicago Cubs. The Cubs are one of the storied franchises in sports, and Wrigley Field is considered a kind of national treasure, the way Fenway Park in Boston is. Some people speculated that because of his run-ins with NBA management, baseball's franchise owners, who have to approve any sale of a franchise, might reject him. They might not want someone in their exclusive circle who might be a troublemaker. I haven't talked with Mark about this and don't know if he is even concerned at all about this perception that is out there.

My point is essentially this. Doing the right thing and understanding and conforming to the rules of the game are important morally and also pragmatically. Too often we think that we don't get rewarded for playing fair and by the rules. We think that we only get punished (sometimes) when we break those rules. What I've learned is that when you look long term and see the bigger picture, knowing and playing by the rules has potential benefits that far outweigh any negative consequences. Doing right is its own reward, and if you continue to do right, those rewards may be multiplied. That's what is written in Derek's rule book, and it's one that I don't need to study because I carry it in my heart and mind all the time.

CHAPTER EIGHT

Dribbling:

The Ultimate in Ups and Downs

When I quoted the original thirteen rules of basketball, you may have noticed one thing was completely missing—dribbling. In the game's infancy, players just passed the ball to one another. As soon as a running player caught the ball, he was expected to stop. The only way to advance the ball was to pass it off. What I've always thought is cool is that players figured out that a player could pass the ball to himself to advance toward the hoop. The inventor of the game didn't come up with it; the innovation was born of necessity and ingenuity by the guys who actually played the game. Some people in the early twenties wanted to eliminate passing to yourself, but the National Association of Basketball Coaches was formed to oppose that ban on dribbling. I can't imagine the game without dribbling. It's amazing to me that the early act of just bouncing the ball a few inches ahead of yourself, then picking it up and repeating, has evolved into the kinds of ballhandling displays you see every day in the NBA and in the NCAA and elsewhere.

I remember watching as a kid the Harlem Globetrotters on their Saturday-morning cartoon show, *The Super Globetrotters.* They were crime-fighting superheroes who always settled their dispute with the evil villains with a basketball game. I also saw the Globetrotters live and on television and, like nearly everybody else, loved the dazzling displays of dribbling that Curly Neal would put on. Meadowlark Lemon was the big-time clown of the show, but the antics of the shave-headed Curly caught my attention. Because of the kind of training that I had, and the emphasis on the basics and the fundamentals, I never really tried to imitate Curly. Sometimes just messing around with the guys I do a few between-the-legs and behind-the-back things, but more important to me is just being a consistent ball handler who doesn't turn the ball over and doesn't get stripped. I have some decent moves and I don't pound the ball mechanically the way you see some of the big men doing, but dribbling as a show or an art form isn't a part of my game.

When I do clinics or speak to a group of young guys and girls, I frequently start off with a ball in my hand. I'll drop it and let it bounce back up. I use that as a demonstration of the ball's natural resilience and ability to bounce back up. I tell them that that's how they need to be. A lot of times, we get in the way of our natural ability to move past the inevitable bad things in life. I don't know of anyone who hasn't struggled or gone through tough times. Those ups and downs continue to repeat themselves in my life, and I've seen people in my profession and in my personal life who have let those down times defeat them. I think that a lot of that has to do with them and their inability to get out of their own way and allow the natural process or their natural ability to recover from those down times.

I see young kids learning to dribble and I see parallels between their struggles to maintain control of the ball and the kinds of things we do as adults that prevent us from coming back from a down period. When you're young and learning to dribble, you tend to keep your hand going down as the ball descends. It's almost as if you don't trust that the ball is going to come back up to you. It will. You just have to be willing to let go a little bit and let the ball do its thing. In my life, it took me time to learn that simple principle applies off the court too. I've always had a strong faith in God, but like a lot of people I've had trouble with the idea of letting go and trusting that the plan He has for me will take me in the most positive direction I could possibly go. I think that when Tatum was diagnosed, some of the illusion that I was in control faded. Candace and I had used in vitro fertilization in an attempt to better control the fate of our child. I'm not suggesting that God gave Tatum eye cancer to teach us a lesson about not messing with His plan. I don't mean that at all. What I do believe is that in life you receive a series of messages in various forms. Those messages are telling you what you need to work on to achieve the kind of peace of mind and happiness that we all want. I think I needed to learn to control what I could reasonably control and to surrender the rest.

For my whole professional career I'd been trying to position myself to play more minutes, be the coach's guy in crunch time, fully be the leader of the team out on the court, and all that. I was making my way toward that in fits and starts, getting close to it, then having something come up that set me back. Dealing with Tatum's illness made me stop, take stock of things, and put things in perspective. I thought that I had before, but this was God, the universe, and everything else telling me that I was deceiving myself. I wasn't living a lie. I was concerned about being a good husband and father and good citizen of the world. But a lot of those lessons I had learned about working hard had distorted things a bit. I always seemed to feel that if I just exerted more effort, eliminated more distractions, focused more intently on the game, and did all the right things nutritionally, spiritually, and physically, I'd get what I wanted. Funny thing was, as the old Rolling Stones song "Satisfaction" said, sometimes when you try real hard, you get what you need. And what I needed to realize, and what Tatum's cancer helped me realize, was that God had an idea of what He wanted for me and of me. I learned that I could be of service to others in a way that I had never understood before. And it had just a little bit to do with basketball.

Because of my prominent position (prominent in the sense that I had easy access to the media), when I spoke to TNT sideline reporter Pam Oliver after that play-off game back in 2007, the words I spoke about Tatum's disease spread worldwide. There was no script, I hadn't thought out days or weeks in advance what I wanted to say, I simply let go and spoke from the heart. My emotions got the best of me, but I'd say that my revealing my emotions revealed the best in me. Since then, Dr. Abramson has publicly said that my speaking out about retinoblastoma has done more for the field and more for patients and their families than he has, and that the impact has been "enormous and profound." I think that Dr. Abramson underestimates what he's contributed over the years and overestimates what I did. I was just the messenger, and the words that came to me were placed in my heart by someone else.

What neither Dr. Abramson nor I can deny is that people from around the world—Germany, Vietnam, Saudi Arabia, England, Italy, India, and Israel—have all come to Memorial Sloan-Kettering Cancer Center in Manhattan to see Dr. Abramson and his colleagues. In an interview in the *New York Times,* Dr. Abramson said that when he asked these people why the had come, they said that it was because of Tatum and the story they'd heard about her. Candace has also told me that when she's in the waiting room at Sloan-Kettering or at L.A. Children's Hospital, she invariably gets recognized. At nearly every one of those follow-up visits, other parents have told her that they've seen me and heard about Tatum. I'm deeply gratified by that, and thankful that many more families have been able to take advantage of the wonderful work that Dr. Abramson and his people do. Even though at the time we never asked, "Why us?" or "Why Tatum?" I now understand why. When I read the newspaper stories about Dr. Abramson and his work and hear similar stories of the good word being spread, I know God decided that these things should be so.

I can't even begin to count the number of times I've dribbled a basketball in my life. Over time I came to do it as unconsciously as breathing. It would only be a slight exaggeration to say that I can do it in my sleep, and I can do it with my eyes closed. In looking back over my basketball career and how I got to this place, I believe that in many ways I was living as if my eyes were closed. Now that I no longer live that way as frequently, the difference is clearly noticeable.

If you ever watch an NBA game and just follow the ball being dribbled, the hypnotic effect will have you drifting off in no time. Though referees watch our dribbling for rules infractions, most of you probably don't pay much attention to it. Just as it has become a nearly automatic reflex among us, the same is true for fans. It's one of those little things, one of those fundamentals, that we don't notice until something goes wrong with it. As my years in the NBA added up, I found myself sometimes dribbling away unconsciously. Not until Tatum's health crisis did I get knocked out of my routine. I thought that I had got where I wanted to be in life—I was finally married to the woman I'd loved for a long time, I had children, I was playing again for a top-notch NBA team, I was a respected veteran player, I was the head of the NBA Players Association—and life was very, very good. I can't say that I was complacent because I was still working as hard as ever to get back to the NBA Finals and to win a championship, I was still exploring new ways to keep my body fit, I was still thinking about and exploring avenues that I might pursue after I was done playing the game—but all those things were about me, my family, my teammates, and my fellow players. Nothing wrong with that, but speaking out in Utah that night and all that has happened since made me realize the truth about ripple effects and just how far out from the impact point they can travel.

So writing this book and thinking back on all those ups and downs is a way for me to learn something about myself and my life, and hopefully for you to learn something about you and your life. I've started to think more about the why of these events and what they mean. Sometimes being a professional basketball player can mean that you're like the Bill Murray character in the movie *Groundhog Day*. We work hard to develop a daily routine—waking at a certain hour, eating many of the same things, going to practice or a shoot-around at a certain time, going back someplace to nap, arriving at the arena a certain number of minutes before game time, going out on the floor at X number of minutes before tip-off. We're all about routine and consistency and getting to the point where we don't have to think so much, we just respond and let our body do its thing. It's a great feeling when our body does what we've trained it to do, and when it doesn't—whether because of injury or whatever—it can shake us up a bit. That's why I think it's important for me to have taken the time to reflect on these events and to see the pattern that has emerged.

I sometimes feel like saying, "Not again!" when I have to prove myself capable of being a full-time player, of being the guy to be there when the outcome is on the line, the one whom the coaching staff trusts to help take us all the way. Now instead of asking, "Why me? Why am I in this position again?" and having that be a lament, I ask those questions because I'm wondering, what opportunity is being presented to me? What can I learn about myself, my faith, and my place in the world and not just the lineup? More important, what can I pass on to others? We all want to make strides toward the same or similar goals. If I can pass the ball off to you, maybe you can come up with some innovation, some new way doing things that will get you nearer to where you want to be.

I was fortunate to come into the league and receive similar kinds of "passes" from other Lakers. In particular, Shaquille O'Neal, Byron Scott, and Nick Van Exel helped me out. Shaq came to the Lakers from the Orlando Magic during the same off-season I was drafted, and we had an interesting relationship. We were both new to the Lakers, but Shaq had already been in the league for four years. Two and a half years older than me, Shaq enjoyed thinking of me as his little brother, and I didn't mind having him as a kind of big brother. Shaq didn't necessarily like yes-men hanging around him, and the big-brother thing only goes so far. He wasn't looking for me to be a puppy dog following him around or a puppet whose strings he could pull to get whatever he wanted. He treated me more as an equal, but since he had some experience in the league, he could share some of his insights about the written and unwritten rules of the game and how to conduct yourself as a professional.

We both had an ex-military man who was present in our lives and in our development. I got to know Shaq's stepfather, and he reminded me in some ways of my father. Shaq and I also shared having a mother who was actively involved in our lives and to whom we were devoted. My move to Los Angeles represented the first time that I was going to be away from Little Rock and friends and family. Most guys had gone to college at a greater distance from home than I had, so the other rookies around the league and on our team (including Kobe Bryant, who was drafted ahead of me straight out of high school) had an advantage on me. True, Kobe hadn't gone away to college, but he'd lived in Europe. Kobe and I had a more distant relationship. I was twenty-two and he was only eighteen, and I think he was more guarded in lots of ways than I was. I can't imagine what it was like for him or understand fully what he was going through. Being a top pick, coming out of high school, having people expecting such great things from you, it all had to be even more unreal to him than it was to me.

At twenty-two, I went from having no money to making a really good salary. A lot of that money was going to be eaten up by taxes, but I didn't have much of a clue about that at the beginning. The NBA recognized that many of the players coming into the league needed help transitioning to adult life. As a result, in September I attended a four- or five-day program before I went to Hawaii for training camp. The Rookie Transition Program provided us with information about all aspects of life as a professional athlete, from health and nutrition to finances, personal relationships, and league policies regarding drugs. It was a lot of information, and not until you bumped up against some of those things could you make sense of it all. As excited as I was about getting a chance to play in the NBA, I was equally excited about living a more independent life. One of the first things I did was to purchase a new car for myself—the first one of my own I'd ever had. I'd always had a thing for the Lexus LX 450

SUV, so that's what I got. Figures, doesn't it? A utility vehicle. No Ferrari, Lamborghini, or Porsche for this guy. Still, it was what I wanted, and it was practical, since I'd be driving out to L.A. to find a place to live and I had to take some of my things with me.

I found a three-bedroom apartment in Marina Del Rey through the help of the Lakers and a real estate agent. I needed the three bed-rooms because my best friend, Clarence, and my cousin Anthony were to live with me. Clarence was my age, but he hadn't gone to college and was still trying to figure some things out. Anthony had just graduated from high school. He and I had been close and I was a kind of big brother to him. He hadn't settled on a path for himself either. My aunt Christine and my uncle John were a bit concerned about his moving away, but I talked with them and assured them I would be on top of things and that he'd get himself into school out there. They agreed, and the trust they put in me meant a lot. Having those two guys with me also helped me. That little bit of back home would help keep me steady and in check. Making it possible for Anthony to experience life outside Little Rock and enlarging his vision of life's possibilities was something I was glad to do.

It was amazing living in the Marina City Club right on the water with a city view from my eleventh-floor apartment. I got to furnish it once I got there, and going out and buying all those things plus a home-entertainment center and a pool table was a lot of fun. Not many guys from the team lived nearby, but I didn't consider that a priority. What was great was that it was close to Los Angeles Interna-tional Airport and to our practice facility at Loyola Marymount Uni-versity. I decided early on that I was going to take advantage of what Los Angeles had to offer, and being in a big city for a prolonged pe-riod was a first for me. I think we got to meet just about every carry-out deliveryman and most of the hosts at restaurants in our first few years there. I was mostly anonymous at the beginning, and that was okay with me. I had enough going on in my life not to worry about whether enough people were recognizing me when I went to clubs or parties.

Getting to know the Lakers was a bit easier than getting out and meeting people in a big city such as L.A. Interestingly, almost from the beginning, my teammates seemed to understand the type of person I am. In most every professional sport, rookies go through hazing at the start of the season and sometimes throughout the entire season. The Lakers made you get up in front of the whole group and perform something they asked you to do. Some guys had to sing their school fight song, some had to dance. At our first official training-camp practice, I was told to get up and recite as many lines as I could from Dr. Martin Luther King Jr.'s "I Have a Dream" speech. Instead of having me do something silly or funny, the guys asked for, and got, a serious rendition of a milestone oration in American history. I had been a speech communications major in college and had to do a lot of speaking, and I knew most of the speech's important and most memorable lines. What struck me then is that the guys keyed in immediately, even before they knew me, that I was a pretty serious person. The coaches were also all there, and I sometimes wonder if it was their idea to have me say that piece.

A number of guys were in camp competing for one of the precious spots on the roster. I was assured of being on the team, but whether I got any playing time was another matter. Nick Van Exel had been the starting point guard, and Rumeal Robinson was also in the mix. Just before our preseason opener, I got word that Coach Del Harris wanted to see me. I wasn't too concerned, we weren't going to be making any cuts or releasing guys that early, but I was curious to hear what he had to say. He asked me to sit down, and he said what I already pretty much knew—Nick Van Exel was going to be starting at the point. I wasn't as prepared for what he said next: "And you're going to be the number two behind him." I thanked him and said I appreciated knowing where I stood. A lot of times coaches don't want to let you know where you are in the rotation because they're afraid you might get complacent. Well, that wasn't going to happen to me.

That was wonderful positive feedback and the kind of open communication that I had always hoped I'd get. I wondered if this was how all professional organizations ran, and this businesslike approach of "Here's the reality so you don't have to guess what's going on" was great. That eliminated any anxiety I was feeling, but on opening night at the Great Western Forum, my system was flooded with nervous energy. Again, things could not have gone better for me during my first regular-season NBA game. Instead of my having to sit around most of the first quarter worrying and wondering and getting cold, Nick Van Exel picked up his second foul a minute and a half into the game. I was inserted into the lineup and finished the game with 11 points and 3 assists. Not a spectacular performance, but a very, very solid one. Getting those positive strokes from Coach Harris really helped, and I was determined not to let him down and to show that he was right in trusting me. They let me know what was expected of me, set a goal or standard that I needed to achieve, and I went out and performed at that level and higher.

All that sounds pretty simple, yet in sports and in business those simple things are too often forgotten. Adjusting to NBA life and the travel was somewhat difficult, but I was more concerned about making the transition to coming off the bench. I'd just spent four years getting the vast majority of the playing time, and when you start a game, you always know when you're going to be expected to perform. You can set your routine by that, and I had to develop a new routine based on not knowing when I would go in or for how long. That transition was fairly easy since I'd spent a lot of my time in AAU ball as a reserve and not a starter. I drew on those past experiences. I looked at my situation as if I were an entry-level employee. I'd earned a job with the team, but I had no sense of entitlement. I knew that if I was going to move up, it would be based on merit. I liked that. I didn't have to worry about if the guy ahead of me was playing just because his father was the assistant coach or any other kind of political stuff that had bugged me when I was coming up.

That's not to say I was happy coming off the bench, far from it. I wanted to be out there, but I wasn't expecting anyone to hand me anything. In a lot of ways, being on the bench was good for me. I could watch the game from a slightly different perspective—literally since I was sitting off to one side and was not directly in the action—and that allowed me to see things that I might not otherwise have seen. The flow of the game and some of the opposition's tendencies were easier to spot than they might have been if I had been out there on the court with lots of other things to see and to do. As a result, generally when I went into the game, I was able to make a significant play of some kind—get a steal, deflect a pass to create a turnover, get an assist, take a charge—all because I'd been taking note of things while I was on the bench. As a point guard, you have more responsibilities than some of the other players in terms of leadership and running the team. You have less glamorous duties, but understanding your function and how you fit into the whole enterprise is an important part of success no matter what you do. Seeing the big picture from the point-guard position and being able to take advantage of the other team's weaknesses and tendencies, and being able to put our game plan into motion, gives me a lot of satisfaction.

That first year was all about learning the ins and outs of the game at that level and recognizing that I fit in. I did belong there. I had enough game to compete with all these guys. I wasn't at the level of a Michael Jordan; then again, who really was? I did have one nice exchange with him that year. We were playing in Chicago—I was a little disappointed that Chicago Stadium had been replaced by the United Center, just as I was that the Boston Garden had been by the Fleet Center—and I had been assigned to guard him. During a stop in play for a foul, he stood next to me and said, "You work hard. Keep it up." I appreciated that small bit of recognition, and I think that was typical of Michael Jordan and some of the other veterans around the league. More than a few of those guys took seriously the idea that they were at the top but it would be for a relatively short time, then the next generation of players were going to come along and take over. We couldn't really ever replace Michael Jordan, Charles Barkley, Magic, Bird, or the rest in one sense, but in a lot of others we could. Those guys had really helped build the league into what it was, and they didn't want to see their work go down the drain.

I had a real appreciation for the league and its history, and I'm pleased that today a lot of the younger guys seem to have regained some of what was lost when people were talking about brawls and drug suspensions and all kinds off-court activities and scandals instead of the great game that it is. I'm probably more pleased that I see this happening in society. To me, one of the cool things about the recent election of President Obama was how he seemed to transcend generations and also recall the past. I heard younger people talking about Dr. King and Abraham Lincoln and how the near past and the distant past were linked. I've always loved the traditions in sports, such as the green jacket at the Masters in Augusta, and other things that span from the past to the present. In just about every town we played in, I'd think about what other NBA greats had been in that building before me—Willis Reed in Madison Square Garden, Dominique Wilkins in Atlanta, Dave Bing in Detroit. The list went on. I think that by knowing about that history and remembering it, I wasn't losing sight of the here and now, but reinforcing the idea that I was part of something bigger. The game wasn't about me.

I've been privileged to play alongside two of this era's greatest players, Kobe and Shaq. I said before that Shaq and I had a good relationship, but it didn't start out that way. Shaq loves to tell everyone the story of how we "met." Before the Lakers had their own practice facility, we worked out at Loyola Marymount University, where the great college star Hank Gathers went to school. He died on the court, and later that year his friend and teammate, Bo Kimble, in one of the most moving acts of sportsmanship I can ever remember, shot every free throw in his NCAA tournament games left-handed in memory of Hank.

Before our training camp began, I went to do some work at Loyola. Coach Harris was there, then Shaq showed up. He was stretching while I worked on some things. Coach Harris wanted Shaq to run some pick-and-roll drills, so coach asked me to help out. Shaq just started doing his thing, basically not even acknowledging me, assuming that I was just some Loyola player. He had no idea who I was. When Coach Harris introduced us after the workout, Shaq was mortified. He didn't let on much though, just saying something in the way that only Shaq could, "Oops!" and laughing nervously. Privately he told me he would make it up to me, and he did. The funny thing about it is, Shaq was the guy least likely to put his nose in the air around anybody. He was always a great teammate and didn't treat any player any differently whether he was an All-Star or a free agent signed to a ten-day contract to fill out a roster.

Kobe and I enjoy a great relationship today. That didn't develop instantly. Our first year, I was a little bit envious of the guy. Who wouldn't be? He was our top draft choice in 1996. Still, I kept thinking, "How can a guy out of high school be more ready to play in the NBA than me?" Kobe exuded the confidence that he was not only good enough to be in the NBA but to be the most dominant player. He was refined in ways that I could never have been at age eighteen by virtue of his background. He seemed pretty aloof and didn't hang out with the guys much (which I can see now was understandable given the age differences), but we were sometimes forced to interact because we were both rookies getting limited playing time. Because of that, the day after a game when the rest of the team had an off day, we went to the gym to practice. A few times it was the two of us, or maybe Rumeal Robinson or Travis Knight would join us.

One day in Milwaukee, Kobe, Corie Blount, Travis, and I went to practice. We shot around for a bit, then played some two on two. After Corie and Travis checked out, Kobe and I were left. We decided to play some one on one. After a bit, things got a little physical. Along with the usual bumping by the defensive player, Kobe kept using his off hand to hook me to get by me. I was used to defenders bodying me up and stuff, but I didn't like what Kobe was doing. He'd been around NBA players for a lot of his life because of his dad, and he'd picked up a few tricks. But in my mind those tricks were fouls and the offensive man shouldn't be putting his hands on me.

I told him he was fouling me and he didn't say a thing, just looked at me with that Kobe glare. I was not going to back down, so the next time he tried to hook me, I fouled him—hard and with a push. He didn't say anything, just took the ball out again. I fouled him again. Things went from heated to boiling. We got in each other's face about who was pushing whom. Finally we were chest-to-chest jawing at each other, and even though Kobe is six inches taller than me, I was not going to back down. Besides, I weighed nearly as much as the skinny little dude. I'd had enough and I said, "You hook me like that one more time, and we're going to go? Understand me?"

Kobe spat back, "Why wait? Let's go at it right now. Okay?"

"Okay."

Fortunately, it didn't come to our punching each other. We let it drop, and I think we both looked at each other a little bit differently after that. We had tested each other and we'd both passed and earned each other's respect.

I felt good about my first year. I played in eighty games including the postseason, averaging about twelve minutes and 4 points per game. We won fifty-six games that year (after winning fifty-three the previous year) and finished just as we had the previous season—second in our division and fourth in the conference. The play-offs were everything I'd heard they would be. The intensity was notches above what it was in the regular season. Fewer fouls were called, the guys were much more physical, and the electricity in Los Angeles and everywhere else we played was palpable. In the first round we beat Portland 3-1, and I got few minutes, but we stuck to the same rotation. I expected that would be the case in the second round when we faced the Utah Jazz. We'd lost in the first round of the play-offs the previous year, so advancing was good. I was really looking forward to playing against the Jazz, but then one of those down times had to come along. Throughout the year, the coaching staff couldn't figure out what to do with Kobe. He wasn't yet physically developed enough to match up well against shooting guards in the league. He wasn't a true point guard either. During the regular season he'd averaged a few less minutes than me, but he hadn't played at point guard.

In that series, Kobe was chosen to take my place in the rotation. No one said anything to me, but I didn't play a single minute, and we were swept by the Jazz. That was hard for me. I felt that the year had been so positive, and then it ended on such a negative note for the team and for me. I wasn't the only one puzzled, and some newspaper stories and some rumors swirled around that Kobe's agent had put pressure on the team's management, who put pressure on the coach, to figure out a way to get him more minutes. The reasoning likely went something like this: You picked him with your first selection. You've invested a lot of money in him and think he's going to be a part of your future. I represent other players in the league who will become free agents. They're going to listen to me about good opportunities.

I can't say for certain those conversations took place, and I'm no conspiracy theorist, but stranger things have gone on. At the time I was confused, and that off-season I found myself in a familiar place. I had done well, but I was going to have to do more to solidify my standing on the team. I thought I'd proved my value, but the word *proved* is past tense: I was going to have to keep proving it. In retrospect, I should have learned some other lessons, and I kind of did but not fully. They are: Control what you can and don't worry about the rest (in other words, my paying any attention to those rumors and speculations was a waste of time and energy). Everyone wins when the team wins. You can control performance and results, so work on improving your performance. Make yourself invaluable in some way.

I had already figured out the last one. When I got to the pros and looked back on some of what had happened in AAU ball and high school, I realized that a lot of times coaches wouldn't start me or play me the minutes I deserved or whatever because I was not likely to complain. They could treat me in a way they might not have treated someone else because I wasn't going to rock the boat. With the Lakers, though, rocking the boat was not something I wanted or needed to do. I understood that as I moved up the ladder, there were fewer and fewer spaces on the rung. Why would a team keep a guy if he was a "troublemaker"? Finding a backup point guard wouldn't be that tough. So I made myself invaluable by being a good teammate and a team player. That didn't mean that I wouldn't eventually go to a coach to respectfully ask for more information about some decision, but I wasn't going to take my questions to the media or to the locker room and poison it. That too was a waste of energy. Worrying, kicking up dirt, and all that other stuff was unproductive. I'd always been taught the old-school way—keep your mouth shut and let your play do the talking.

At that point, and more so at other points in my career, I was angry about suspect decisions regarding me. But I learned not to act out of anger and not to speak out of anger. I needed to step away from the situation. In the season, that was especially true. Another game was always in the pipeline, and the worst thing I could do was let my anger, confusion, disappointment, etc., carry over from one game to the next. The same was true with one season to the next. Fortunately, I had time to work things out in my mind and approached my sophomore season with a clean slate.

As badly as my first season ended, the next season the ball came bouncing up for me. As so often happens in the game and in life, that bounce back up for me came at the expense of a bad bounce for someone else. At the start of the 1997–98 season, Nick Van Exel had problems with his knee and couldn't go at the start of the season. Everyone hoped that rest would help. That meant that I was going to be the starter as the season opened. We were in Indiana playing the Pacers, and the game was going to be the opening-night broadcast for TBS. Bryan Burwell came up to me moments after I learned that I was going to start and I said, "I'm just here to help us win. I'm not concerned at all about my statistics." Well, I think not being concerned with them helped because I once again took advantage of an opportunity and started off well by scoring 20 points that night, by far my greatest point production as a professional to that point.

Some seasons seem to be a blur to me, but I have such a clear recollection not of that whole game, but of one play. Late in the fourth quarter, we were up by just a few points and I brought the ball up court. I dribbled to the wing and fed the ball into Shaq on the block, and as expected, they double-teamed Shaq and I was open. As he did thousands of times in his career, Shaq kicked the ball back out this time to me for a wide-open look. I rose up, and halfway there, I knew the shot was good, and it was. It was just as we'd drawn it up, was just as we'd run it hundreds of times in practice. That basket seemed to break the Pacers' spirit, and we went on to the victory. I can still picture that jumper floating in the air, almost seeming to hang suspended at its apex before coming down softly. After the game, I did a TBS interview, and we joked about my pregame statement. Just imagine if I had cared about my stats.

I continued to play well at the start of that season, including scoring 18 points against the Knicks on national television. Oddly, maybe the highest compliment I was paid was against the Knicks in New York. I fouled out, but the Knicks crowd was so glad to see me leave, their taunting and singing told me just how effectively I'd been playing. The following Monday, in an NBA recap in *USA Today,* in their power rankings, they asked if Derek Fisher was the best backup point guard in the NBA. The sports information department at UALR sent me a copy of that, and it felt good to be getting that kind of recognition in a national publication. Even more gratifying, we were doing well. We won our first eleven out of the gate, and the longest losing streak we had was three games (which occurred twice). We ended with a regular-season record of 61-21. We beat Portland again in the opening round and faced Seattle in the Western Conference semifinals. We lost the first game on the road, then swept the next four games to advance to the conference finals against the Utah Jazz.

If I'd thought that the earlier rounds of the play-offs were intense, the conference finals were frenzied. With so much media coverage and so much excitement about the matchup to see who would go to the finals, the buildup and anticipation were almost painful. I was so eager to get out there and play. I was starting every game in the play-offs, but splitting the minutes with Nick Van Exel. He had been great all year about the situation, even telling the coaches that he was okay with coming off the bench because he didn't want to disrupt the chemistry that I'd developed with the guys as a part of the starting five. That was the kind of selfless action that you need to be successful, and his putting the team's interest ahead of his own reinforced what I'd always been taught and believed.

Unfortunately, all that hype meant nothing once the series began. Getting swept in four games was painful. Worse, we contributed a lot to our demise with bad fouls, turnovers, missed free throws, and a bunch of other lost opportunities. Going back over each of those games in my mind was not fun, but I felt that I needed to do it. Taking ownership of a loss is important. When you do that, you turn some of that negative energy into positive. We couldn't just forget about it, we had to look at what had gone on to see where we needed to improve and figure out the why of our poor performance. Losses are sometimes referred to as setbacks, but that's true only if you let them be so. I think you often learn a lot more from a failure than a success. I don't mean blaming it on the coaches, the referees, or any other externals. If you can honestly assess yourself and your performance and devise a plan to improve, then you'll have more confidence the next time you're in that situation. It's kind of like this: If the problem is X, and I do Y to overcome that problem, then next time the result should be Z—a victory for my side.

The frustrating thing about analyzing the Utah Jazz of that vintage was that a lot of the time you knew what was going to happen on the offensive end—a pick-and-roll between John Stockton and Karl Malone—but they executed it so well and the play so seamlessly suited their unique skills that even if you did a good job defending it, you still couldn't stop it. Having to play against John Stockton in that series really helped my development as a player. Defending against him and the pick-and-roll fed into the most competitive part of my personality. How could we defend against that play? I was definitely disappointed about the outcome of the season, and watching the Chicago Bulls defeat the Jazz with the six-feet-eight-inch Scottie Pippen harassing John Stockton didn't give me much insight. I wasn't going to be able to grow seven inches over the summer, but I had grown as a player in my two years in the league. I'd doubled the number of minutes per game I averaged and just about doubled my scoring average. I knew it was impossible to expect that I could repeat that amount of statistical increase each year in the league, but for the foreseeable future, that was what I hoped to do.

What watching those finals did do for me was to stoke the fires of my desire to be an NBA champion. I also simply loved watching two teams or two individuals go after each other in just about any sport. I loved the purity of it and, when the game or the series was over, to see all that raw emotion spilling out of the guys. I hoped that I'd experience that one day—sooner rather than later. I was angry that we'd been swept, but that would only carry me so far. Eventually, I'd get over the anger and get back to work. I was ready to let the ball come bouncing back up, but something loomed large on the horizon of the 1998–99 season. The collective bargaining agreement between the Players Association and the owners was voided in March when the NBA exercised its option to terminate the 1995 agreement at the conclusion of the 1997–98 season. They reasoned that salaries had gone out of control. That year, the players earned an all-time high of 57 percent of basketball-related income (BRI), and the average salary rose to $2.36 million. The NBA owners wanted to roll salaries back to 48 percent of BRI and install a hard-cap system that would effectively eliminate guaranteed contracts. We couldn't agree to those demands—particularly not the big pay cut at a time when revenues were so high.

It wasn't going to be easy, but we all stuck together, even though we knew that it would cost every one of us a lot of money if the work stoppage went for long. But right was right, and we stood strong under the leadership of our president, Patrick Ewing. Even though many of us had guaranteed contracts, the owners refused to pay. We took them to court over the issue but lost. I was solidly behind our union, but the expectations that I had going into the 1998–99 season made it hard for me to just sit and wait and wonder. The Lakers had traded Nick Van Exel, effectively handing the starting job to me, but I wondered if there would be any games to start. When the date for the opening of training camps passed, then the start of the regular season, then Christmas, and then with the announcement that the All-Star game had been canceled, things looked bleak. We'd been kept apprised of the status of the negotiations and had attended an association meeting in Las Vegas to get the latest lowdown, but basically all we heard was that we needed to sit tight, stay together, and we'd come out on top.

I was working out in Los Angeles, but we didn't have any informal team workouts until finally, in mid-January, an agreement was reached and we could return to work after 191 days out. The lockout was costly, with losses of $400 million in player salaries and close to $1 billion in owner, team, and league revenues. The damage we did to fans couldn't be measured. I remembered thinking that the average person hearing about our salaries couldn't relate to what we were holding the line over, but the six-year deal we signed was fair to both parties. A luxury tax was imposed, but the "midlevel exception" came our way along with increased minimum salaries, up to $1 million for players with ten years of service, and a significantly increased benefits package including a 401(k) plan. As is true in our country generally, a big gap exists between what the superstars make and the salaries of the rest of us. That gap was closed a bit and that worked to everyone's benefit.

The timing of the lockout couldn't have been worse for me. I had signed the league-mandated rookie contract after being drafted, so I was moving into my last year of it. Not being able to play a full season could hurt my chances of having a great season and being in a better bargaining position. Even though we didn't play until February, I was still learning a lot about basketball, but mostly about the business side of things. I tried to keep up with all the negotiation points because I felt that I needed to know what was going on. I trusted the people in positions of power in the association, but knowledge was power as well.

With everything in an upheaval and with an abbreviated training camp and four-game preseason, I should have expected that things would be weird, and they were—except not in a way I'd even thought of. One day before the first regular-season game, Coach Harris asked me about my mind-set. He said that I shouldn't get my hopes up too high. I was in the last year of my contract and the temptation was to try to do too much, to dream too big about the dollars that might come floating my way. He wanted me to keep on an even level and not focus on some big reward at the end of the year. All that made sense, but I'd never before had a coach discuss anything to do with contracts or salaries. I didn't know if I should thank him or if I should have been suspicious. Then he told me that they'd brought in the veteran guard Derek Harper who would play fourth-quarter minutes.

None of this was what I expected to hear or to have be my reality. It was as if I'd been transported back to high school or AAU ball and I had a coach doubting my ability to perform when it mattered. I was confused because the team had traded their starting point guard, had essentially anointed me the go-to guy at the position, but then changed their mind. Maybe with the fifty-game abbreviated season they thought they needed to take a different approach and couldn't afford the time for me to grow in fourth-quarter situations. I wasn't sure what was up, or what Coach Harris was really thinking, but that get-off-to-a-quick-start thing made more sense when we went 6-6 out of the box and Coach Harris got fired. After one game under Bill Bertka as our interim coach, former Laker Kurt Rambis took over. We went 24-13 under him and 31-19 overall, finishing fourth in the conference. We lost in the second round to San Antonio and Tim Duncan, and we'd definitely not made the kind of progress we'd expected after reaching the conference final the year before. The whole season had a nightmarish quality with everything seeming disjointed and out of sync. I wound up starting only twenty-one of the fifty games, and my minutes and scoring average were nearly identical to the previous season. Not much progress there either.

I didn't have those big dreams of huge rewards that Coach Harris had talked about, but I was definitely thinking about my future and what all this meant for me. I wanted to be a Laker, but I also wanted to be a guy who contributed as much as possible to his team's success and who fit well with the team's plans. I tried to chalk up that season's disappointment as a temporary bump in the road, and I didn't want to blame things on the lockout and the change in coaching, but they did contribute. I went into free agency with a lot of questions, as did the organization as a whole. The main question was, who was going to coach the team? Phil Jackson decided to leave the Chicago Bulls after the second of the team's three-peats, sat out for a season, and then signed with the Lakers. I wasn't sure what that meant for me personally and for the team generally. We'd earned a reputation as a talented but troubled team, and no one was sure what that meant in terms of personnel decisions.

I'd been in the league long enough to know that Phil Jackson preferred to have taller/longer guards on his squad. I wasn't either of those things, so I hoped that I wasn't going to be expendable. I also wanted to test the waters to see if other teams had any interest in signing me. I loved Los Angeles and the Lakers organization, but my desire had always been to play full-time and be the guy come crunch time. I was playing decent minutes, but I wanted to play major minutes, and I felt that I was capable of doing that. A couple of teams agreed. Seattle and Portland were in our conference; consequently, they saw me play more often than teams in the East. They'd also seen me play against them in the play-offs, and I think that helped to spur their interest. I visited Seattle and spoke with members of their organization.

I won't lie to you and say that salary had nothing to do with my thinking. I was looking to take a step up on the pay scale from what rookies received and beyond the league minimum. I was also looking for a commitment in terms of the length of my deal—three to four years minimum and a midlevel salary. I thought I'd demonstrated my worth, even though I'd had to do it time and time again, and was pretty adamant about the kind of deal I wanted. To be honest, contracts made me uncomfortable. This is no knock on the guys who represented me, but I didn't like that when it came time to negotiate, I was just going to have to let go and trust the people I'd hired to represent me. That was hard, and another lesson in learning to let go and relinquish some control. Obviously, I would have the final say on the deal, but it felt wrong to me to not be sitting in the same room with the people making these huge decisions about my future. So, when I went to lunch with my representatives, Lakers general manager Mitch Kupchak, and Jerry West, I was sitting among a group of people who in one sense had my best interest at heart, but in another had their own best interests at heart. Later, after Jerry left, Mitch and my team and I sat making small talk, and then Mitch suggested that it was time to get to business and I had to leave the room.

In principle I understood why I was not to be involved in those negotiations. Teams make offers and back them up with statistics, and they make their case to pay you what they consider "fair." Everyone's definition of fair is different, of course, and it would be hard not to take some of the things they said personally. Anytime someone talks about your salary and what you're "worth," it can be uncomfortable. That's particularly true because our salaries are generally public knowledge. Imagine if you knew what everyone at your company earned and how that might make you feel. It would be valuable information to have when it came time for you to negotiate your deal, but in a lot of cases people don't share that kind of information. We didn't have that choice.

While the Lakers worked on their offer, I returned to Little Rock to spend time with family. That was also a strategic ploy, kind of sending the signal that I would have no trouble leaving Los Angeles. Fortunately, I didn't have to put any more of my acting skills to use or really weigh one offer against another. I was on cloud fifty-nine when I got word from my agents that the Lakers had offered me a seven-year deal (with a player option at the five-year mark) with a healthy bump in salary over what I'd been earning. That the Lakers were willing to make a long-term commitment to me, more than twice as long as what other teams were considering, made me ecstatic. It was overwhelming to think that I would be able to take care of my immediate family and extended family for years to come. I'd gone from not being certain that I would even get drafted to having a career in the league—a ten-year career if everything worked out.

That level of commitment convinced me to sign. If I had been more money-motivated, I might have gone elsewhere. That seven-year contract called for me to earn the same amount each year—not even a cost-of-living increase. I didn't consider that at all initially, and I later thought it was an error on our part, but I'd signed the deal and wasn't going to complain at the beginning of it, nor was I going to cause dissension by trying to renegotiate it later. A deal was a deal and what was done was done. I was eager for training camp to start. If the Lakers were willing to commit to seven years, then maybe all those thoughts about not being the big guard that Phil Jackson seemed to prefer didn't matter. I worked out as hard as ever that summer and was thrilled when the season was about to get under way.

I liked and respected Coach Harris, and I felt bad that rumors had constantly been swirling around about his departure. He was a good, solid basketball man and person, but in Los Angeles that just wasn't good enough. With the tradition we had and the expectations that the ownership and fans had, and the whole "celebrity" environment, I think a big-name coach was what everyone was looking for. Along with that big name came instant and undeniable credibility. What Coach Jackson had done in Chicago was amazing. Six championship titles in ten years is a dynasty by anyone's standards, but his detractors said that anyone could have won with Michael Jordan on the team, but no one before him had. I'd always been told to respect coaches just because of their position, but with Phil Jackson, I respected him instantly because of what he'd accomplished. I wasn't alone in feeling that way. When Shaq was in Orlando, he had been beaten by the Bulls and Coach Jackson, and that meant something to him. For Kobe, being coached by the same man who had helped Michael Jordan reach the pinnacle certainly promised something. In the NBA, rings talk, and with Phil's six championship rings, they had to talk awfully loud to be heard over one another.

If the previous season had all the qualities of a nightmare, our first championship regular season under Coach Jackson had all the qualities of a pleasant and satisfying dream from which you wake up feeling refreshed and hoping to fall back asleep so that you can resume it. What made us all so comfortable, after an initial period of adjustment, was that the triangle offense we ran was a proven system. It wasn't just about getting the ball to Shaq or Kobe, but if we ran the offense the way it was designed and intended, the best players would get the most opportunities. Who could ask for anything more than that? Phil also made it clear that we'd better run the offense the way he intended it to be run, and whether you were in the starting five or the twelfth man, failure to do what he wanted would have consequences. Where had I heard that before? He didn't phrase that as a threat to playing time, but rather to our chances of winning. He emphasized that we'd broken down in the past, particularly in the playoffs, and having a system to rely on when things seemed to be slipping away, particularly a proven system that had helped lead teams to championships, would help us to do what we hadn't done in the past.

I don't know if it was the triangle offense that made Shaq so comfortable or if he had just matured in his skills and understanding of the game after eight seasons in the league, but if I hadn't been on the team, I would have bought a ticket and followed the guy to every city to watch him play. He was absolutely, astoundingly dominant in 1999–2000. He averaged 29.7 points, 13.6 rebounds, and 3 blocked shots a game.

So much has been written and said about that year, but the numbers still bear repeating: sixty-seven regular-season wins, a nineteen- and a sixteen-game winning streak, and a longest-consecutive-loss streak of two. Well, I exaggerated a bit about its being dreamlike the whole way. We were 2–6 in the preseason and I can remember being beaten by Utah in one of those games and thinking, "We don't even seem close to being good."

What also helped us get over the hump and win the championship was the makeup of that team. We had a nice mix of veterans and younger guys, and the on-court chemistry among us was exceptionally good. Once we gained traction and learned that the system we were playing under could produce the results our coaching staff said it could, our confidence was high. A lot of teams say that they believe they can win every game, but we truly felt that way. We were also a hardworking bunch who managed to stay focused for the full eighty-two games of the regular season and into the play-offs.

The season wasn't particularly dreamlike for me. I began the season in the starting lineup but was soon replaced by the veteran Ron Harper, who had played with Phil in Chicago. I had so much respect for Ron and what he'd done and what Coach Jackson had done and what they'd done together that I didn't complain. I wasn't about to throw a party to celebrate the move, but I accepted it and knew that I was going to have to improve some things in my game if I wanted to be out there more. In the triangle offense, there isn't a true point-guard role as there is in other types of offenses. If I was going to be the guy in that offense, I was going to have to improve my outside shot. With Shaq down low and a lot of teams double-teaming, that meant that perimeter players would be left open. If you couldn't knock those shots down, then you weren't doing what was asked of you in that system. I only hit 34 percent of my field goals and only 31 percent of my threes. I was going to have to improve that.

The play-offs that year were enough to keep us and the fans up all night from the anxiety and the elation. Going to five games against Sacramento was tough. All our hard work and all our success in the regular season could have gone down the drain. All of those clichés like "That's why you play the games" and "It ain't over until it's over" applied in this case. Sacramento didn't have nearly the kind of season we did, but taking us to five games kicked our collective sense of ur-gency into gear. That was a good thing. In the past, we might have panicked, but we played that fifth game as if we understood what was at stake and what we needed to do to win. We stayed in control, and that was a good lesson for us all to learn.

No one can really prepare you for what it is like to play in the NBA Finals. I've already talked about the ups and downs of the Sacra-mento and Portland series, but the finals are a whole different ball game. As much as you try to tell yourself it's just another game, it isn't. With all the NBA Finals banners draped in the Staples Center, with it emblazoned on the court, on the sideline chairs we sat on, and even on our uniforms, everything let us know that this was indeed something special. I remember as a kid watching the finals on televi-sion, and during the pregame ceremonies they'd show players on the sidelines listening to the national anthem. I noticed a lot of guys rocking back and forth, and that was a product of all the adrenaline flowing through their systems. I could barely keep myself still and focused on the anthem's lyrics the first time I stood on the sideline during game one.

Like us, the Pacers had their share of trials and tribulations.

They'd been to their conference finals four times until they finally broke through to make it to the finals for the first time in franchise history. Coached by Larry Bird, some tried to tie this series to the old Celtics-Lakers rivalry, and as much respect as I have for what those guys accomplished, this was a different generation of players. We started off strong in the opening quarter, jumping all over them for a 33–18 lead. Sitting on the bench, we all noticed that the Pacers had decided to play Shaq straight up with Rik Smits—no double teams were coming—and Shaq made them pay with dunks and several really nice turnaround jumpers. Kobe was on fire as well. The triangle offense and Phil's philosophy paid off for us when the Pacers decided that they had to double down on Shaq. Just as Kobe had found Ron Harper free in that nail-biter in Portland in the conference finals that year, Shaq waited for the double to come before kicking the ball back out to Harp for an open three. At halftime we were up 55–43.

The Pacers took it to us in the third quarter, eventually drawing within 2 points. That's when Shaq essentially took over. Whether it was blocking shots, grabbing free throws, or scoring, Shaq played like a guy who really wanted a championship ring. He punctuated his 43-point game with an exclamation point when in the closing minutes Ron Harper went up in the right corner looking for all the world as if he were putting up a three. Instead, he lobbed the ball to Shaq. The pass went over the rim to the far side, and Shaq went up with one hand. The pass was long, and Shaq had to bend backward while in midair to bring it in. Instead of just coming down with it, he cradled that ball in his hand and, using his arm like a catapult, swung the ball forward and down for a dunk that had all of us on our feet before he finally came down.

We knew that the Pacers would really come after us in game two and that we couldn't count on their star, Reggie Miller, shooting 1 for 16 as he had in the opening game. Phil told us that we would have to match their intensity right out of the gate, but even though we knew what was coming, we still weren't able to stop them right away. Worse, in the second quarter Kobe rose up for a jump shot and came down on someone's foot, spraining his left ankle. He hobbled off the court and into the locker room. That was about as quiet as I've heard the Staples Center. We knew the Pacers sensed that they had an advantage with one of our starters gone, and we openly talked about the need for us to turn the tables on them. We were so effective at doing that, the Pacers resorted to the Hack-a-Shaq, and he went to the line thirty-nine times in that game, converting nearly half of his free throws. But not until late in the fourth quarter with about a minute and a half to go and us up by only 99–96 were we able to put them away. Rick Fox had the ball out top and fed the ball to Shaq coming across the lane. Robert Horry was cutting toward the basket, and Shaq hit him with a beautiful pass and Horry used the rim to keep the defenders off him and made a beautiful reverse layup and was fouled.

Always an adept passer, Shaq showed that he could do more than just kick the ball back outside in the face of a double team. We also showed that as valuable as Kobe was to our efforts, the supporting cast could do more than just hold a lead, keep a game close; we could all step up and deliver when needed. Holding our home-court advantage was huge, and having won the second game largely without Kobe gave us the kind of confidence a championship team needs, especially going back to Indiana. I remember greeting Shaq and the rest of the guys at the end of the game and saying, "Two down. Two down. Two to go." We were halfway to the crown.

As fired up as our fans had been, the Pacers fans were equally boisterous. Walking onto the floor at Conseco Fieldhouse, we were greeted by a deafening throng of blue and yellow. With Kobe unavailable, I knew my minutes would increase, and I played a solid game, going 3 for 5 from the floor with 10 assists. That wasn't enough to offset Reggie Miller and Jalen Rose, who had solid games for the Pacers, and we lost 100–91. At one point we had been down by 18, and turnovers really hurt us.

Game four was pivotal and lived up to everyone's expectations. The Pacers knew they could make it a series with a win, and we sensed that a 3-to-1 lead would be huge for us. In a lot of people's minds, Kobe's role was the probable key to the outcome. In a pregame interview Kobe was asked if he could think of any circumstances that might keep him from playing that night. He paused, smiled, and asked, "Are there any snipers in the room?" That's the attitude it takes, and we all shared that feeling that we were going to have to take out the Pacers' and their fans' hopes.

The game was a play-off classic, filled with the kind of drama we all imagined as kids. That we were playing out that dream in front of eighteen thousand fans and millions around the world only made our 120–118 overtime victory sweeter. As in game three, the Pacers came out and were more aggressive than we were. Every loose ball went their way, and in one sequence, Mark Jackson dove to knock a ball loose, and Reggie Miller went to the floor, wrestled the ball away, and from his back made a pass for a breakaway layup. The fourth quarter was a classic, with ten lead changes.

With the game tied, the former Laker Sam Perkins launched a three from the wing. The ball hit the rim and bounced about as high as any shot I'd seen. The smallest guy on the floor, the Pacers' Travis Best, somehow got the rebound from Shaq, Kobe, and Robert Horry. Best passed the ball out to Reggie Miller, who calmly stepped up and knocked down a three, giving the Pacers the lead. That play typified the kind of hustle and cool, dead-eye shooting of Indiana in that game. That play could easily have been a backbreaker; instead, we stayed resilient. We led by 3 in the last minute, then Sam Perkins, whose heavily lidded eyes made people think that he was sleepy, found himself open in the right corner. As he had done so many times for the Lakers, he nailed the three and the game was tied. We each had a shot to win in regulation, and I was almost certain that when Shaq got the ball down on the block and went up with a jump hook, we'd won. Instead, the ball grazed the front of the iron and rolled off. We ended regulation tied at 104.

Early in the overtime, it looked as if this wouldn't be our night. Jalen Rose put up a jump shot from the wing. The rebound went long to the weak side. Shaq went up for it, but he got tangled with the Pacers' center, Rik Smits, and was whistled for his sixth foul. He'd played forty-seven minutes and scored 36 points; he was gone and so was, in a lot of people's minds, our chance of a win. We still had a long way to go, and in that overtime Kobe, at age twenty-one, showed that he didn't have a long way to go to establish himself as one of the games superstars. Kobe and Reggie Miller traded threes late in the overtime and the game was tied. Conseco Fieldhouse was rocking when Reggie's three went in. On the next possession, Kobe came downcourt, faked a drive, and pulled up for a twenty-two-footer that was pure. With twenty-two seconds left, we were up by 1. With fourteen seconds left on the shot clock, Brian Shaw slashed across the lane and put up a floater. The shot was just off, but Kobe came over from the weak side, grabbed the rebound out of midair, and put the ball in with a kind of over-the-shoulder reverse hook. With 5.9 seconds left, the Pacers trailing by 2, called a time-out. The crowd was waving towels and chanting, "Beat L.A.! Beat L.A.!" and we knew that one defensive stop, which likely meant preventing Reggie Miller from scoring, and we would be one game away from a championship. Phil told us in the huddle that he'd been in this situation before and told us what the Pacers had run—a play to free Reggie Miller for a three.

When the teams left the bench to play it out, Reggie went to the scores' table and applied talcum to his hands. I know that I wasn't the only one with my eyes on him. Jalen Rose inbounded the ball to Mark Jackson at the top of the key. He took a few dribbles to his right, then found Reggie a few yards above the right baseline just inside the arc. He stepped back and put up a high-arcing jump shot. I remember that the ball didn't have a lot of spin on it, and it kind of knuckled up there and fell just short, bouncing high off the iron as time expired. Game four was ours.

We suffered a huge letdown in game five, and the Pacers smacked us 120–87, forcing a game six back in Los Angeles. Phil told us in the locker room before the game that it was important to stay focused and not get too giddy with the prospect of being one game away from realizing a dream. Easier said than done. We'd had trouble closing out series throughout the play-offs, and with Reggie Miller raining down threes on us (and even a 4-point play when he was fouled on a trey), Phil was not happy. He called us out by saying that he didn't like that a championship team could suffer its worst defeat of the season and lose by 33 points in a game in which the title was ours for the taking. He didn't need to say it since we all knew it ourselves. Nothing was going to be handed to us, and we had to prove to ourselves and to everyone else that we did indeed have what it took to win it all.

We'd been criticized all year and hung with the label of talented underachievers and immature guys in need of a gut check. L.A. was starved for a title. It had been a dozen years since the last one, and as a group we'd experienced our share of failure. We wanted to experience a kind of redemption together. As someone said, "Before there could be a celebration, there had to be a competition." The Pacers gave us all we could handle, especially in the early going. We didn't crumble. We'd been through so much that season, particularly in the play-offs when we won elimination games against Sacramento and Portland, that we knew we could pass the test.

If the Pacers were going to push us, we'd respond. I could sense a difference in us in the second quarter. Robert Horry came over from the weak side to swat away a sure Jalen Rose layup. The ball ended up in my hands, and I took off down the court. Shaq, as he always did, was running hard downcourt. I found him with a lob pass and he put it in. That's what I loved about the game, the uncertainty of it all. What looked to be a sure basket on one end turned into 2 points for us. That was my only assist of the game, but knowing that we had guys who would battle like that at both ends of the court gave me even more confidence. Though we ended the first half down by 3 and entered the fourth quarter down by 5, I sensed that we were in a good place mentally—in spite of Mark Jackson's throwing up a midcourt prayer and having it answered at the end of the half.

I think what separates a fan from a player is that sense that despite appearances, the game is under control. We were executing the way we wanted to, and though Kobe was having an off night shooting, he was getting good looks. We weren't forcing anything, and Shaq was doing his thing. In the fourth quarter, when I found myself open at the top of the key for a three, I didn't hesitate, I took it. A few minutes later, Rick Fox did the same, knocking down a huge three-pointer. Later when I watched a tape of the game, I heard the announcers talking about those unexpected contributions. I can understand classifying those efforts that way, but the truth is, I did expect those things of myself. It seemed as if my entire athletic career had been building toward moments like that—being in the game in the fourth quarter with the team down, knowing that we needed a spark. Sure, it wasn't a buzzer beater, but it helped ignite our comeback.

As you might expect, even though we took the lead in that fourth quarter, the Pacers weren't going to just roll over and let us celebrate. With five minutes left in the game, Jalen Rose hit a three from the corner to tie the game at 103, capping a 7–0 run. We were being tested again, and not just Kobe and Shaq would have to contribute. It would have to be all of us. Robert Horry had 8 in the period, and Kobe and Shaq held fast.

The ending was magical and abrupt. All of a sudden the game was over, the series was over, and the season was over. As overjoyed as I was and as surreal as it all was, when I did have a moment of clarity, my thoughts were about not having a practice the next day and no game to prepare for. It felt so strange after such a long odyssey. When the buzzer sounded, my joy was replaced for a few moments by a bit of empathy for the Pacers players. I'd been in their shoes before, not having lost in the finals, but having come up short nevertheless. I walked to their end of the court and shook the hand of everyone on their team I could. Then I sprinted to the far end of the court where Lakers family members were seated. My mom was there, and with aid of one of the security guards, I got off the ground high enough that I could wave to her. After that, I went into the locker room and joined A. C. Green for a brief but heartfelt prayer of thanks, a recognition that what we'd accomplished we'd not done alone. We also got to share our victory with the people of Los Angeles with a parade and a rally. I enjoyed those moments so much. I always knew that the vast majority of our fans couldn't afford tickets to our home games, so being able to see them along the parade route and in the parking lot meant a lot to me. I thought I was happy until I saw some of these folks.

It took weeks for the reality of it all to set in, but it would only do that in fits and starts. I took a few weeks off, then resumed working out in July. I had been experiencing some pain in my foot throughout most of the 1999–2000 season, and I thought that some off-season rest would help it. I'd had X-rays taken during the season, and only bone spurs showed up. Just about everybody in the league developed them to some degree. I kept playing through the pain with the help of cortisone shots. I basically sat for the last week of the regular season so that I could be ready for the play-offs. Phil, the team doctor, and the rest of the training and medical staff all agreed that was the best approach. The pain got so bad at one point in the Portland series that I sat on the bench and said a prayer asking that God help me find the strength to go on. He did, and I was glad for that. At the end of the season, we all went through physical exams, and to my pleasure and surprise, I now felt no pain at all. X-rays and a general examination couldn't find anything, so I was cleared to do my thing in the off-season.

I hit it especially hard that off-season, hoping that I would get a chance to play a more significant role in the team's success the following year (I already told you what I said to Kevin Garnett that summer), and one day in September I went to the University of California at Los Angeles to play five-on-five with a group of other pros. When I made a move to the basket and planted to do a reverse layup, I felt that familiar pain in my foot. I wanted to keep going, but my body told me this was not the time. I called the team's medical staff and they got my foot scanned. That CT scan revealed that I had a nondisplacement fracture of the navicular bone. In simple terms, I was going to need surgery, then be on crutches for fifteen weeks before I began full rehab. As a result, I was out for almost the entire 2000–2001 season.

I'd gone from the high of a championship to being on the injured reserve list for almost the entire season. I was really down, and I hated not being able to play ball. On top of that, to see us struggling a bit that year in the regular season was hard. We never got on a tear the way we had the year before; our longest winning streak was only eight games, but we never lost more than two in a row. Whether it was the hangover from the championship season, or if we thought that the lessons our teacher had taught us no longer applied and we could do it on our own, I'm not sure. Winning fifty-six games is a good year in most everybody's book, but all the "What's Wrong with the Lakers?" stories gives you some idea of the kind of expectations we'd created for ourselves. We hadn't made significant roster moves, but Glen Rice and A. C. Green were gone, and the chemistry just wasn't there the way it had been.

I decided that I couldn't stay away from the game completely, so even when I was on crutches, I'd do some shooting drills, knowing that if I wanted to step up to the next level, I'd have to improve my outside shot. After the crutches went away and I was just wearing a protective boot and was unable to run, I still kept shooting, working to refine my release. Rehab was tough, but I was used to hard work, and I was determined to come back from the injury even stronger and more fit than I had been before going down with the fracture. All that shooting paid off when I came back. It's a good thing too, because my first game back postsurgery, I should only have played twenty minutes at most. Unfortunately, Ron Harper and Tyronn Lue were both out with injuries. As a result, I started and played the bulk of the minutes. As I had so many times before, I took advantage of the opportunity, this time to the tune of 26 points, 6 assists, and 6 steals. Shaq made a joke that with all those 6s, I hadn't achieved a triple double but a devil double. Phil caught me on the way off the floor and said to me in the tunnel, "Don't act like you knew this was going to happen." We both smiled and laughed. A winner's reaction.

What I knew from my reading of the Bible was that when we are down, that's when His best work is done. That's when we're more receptive to His message and guidance. When I was really down about the injury, that's when my faith really helped me. Anytime I had experienced failure, a similar thing had happened to me. Just like after that AAU championship game when I didn't play, I knew that I didn't want to experience that kind of pain again, and I had asked God to help me so that I wouldn't. That foot injury and that failure had made me even more humble. The injury especially reinforced the idea that I only had control of so much in my life. Later, when Tatum was diagnosed, I was able to draw on that experience. Yes, the injury and her illness were things I couldn't control, but what I could do in the wake of them was definitely in my hands and God's.

The 2000–2001 season was like the previous season in reverse. We struggled a bit in the regular season, finishing with "only" fifty-six wins, but we got on a roll in the play-offs that was truly impressive. What was most gratifying was that we swept the first three series against teams we'd struggled with in the past—Portland, Sacramento, and San Antonio. Going 11–0 in the Western Conference play-offs sent a message to everyone: we were not going to be denied. A lot of times that season we could have caved in, but we demonstrated that when we really put our minds to it, when we let go of all the distractions, the injuries, the media calling us out, we could take care of business on the basketball court.

Some of the pressure on us was self-imposed. We'd all grown up and some of us had even been in the league when the Chicago Bulls were thought of as a dynasty for winning six championships in eight years. We were also part of a proud and accomplished organization that had won multiple championships, and as we entered the new millennium, we were determined to be the next great dynasty. In the wake of our game-six victory over the Pacers, Shaq had announced our intention to be back and to win another. It was put-up-or-shut-up time, and we were as focused and determined a group as I've ever been a part of. So much was made of Shaq and Kobe and their divergent visions and off-season approaches. Shaq was a veteran coming off an NBA championship, a regular-season and play-off Most Valuable Player selection, and he was told to take it easy and let his body rest. Kobe, on the other hand, had ambitions beyond winning a championship. He didn't let up for a minute after our 2000 victory, determined to become the best player in the league. At times the two of them seemed to be at odds with each other. Most of that was fueled by the media.

As I saw it, we had two supremely talented players, one whose game focused on the patient execution of the half-court offense that allowed us to get the ball inside to him. The other was a more freelance-type player with an all-court game who thrived in the open court as well as in the half-court game. As we all grew up hearing, there is only one ball and it has to be shared. How that translates into who gets credit for our success is another matter.

The situation seemed to come to head against Golden State in a regular-season game. Kobe scored 51 in the game, but he clearly thought that he could carry the team on his shoulders and was trying to do too much. When he shot an air ball on a three as time expired, Golden State won by 2. In interviews after the game, he talked about how much he had improved and how hard he had worked (which was true), and that he wasn't going to level off his game and do what he'd done the previous year. Chemistry on a team is a delicate matter, and with the inclusion of new players (Horace Grant, Isaiah Ryder) and the loss of others (A. C. Green and Glenn Rice), it was a tough road in the regular season, especially with the added distraction of the Kobe-vs.-Shaq saga. We'd been successful the year before doing it one way, and now that this new way with Kobe wasn't working out, everyone (including the rest of the team) focused on that issue instead of on what we could each do to improve as a team. We suffered more than a few embarrassing losses, and as Phil referred to it, the community of our team had broken down.

When I came back after sixty games out, we seemed to settle in. I was given credit for being a steadying influence, but once again, the Lord moved in mysterious ways. In March, Kobe went down with a leg injury, and for the nine games that he was out, we had to figure out a way to win without him. We did. We returned to Shaq as the dominant presence on the floor, and from his position on the bench, Kobe noticed that we were playing as a team and winning. To his great credit, when he returned, he made a conscious decision to trust the rest of us and to become more of a playmaker. We won our last eight in the regular season before that 11-0 play-off run, so in total we won nineteen games in row.

A lot of the reason for that success was our letting go of things and trusting that the ball would come back up to us. We had to let go of ego, let go of the distractions, let go of the heightened expectations, and just do what came naturally to us—winning. When we squared off against Portland in that first game of the play-offs, we faced another test. As the fourth quarter opened, we were only up by 2. Of course, everyone was thinking about the previous year's game seven and our 15-point comeback. Thanks to Rick Fox and Brian Shaw hitting some key three-pointers, generating some turnovers, and playing with the kind of energy that characterized that series winner, we ran off 15 straight points to start that crucial quarter. We never looked back. We knew that we had the Blazers frustrated when in game two, they were whistled for five technical fouls and two players were ejected. We won every way possible, with Shaq going off, and in the Sacramento series when he was in foul trouble, Kobe took over, scoring 48 in game four of that sweep.

Next up, we got the chance to erase the memory of being swept in 1999 by San Antonio in the last games ever played at the Forum. They had the league's best record going into the play-offs, and they all felt as if our title the previous year had been tainted since their starter Tim Duncan had been injured. They'd won the title in 1999, so this was a matchup of the two previous champions. We'd been embarrassed in 1999, and none of us forgot what that had felt like. We opened the series in San Antonio, and Kobe scored an amazing 93 points in those two road wins. He scored in every conceivable way, and a few that those of us watching could barely believe. In game one, Kobe had the ball at the top of the key. He feinted right, then drove left. As San Antonio's interior defense closed down on him, he stopped and lofted a high-arcing jumper. How he even got the shot off was amazing, but what had us all jumping up and down and shaking our heads in amazement was that when the ball bounced high off the front rim, Kobe didn't give up on the play. He followed his shot, rising high above the rim to jam down his own miss. As Shaq said in the postgame press conference, he told Kobe that he was now his idol. Shaq went on to say that he thought that Kobe was the best player in the league.

In game two, Tim Duncan and the Spurs and the thirty-six thousand fans in the Alamodome and Phil's getting ejected for arguing calls all conspired to present us with our first real challenge of the play-offs. Shortly after Phil left the court, I had the ball on top. I saw an opening and drove the lane. I went up and tried to dunk the ball (I know, I can hear all my coaches asking me, "What is wrong with a simple layup?"), but banged it off the back of the rim. The loose ball was up for grabs, and Shaq fought off two Spurs to corral the rebound. He put up a ten-foot baby hook shot that was long. Shaq and Rick Fox battled for the rebound, with Rick crashing to the floor. Shaq scooped up the loose ball and slammed it home. A few possessions later, Kobe found me open in the right corner as he drove the lane. I got the pass and watched as Avery Johnson came out hard on me. With a quick ball fake, I had him in the air, and he went flying by into the Spurs' bench. I set my feet and knocked down the three, capping a 9–2 run immediately following Phil's departure.

We kept the pressure on when we returned to Los Angeles after having taken two on the enemy's home floor. Wining by 39 and by 29 in the next two games sent the message we'd hoped. The Spurs, not us, were pretenders to the throne. Some people have said that the stretch of basketball we played against the Spurs in that series is unmatched by any other Lakers team ever, including all the Showtime championship teams. I don't know about that, but we had a lot of fun and executed about as well as we ever had. All that stood in the way of our back-to-back championships was Philadelphia and the league MVP Allen Iverson and their legendary coach, Larry Brown.

We had a chance to be the first team in NBA history to run the table in the play-offs, and L.A. was at a fever pitch expecting, if not demanding, that we sweep. At the beginning of game one, it looked as if that would be the case. We went on a 16–0 run to go up 18–5. We knew that the game was far from over, but the long ten-day layoff didn't seem to be bothering us—yet. Iverson and the Sixers took over from that point, and though we tried to climb back into the game and did eventually tie it with five minutes to go, we lost 107–101 in overtime.

In the second matchup, I had a much better game, scoring 14 points with 3 assists. We were only up 2 at the half, but surged ahead in the third quarter playing some of our best ball as we had in the first three rounds. We had to withstand a Sixers fourth-quarter run, and when I hit a three from the top of the key to finally put them away, we all felt that we were back in sync. The Sixers proved to be a tougher match for us than most people gave them credit for. With Shaq fouling out in game three, it took Kobe with an assist from Robert Horry's clutch three-pointer from the corner with under a minute left to seal the deal for us. Going up two games to one meant that even if the Sixers won their next two at home, we'd be going back to L.A. to close out the series. We wouldn't need to go back.

When we finally put them away in game five, I felt a sense of accomplishment that was different from the first championship. As much as Kobe and Shaq contributed, everyone recognized the contributions of the supporting cast. It was also a vindication. For as much as we'd been through that season, we hadn't broken. As much as people talked about the Shaq-vs.-Kobe battles, we all pulled together. What people didn't see was the behind-the-scenes togetherness, the willingness and joy of going to battle for one another that made that season and that spectacular play-off run so fulfilling. Putting all of our individual needs and desires aside for the sake of the team was really what it was all about.

That off-season, I did the usual thing and went for my physical. The foot felt fine, but the team did another CT scan knowing my history. I was so sure that nothing was wrong that I went to Las Vegas for a charity event. Mitch Kupchak called me the next day. I could hear something in his voice, then he delivered the bad news. Fracture. Same spot. Surgery. The good news was that we'd caught it right away, and a quicker turnaround time was expected. At best I would miss the season's first few weeks. That was what I set in my mind as a goal. As I was lying in bed following that surgery on July 3, I got a phone call from Jerry West. He sounded more down than me. He told me that he was really sorry about the injury and that he was equally sorry that I wasn't a free agent at that point in my career. I was confused by that at first, but he went on to say that I had done a lot to reshape the image of my value to a lot of teams. I had showed people what I could really do. As he put it, "Derek Fisher has arrived. Shaq did it. Kobe did it. And now you." Those words meant so much to me. I couldn't imagine another general manager telling one of his players that he wished that he were a free agent so that he could go out and get his full market value. And truthfully, it wasn't really the dollar value, but that kind of respect and recognition that mattered to me. I don't think the Lakers ever didn't respect me, but I still desired to play an even more pivotal role in a team's success.

Even when we won the championship the following season and I put up similar numbers in the seventy games I played after coming back from surgery, I still felt that way. I was still in that I'll-show-you mode that I had been in for so long, but that was starting to get stale. I loved that we pulled off the three-peat, but in the wake of the celebrations, things were clearly not going to remain the same.

It would take a couple of years and the dismantling of the team with Shaq's departure and Phil Jackson's hiatus before I could make a move in the direction I wanted to go.

Losing in the play-offs following our three-peat was hurtful, but my last year with the Lakers prior to my reunion was especially difficult. With the arrival of Gary Payton, my role was clearly going to be reduced. I didn't realize just how much. I went from starting every game the previous year to starting just three. My minutes were cut from thirty-five to just a little more than twenty. I can say this about that year. It was a learning experience. One thing I realized in seeing how people reacted to our loss was that everyone—Shaq, Kobe, Phil, and everyone else in the organization—had to continue to prove themselves all the time too. We live in a world and played in a profession in which what have you done for me lately is the norm. At times I got so wrapped up in trying to prove to other people what my value was that it became an end in itself and not a means to an end. The end was being satisfied with myself and understanding fully what my value was to myself, to my family, and those closest to me.

I love sports because you keep score and you can measure performance pretty easily with all kinds of statistics. But living your life by someone else's measuring stick, no matter how objective or subjective it might be, eventually proves unfruitful. In my years in the league, I've finally come to understand more fully that the reward is in the effort. Do your job, do what's expected of you, without expecting anything in return. Find the validation within yourself instead of seeking it from others. For so long before and with the Lakers I had put the game at the apex of my life along with faith and family. Something had to give, and in going somewhere else in the pursuit of what I thought I really wanted and would make a difference in my life, I ultimately realized the value of all my teammates and not just the ones out on the floor.

CHAPTER NINE

Staying Home:

Making Good Choices

One of the fundamental principles of playing good team defense is knowing when to stay home and when to leave your man to help a teammate whose man has either got around him or needs to be double-teamed. You never want to give an opposing player a clean look at the rim or a clear lane to the basket. In time, you develop a kind of sixth sense about what a player driving to the basket might do—pass off or take the shot. Understanding the opposing team's offensive scheme and having good court vision (being able to see a play develop even before the opposition has fully executed the play) help enormously in developing this kind of extrasensory perception.

I sometimes wish that I had as refined an ability to see things developing off the court as I do on the court. Only sometimes. As I got older, I learned to like surprises, but my failure to see the big picture off the court has sometimes led to my hurting other people and being hurt myself. Writing this book has helped me in lots of ways to see patterns emerging and to better understand how that powerful hand of God has been at work in my life in ways that I could never have imagined at the time and am in awe of now.

For example, I made several decisions right when I joined the Lakers that, completely independently of one another, ultimately made all the difference in my life. I knew that adjusting to life in L.A. and in the NBA was going to require me to draw on resources that I thought I had but wasn't certain were as refined as they needed to be. That's why I asked my friend Clarence (we call him Chuckie and that's how I'll refer to him here) and my cousin Anthony to come and live with me in Los Angeles. I also mentioned that I moved into an apartment in the Marina City Club, which had two towers. I looked at units in both structures, but ultimately chose one on a high floor in the west tower. I liked the view of the city from that unit and that building.

All of that sounds pretty mundane, but, as a result of that decision, I met the person who came on board what I might once have characterized as "my" team, but who is in all things truly my partner in forming something bigger than each of us individually. I wasn't the first among the three of us to meet Candace shortly after moving into the building. The strange thing is that Chuckie and Anthony met her at all. The Marina City Club wasn't the most upscale address, but as far as rentals went, they were fairly pricey. As a result, and because of their location, they were mostly rented by whites. So when Candace noticed Anthony and Chuckie in the parking garage of the building, she said hello. She lived in the same tower as we did, one floor up from us in what were the penthouse apartments. Certain elevator banks served certain sections of the building, and since Candace lived in the same section as we did, she used the same elevator as us.

Most couples could probably look at all the choices they made that led to their eventually meeting, but in big cities such as L.A. and in areas such as the one we lived in, there seemed to be more to this than merely coincidence. I know about Hollywood and scripts, and this isn't the kind of meet that you would expect to see in a romantic comedy. Chuckie and Anthony and Candace and one of her friends developed a friendship, mostly based on proximity, and they all hung out casually after a few more of those incidental bumpings into one another.

The first time I met Candace, she saw me in the parking garage and waved. Knowing that not that many African-Americans were in the building, I assumed that the woman who waved was Candace. I stopped walking as she drove by. She rolled her window down, and here's how charming I am. I stood there a few feet away from the car and didn't even bend down so I could see her face clearly as she sat behind the wheel. We both kind of felt that we knew each other since we had both heard about the other. Chuckie and Anthony had taken to inviting people up to our place (Chuckie had got a job at an athletic-footwear store and invited coworkers) to watch Lakers games on television. Obviously, I'd never been there for those things, but toward the end of the season, one of the parties ran late and a few people were still hanging out when I got there. My girlfriend was in town and had gone to the game, so a bunch of us were just hanging out for a while. Candace was just one among that crowd.

At the end of my rookie year, I realized that the long-distance thing just wasn't happening for my college girlfriend and me. I was only twenty-two, I was living in L.A., and the single life was pretty appealing. I didn't go out a whole lot, but I did know that a lot of beautiful and interesting women were in L.A. I had spent every year of my life to that point in Little Rock, and here I was in a cosmopolitan city with women from all over the country and the world to meet, and I was feeling major guilt if I even talked to any of them. I was direct and honest, and even though it hurt her to hear it, I told her that I just wasn't ready to settle down and be all serious in a relationship. Part of that was because I wanted to pursue other opportunities and part of it was the distraction. I felt bad because I cared about her, but I had to do what my heart told me to do.

After that, I started to hang out with Chuckie and Anthony and Candace and her friends. We would go out as a group of about ten people, and I'd usually arrange for a limousine so that we could go out and have a few drinks and not worry about anyone having to drive. Also, my face was starting to get known around town, and I could get them into clubs more easily if they were with me as we got out of the car together. Here's how much of a player I am. This went on for about a year and a half. I noticed Candace and thought she was cute and interesting and fun, but I barely spoke to her during that time. One night toward the end of my second year in the league, the usual group was out at a club in L.A. We were all sitting around a large table. Candace was sitting pretty far away from me, and one of her friends was right next to me. The music was pumping and the lights were flashing, and I knew Candace couldn't really see me and I knew she couldn't hear me, so I said to her friend, "What's her story?" Her girlfriend asked, "Who? Candace? Why? You like her?"

Here's more evidence of how naive I was when it came to women. I told her girlfriend that yes I did, but I never expected her to go to Candace and tell her what I'd said. Later on we would both laugh about this and how it was almost as if I were back in third grade handing that "Do you like me? Yes or no?" note to the little girl in my class. Candace also told me that she didn't believe her friend, but her girlfriend was like "What do you mean you don't see it? Haven't you noticed how he looks at you?"

After that, I started talking with Candace a bit more, trying to gauge her interest in me, buying her drinks, trying to impress her, but she seemed to just keep treating me as she had for all those months before. Friendly and polite and all that, but definitely not sending any kind of overpowering signals. I knew that Candace had a son from a previous relationship. I didn't know all the details, but I knew his name was Marshall.

I started to pursue her a little more aggressively, at least for me, by buying roses from the flower girls at the club and asking them to deliver them to Candace without telling her whom they were from. Slick, right? She figured it out of course, and I was glad that she knew. One night I came up with another plan. I tracked down a flower girl and bought her entire supply of flowers. I asked the woman to deliver them three at a time at intervals all night until her supply was gone. That seemed to do the trick. To that point, the two of us had never spent any time alone one-on-one, and it took about another six months before she really was ready to trust me. She had a child and wasn't into game playing, and she wanted to be sure that I was genuinely interested in a relationship. I was, and we started to date at the end of the season in 1998.

I was into Candace and getting to know her better, but that she had a son troubled me. I had nothing against Marshall, but all those old-fashioned things I'd been taught about marriage and children and all that made me hesitate somewhat. There were also practical considerations. She had a child and responsibilities to him, and that might sometimes get in the way of our being together. I don't like that I thought that way back then, but it's the truth. After a while, I had to get real with myself. I wouldn't have been alive if my mom and dad had thought the same way that I did. I also knew a number of people, people whom I was close to, who had children outside of a marriage. If I was being so judgmental toward Candace, then what did that mean about what I thought of my sister, who had a baby right after high school? What about my good friend Corliss Williamson, who had a son while in college?

What ultimately made me decide that I was way off base was when I saw how judgmental I was being and how un-Christian my ideas were. Who was I to hold those kinds of beliefs? I was glad that I came to that reversal because Candace really was a great person, and she added so much to my life. She was raised in Los Angeles, and her parents split like mine, but she retained a great relationship with both of them. She was also a lot more worldly than I was. She laughed when I told her that to that point I had only been on public transportation once in my life. I couldn't believe that she took a city bus to school. She'd been in L.A. through the Rodney King riots, had endured earthquakes, had traveled around the country with her family and independently, and not just to play in basketball games as I had. She'd been to museums, to dance performances, and the theater; she'd gone to college and lived on her own and had to budget money and pay bills and do all the things that made me realize that in a lot of ways I had been sheltered from the everyday reality of life that most people experienced.

She is almost two years older, but was far more mature than I was. Having responsibility for a child will do that to you. She knew that life was about more than playing a game and having fun and hanging out. Truth is, I didn't. I also thought that at the age of twenty-four or twenty-five I had it all figured out, but I really didn't. I wanted the responsibilities that come with being a man, but I wasn't doing the work that was necessary to really say that I was a man in all facets of my life. I wasn't the kind of guy who wanted to run around all night and chase and bed a different woman all the time. Those kinds of temptations are out there when you're a young, fit guy making a lot of money and playing a sport. People assume a lot of guys gave in to all that temptation, and quite a few of them looked at Wilt Chamberlain and his claim regarding all the women he'd been with and thought, "I could do that." I couldn't. I was a serial-monogamy kind of guy, and just because I was, I sometimes thought I was ready for the commitment of marriage and family. Other times I thought that was the last thing I wanted at that point in my life. I also knew that the last thing I wanted to do was to get really, really serious with Candace and develop a close relationship with Marshall and then not be able to follow through and be a presence in his life for the long run. I also knew that I had responsibilities beyond Candace and Marshall to my family, including my daughter Chloe. Supporting financially, partly and in full, a number of people I really cared about was something I took seriously. I was happy and proud to be able to do it, but would getting married and having a family of my own interfere with my ability to do that?

A lot of those questions were running through my mind while I was dealing with all the ups and downs of my career. My relationship with Candace, if I were to create a line graph of it, had similar if not identical high and low points to those of my career. That was because I took my work home with me. I suffered with every loss and agonized over them, and every coach's decision and injury and feeling that I wasn't where I wanted to be in my career weighed so heavily on me. I wasn't the best communicator, and when I knew that Candace was bearing the brunt of some of my disillusion or disappointment, instead of letting her in and allowing her to help me figure things out, I pushed her away. I didn't like feeling that I was hurting someone or disappointing someone, so for the next few years Candace and I were very much an on-again, off-again couple.

I'm not proud that I didn't adequately take into account what that must have done to her and to Marshall. I beat myself up plenty, but I didn't want to fully face what I was doing to her and how I was hurting her. Sometimes the split lasted a few months, but during the 2004 season, it seemed as if the breakup would be permanent. I was at a crossroads in a lot of ways. My contract was up with the Lakers, and I was back in the free-agency world. The team was in turmoil, and it seemed as if everything was going in different directions. Shaq went to Miami, Coach Jackson went into hiatus, and the great run that we had was clearly over. I figured it was best to clear out and pursue what I'd always wanted. Several teams expressed an interest in me, and a couple told me what I'd always wanted to hear: "You can be our guy here. We'll put you at the point and let you run the team. You'll be the guy to help us close out games."

Ultimately, I decided that I would go to Golden State and accept the challenge of being a leader there. That almost didn't happen. After all the upheaval of that summer, I was ready to sign and eliminate a few of the many unknowns in my life. When my agent called me to outline the details of their offer, I told him I was good to go. He let the ownership know that a deal was in place. A few hours after that, I got a voice-mail message from Kobe Bryant. He said that he wanted to talk to me and that he hoped that I would come back to the Lakers. I tried to call him back, but couldn't reach him. He might have been able to persuade me to stay except for one thing. I'd given my word that I was going to the Bay Area to sign with Golden State. I couldn't back out on that, and I didn't.

It would be an understatement to say that things didn't work out with the Warriors the way any of us hoped they would. For various reasons I started fewer than half the games the two seasons I was there. My numbers were decent and I averaged more points per game than I did in L.A., playing fewer minutes in some cases. It was good to be one of the offensive options, but something wasn't right. I could tell from the start. I'd signed a big contract, I was making more money than ever, I was supposed to be in the position that I always wanted to be in, but I was really, really not happy. The old line about being careful what you wish for was ringing in my head. I felt empty in a way I hadn't before in my adult life. What was the point of working so hard if I felt so unfulfilled?

I'd always been a reader, and at the start of that year I'd undertook to reading a number of self-improvement and personal-development books. At the time, I was reading Dr. Gary Smalley's book *The DNA of Relationships.* I saw so much of myself in that book. I was at a kind of crisis point in my life, and I somehow found that book and realized that the approach I took on the court was getting in the way of my being successful off the court. I was so used to working hard and taking a problem/solution approach to everything that when Candace approached me about something, I immediately went into the tell-me-what-it-is-and-I'll-fix-it mode that had worked so well for me in developing my off hand, perfecting my free throw stroke, etc. What she wanted was to be heard and not diagnosed and analyzed and to have a five-point plan implemented. I also couldn't be the take-charge kind of person I was on the basketball court. I needed to listen to her and not just do something.

What I also realized was that not everything was about me: sometimes how she was feeling and responding didn't have anything to do with me. And finally I learned that unlike on the court where my actions were all that mattered, with Candace what I said mattered as well. I was of the belief before that "Hey, I'm helping out around the house, I'm doing this and I'm doing that, so why do I have to say I love you? Can't you see I do based on all the stuff I'm doing for you?" All that emphasis on doing I'd had in place since I was a kid had been my undoing in my relationship with her. Instead of trying to shoulder more responsibility, I needed to learn to share the responsibilities and figure out ways that the two of us could manage the tasks we needed to be together happily.

So, I called her late in 2004. We hadn't spoken since May of that year. I told her about what I'd been thinking, and she knew that I'd loved her for a long time and that I'd finally stopped putting up obstacles. The ups and downs weren't going to be over, but I was firmly committed to riding them out together. In February of 2005, we got married. Our wedding day—February 19—was over All-Star weekend, and we had a nice backyard ceremony at the house I still owned in Encino. My uncle George Johnson officiated.

Things just seem to have a way of working out for me since then. Even though my time at Golden State wasn't the best for me, that we missed the play-offs in 2006 meant that I was home in the late spring and early summer to be with Candace full-time as we awaited the arrival of the twins. Otherwise, I might have been preparing for the finals and not there with her during that last critical month. I had a good time putting together the nursery, even if being left-handed meant that assembling the crib got a bit frustrating. We were also blessed that Candace's mom could be there for the birth, and I was surprised to walk into the hospital and find my mother sitting there. Everyone else was in on it but me, and I was so glad to see her.

Since marrying Candace, I've experienced a peace that I never had before. I still take the game seriously, and I do hate losing, but I use the long drive or flight home to let go of that. I definitely have learned to keep things in perspective. I play a game that I love and one that I have been so blessed to be a part of and that entertains millions, but when I come home, neither the twins nor Chloe care about the minutes I played, they just want to play with me. Instead of reading the paper to see what people think of my performance, I read *Five Silly Monkeys, Brown Bear, Brown Bear, Mama Llama,* and *Daddy Hugs.* The game continues to sometimes confound me with all its ups and downs and dramas. But play-off losses don't define my life. I've gained so much more than I can ever really begin to count.

In the wake of Tatum's diagnosis, I understood that box scores only tell one small part about anyone's life. I started out this book by saying that all the experiences I've had helped us to be in a position where Tatum's eye could be saved. In reality, a lot of me was saved as a result of all those experiences as well. At more than one point, things could have taken a very different direction for me. Thanks to my parents, my coaches, and my extraordinary wife, I'm at a place now where I am playing better than ever. There is no logical explanation for how that can be. When I should be on the downside of my career, the ball seems to be bouncing back up to me more easily than ever. Having let go of some of the concerns I had and the need to constantly be in control of everything and to take care of business, and instead leaving the rest up to someone far greater than me, has made all the difference. Having all those teammates on my side and knowing that I don't have to do it all feels better than I ever thought possible.

Knowing that I had helped myself by finally committing fully to my life with Candace gives me a lot of satisfaction. Having a family to come home to after games has really helped me with my priorities and allowed me to really see what is important. It's ironic that we use the term *court vision* in talking about basketball and in general we use the word *see* to talk about understanding. I was well on my way to putting things into the proper perspective when Tatum's diagnosis rocked our world. I've already talked about that dramatic first procedure and the game that followed. A lot of people know elements of that story, but that was just phase one of her treatment. Unlike in playing good help defense, I had no moment of indecision about whether to stay home or to go help out. In a sense, I did both. The second treatment was scheduled for May 30, the same day that the Jazz were going to face off against the San Antonio Spurs in game five of our Western Conference Final. Our backs were against the wall, trailing San Antonio three games to one and facing elimination on the road.

We stuck to the schedule that Dr. Abramson had recommended and were in New York. The second time through the process was a bit easier, and we had worked out the details so that I could make it to San Antonio in time for the game. Fortunately, the procedure went well again, but the results of the game were not as good as they had been against Golden State. We lost, falling short of the finals and a chance at an NBA championship. I was disappointed, of course, but I had more important things on my mind. I needed to get away from the game completely and focus solely on my family and Tatum's treatment. From the very start of our working with Dr. Abramson, we had a lot of questions on our mind about follow-up care. Once it became clearer that the treatment was having some positive effects, those questions became more prominent in our thinking: What will we have to plan for in terms of Tatum's diet? Exposure to the sun? What additional treatments and appointments would she need? Would we continue to have to go to New York for every visit? We would go to New York if there was no alternative, but what were our options? We wanted to be sure that we did everything we could to maximize the chances of a successful outcome for Tatum. Nothing else mattered.

By the end of June, Tatum had undergone the third and final treatment Dr. Abramson thought would be necessary. We were all very aware of the level of toxic chemicals an infant could take, and monitoring the tumor would guide us on whether she would need additional treatments in the immediate future and long term. That meant we would have to be constantly vigilant—again, knowing when to stay home on defense or when to make the move to help elsewhere. The priority was always to defend Tatum and my family to the maximum of my ability. Finding the right doctors and the right after-care mattered more than anything else. I was not about to abandon my responsibilities or shift too many of them to Candace just so that I could continue to play basketball. If the best thing for me to do was to retire so that I could be with my family full-time, I was prepared to do that. That didn't mean that was what I wanted to do, but we had to consider all scenarios.

Fortunately, Tatum's response to the treatment was so good—both in terms of the tumor and her general well-being—that we were all able to stay very positive. She was a little fatigued after the treatments, but that could just as easily have been from the changes to her schedule and the travel as the chemotherapy. Seeing that she was doing well made it easier for us to remain upbeat and focused on a good outcome. I think that was critical to the success of the treatment. Today, two years after her last treatment and with no signs of the tumor and no indication that the cancer has spread, we remain optimistic but take nothing for granted. We also haven't allowed ourselves now or back then to feel sorry for ourselves, nor have we been stuck on high alert. We're not at the edge of an emotional cliff, and we take it the proverbial one day at a time and remain grateful and prayerful for all the blessings we've received.

The Utah Jazz organization and the people of Salt Lake City particularly and people around the country generally were wonderfully supportive of us. I can never repay Jazz fans and management for the kindness and consideration they extended to my family. It's both funny and sad that a few people have looked at the situation we were in and thought that I had somehow orchestrated all of it to get out of Utah. Nothing could be further from the truth. I had a contract with the Jazz that would have paid me in excess of $20 million. I was playing for a team with a wonderful combination of youth, athleticism, and veteran savvy. I was playing for a Hall of Fame coach in front of an adoring mass of devoted fans. If it weren't for Tatum's cancer, I could easily and happily have ended my career in Utah.

Unfortunately, in terms of my basketball career, I had to make a decision based on what was best for my family. So after considering the options and consulting with Dr. Abramson about possible locations where Tatum could receive the best after-care, I approached my agent at the time and told him that I would list the cities I would consider playing in based on the kind of medical facilities available there. Based on what Dr. Abramson told me, and he did this reluctantly, Salt Lake City did not have a pediatric oncologist with experience in the kind of tumor Tatum had. This is no knock on the doctors and medical centers in Salt Lake City. But we needed a relationship with specialists familiar with the specific disease Tatum had, and only a few places in the country had such doctors.

Obviously New York and New Jersey were on that list because that would mean that we could easily see Dr. Abramson. Cleveland and Boston were also possible because of their proximity to New York and because of the treatment options available there. Golden State, Miami, Memphis, and Los Angeles were also possibilities.

I broached the subject of leaving the Jazz in a face-to-face meeting with General Manager Kevin O'Connor. I took him through my thinking about Tatum's after-care and stressed that I did not want to live in one city and have my family be in another. Being an absentee/part-time dad was not something I ever wanted. I wanted and needed to be home for my wife and our kids. As he had been throughout Tatum's health crisis, Kevin was supportive and said that he, of course, understood and that he would find out from ownership what might be done to achieve our mutual goals. A few days after that meeting, discussions centered around the possibility of trading me to one of the cities on my list. If you know anything about the economics of the game and how it influences personnel decisions, midlevel exceptions, salary caps, and all that, then you know how incredibly complicated this could all get. As much as I wanted the Jazz to benefit somehow, I knew that I couldn't let basketball decisions dictate where my family and I ended up and what doctors we would be forced to see.

As much as I'd learned about letting go and not trying to control everything, in this area I had to exert total control. Cancer is powerful and all-controlling. I knew that I had to do what was best for my daughter's health and for my family. The choice of where we went had to be mine and based on doctors, quality of life, comfort level, and access to our support system. I wanted to choose and interview (meet face-to-face with Tatum's doctors) and not sit passively by while other people made life-altering decisions. I don't for a minute blame the other people involved for thinking of basketball. That's what they are paid to do, and if I were in their shoes, I would have been trying to look for a similar win-win situation. But I couldn't settle for just any old kind of win. I had to have complete dominance over what I can't even call a "game." This was far more important than that. I began to push for the Jazz to grant me a complete release from my contract. My agent wasn't too thrilled to hear that, and he recommended that I at least press the Jazz for some kind of buyout/settlement. I knew that wasn't going to fly. Why would the Jazz pay me anything to leave the organization?

In the end, Larry Miller, the Jazz owner, agreed to release me from the contract. To his credit, he didn't hesitate. He knew that I had to do what was best for my family. Again, I can't thank the Jazz organization and the people of Salt Lake City enough for what they did for my family and me. Walking away from the security of that long-term deal was difficult. I was going to be leaving a great group of players and an organization that treated me wonderfully throughout my time there and really stepped up with big-time help when we all needed it the most.

Being a free agent was a bit scary. I felt that I still had a lot of basketball life left in me, but you can never be too secure in this game. With our list of cities in hand, we started discussions with a lot of teams. Not all of them needed my services as a point guard, and not all of them were likely to value what I brought to the position. I knew that going in, but as I talked to more and more teams, Los Angeles and the Lakers remained a prime choice. Dr. Abramson had said that another expert in the field, someone he knew well and would feel comfortable handing over treatment of Tatum to, was in Los Angeles. Dr. Abramson was reluctant to just turn over treatment to anyone, and he insisted that he continue to be consulted and remain actively involved in treatment decisions. I appreciated that about him. He was going to both stay home and help, just as we all were. We'd developed a strong relationship, and even though ultimately Tatum's treatments and evaluations would take place at Childrens' Hospital in Los Angeles, Dr. Abramson remained an active presence in our lives and in Tatum's care.

Los Angeles made sense for another reason. We were all familiar with the city, and Candace's family lived there. I'd still also be close to my daughter Chloe. I wanted to be as active a presence in her life as I could possibly be. We had to consider proximity to our support system, and that factored heavily into our decision. I can't lie and say that we didn't think about finances as well. We had walked away from a lot of money, and we had college tuition and retirement to think about. Of course, I also wanted to go somewhere that was a good fit for me on the court. In my discussions with Mitch Kupchak of the Lakers, I was encouraged to hear that if I signed, chances were I would see big minutes. The Lakers definitely needed a point guard, and I was a known quantity to them and they were a known quantity to me as an organization. The team, however, was vastly different from the one I had last played for. While Phil Jackson had returned from his one-year sabbatical and we would be playing the same offensive and defensive schemes, the roster had completely changed.

All that said, I was looking forward to be heading back to Los Angeles. You can go back home again, and the 2007–8 season proved that not only could you go home again, you could thrive. Much has been made of my decision to walk away from the big money I would have earned in Utah. No one likes to take a pay cut, but I never questioned if I had done the right thing. All the factors I talked about—doctors, quality of life, proximity to family—trumped everything else. The Lord does move in mysterious ways, and I'm grateful that He saw to it that things worked out so well for us off the court in returning to the Lakers, and on the court as well.

As the saying goes, "You can't tell the players without a scorecard," and that's how it was for me at first. Of course, Kobe was still the main presence on the team, as he had been when I last played for the Lakers, but the only other players remaining from our 2003–4 team were Brian Cook and Luke Walton. I'd played against most of the guys, but being a teammate is another matter. As a point guard, you are a kind of coach/leader on the court, but I knew that I couldn't just walk into the locker room and take command. I fell back on my skills as an observer in those first few weeks back with the Lakers, noting our strengths and weaknesses and the various temperaments and tendencies of our guys. I liked what I saw. I liked it a lot.

Though the team had struggled the year before, finishing with a 42-40 record and getting bounced out of the play-offs in the first round, I sensed a real commitment to excellence. I also noted that Kobe was taking a more active leadership role. I knew that he hated losing as much as anyone I'd played with, but I think that he'd been in the league long enough and grown up enough to emerge as someone we all respected and looked to who could take us where we wanted to go. The promised land of an NBA championship is always out there for every player; it just seems as if you can get to it more easily from L.A., despite its legendarily awful traffic. I liken my return to L.A. and having to deal with road congestion to what it was like on the court as well. I was familiar enough with everything that had to do with Los Angeles and Lakers basketball that I knew some of the ins and outs of the game the way I did the freeway system. When I was first with the Lakers, we were clearly going to get to the finals and win by taking the Shaq or the Kobe freeway.

Last season, I think we all recognized that we needed another major option besides Kobe, and our in-season acquisition of Pau Gasol gave us another avenue. Though not as dominating a physical presence as Shaq had been, Pau was a versatile player with a floor game typical of a big man from Europe. His ability to play both inside and outside was crucial to his meshing with the team, and with all five starters averaging in double figures for the regular season, we won fifty-seven games. We won the Pacific Division and headed into the play-offs as the number one seed in the Western Conference. Kobe earned the Most Valuable Player award and was more than deserving of that honor. As much as his critics have got on him, I don't see how anyone can question his desire to be the best and to win, and in my mind, 2007–8 demonstrated again how his fierce determination could provide the kind of leadership that brings out the best in everyone around him.

In 2007–8 I had the opportunity to do what I'd always wanted to do with the Lakers—to be the starting point guard running the show through thick and thin. As always, expectations were high in Los Angeles, and losing the first game of the season against the Rockets and only going 9-6 in November had people outside the organization on edge. They were thinking that we could just dominate, but a 10-4

December and a 9-5 January didn't have people dancing in the aisles. We were playing solid but unspectacular basketball, and though we didn't run off a long string of victories as we had in my earlier glory years with the Lakers, we were making good strides at becoming a better basketball team at both ends of the court.

Our front line was banged up, and then when Andrew Bynum went down with a knee injury, we clearly needed some help in the front court. That help came in the February 3 trade that brought Pau to us in exchange for Kwame Brown, Jarvis Crittendon, and two draft picks. It was no coincidence that we had our best month of the season in the wake of that trade, going 13-2. Pau brought great energy to the team and he fit in well. Knowing that the organization was going to do whatever it could to ensure our success also gave us a boost. And believe it or not, the brief break for the All-Star game helps.

The NBA season is no sprint, and the marathon requires you to go to different places to tap various energy reserves. The inevitable "slump" hit us in March and had our critics crying foul. I'll admit that a 9-6 March isn't the greatest, but while someone once said that April is the cruelest month, for me it's always been March that has fangs. By that time, we've been at it for seven months, the play-offs are still six weeks away, and that dip in energy seems inevitable. You can't sustain the kind of high we were on in February for the whole season, and that little slip was offset by a 7-1 end of the regular season in April. We were like runners who saw the finish line, and that ray of hope was enough to bring us home strong.

One game in particular gave notice to the NBA and to ourselves what our new lineup was capable of. We traveled to Orlando on February 8, 2008, to face the Magic. Our records were similar, 31-17 for us and 32-19 for them. Dwight Howard, one of the bright young superstars in the game, was having a terrific year, and we knew we had to contain him if we had any hope of victory. Orlando came out smoking in the first quarter and put 44 points on the board. It wasn't as if we'd been run over by a bus, but it had gone past our stop without us getting on board. We did put up 33 ourselves, and the up-and-down action of that game was admittedly fun, but the basketball purists and defensive preachers weren't happy with that 77-point display in the first twelve minutes. The Magic were raining down threes on us, making seven of them from beyond the arc. Everyone was getting in on that action, and when a team is shooting that well from outside, even when you're putting a hand in their face, you just have to tip your hat to them and know that eventually they are going to cool off. For my part, I had four assists in the first quarter, all to different players. It was nice to have other options, and for the first time since his acquisition, I was getting a better sense of where Pau wanted the ball and where he could score from. His ability to hit those mid-range jump shots as a seven-feet-tall player was impressive.

And the Magic did cool off. We held them to only 19 points in the second quarter while we put up 31 to lead by 1 at the half 64–63. We also saw Pau's floor game and his ability to get up and down the court, which led to a couple of fast-break layups and a particularly emphatic dunk. No knock on Shaq, but Pau's versatility was something very different from what I'd experienced before. That game gave us a glimmer of what was to come the rest of that month and the rest of the regular season and into the play-offs. We played dynamic up-tempo basketball and won 117–113. We had an 11-point lead after three quarters and were outscored by 7 in the fourth, but we managed to hold on. That pattern of nearly letting leads get away would eventually catch up to us. With Kobe scoring 36 and Pau adding 30 and the rest of the starters in double figures, we were an offensive juggernaut. We all knew that come play-off time, defensive stops were going to have to come more into play.

In the play-offs, a similar pattern of what our critics called our "coasting" was best exemplified in the second round. We faced my old friends at Utah once again, and in the first five games each team held their serve on the home court. We narrowly lost both games in Utah, losing the second there in overtime, and heading into game six at the EnergySolutions Arena, we were riding high confidence-wise. We demonstrated that confidence in the first quarter, jumping out to 13-point lead 33–20. We followed that up with a strong second-quarter effort to go up by 19 at the intermission 62–43. None of us thought that Utah was going to roll over in the second half. Jerry Sloan's teams just didn't do that kind of thing, and we knew that with their backs against the wall in a potential elimination game, they were going to get after us hard in the second half. We held them off and they trailed by 16 going into the fourth quarter.

Kobe, who had tweaked his back in game four, wasn't feeling great, but he was playing that way and, bad back and all, helped us to hold off a furious Jazz rally that saw them cut our lead to 2 with less than two minutes to play. Kobe's 12 points in the fourth helped us to hold on. Fortunately for us, we hit 31 out of 38 free throws, many of those down the stretch when the Jazz took to fouling us to preserve the clock. That old fundamental skill made the difference in our 108–105 escape.

What can I tell you? The rest is history. We took a hard-fought and close series from the Spurs, winning in five games, with both teams winning a blowout game and the others being tightly contested. That set up the dream matchup that everyone on the coasts was looking for: Lakers-Celtics. I don't have to tell you about the storied history of the two franchises, and if you didn't know any better, you would think that MagicBird was a rare type of species found in the Amazon that picks fruit from the trees and drops it into its nest in spectacular fashion to feed its young. We were both top seeds in our conferences, and that was the first time since 2000 that both number one teams had reached the finals. In fact, it was the first time since 2003 that either top seed had made it to the finals. This was our first time in the finals since 2004 and the twenty-ninth time overall. This was the first time for the Celtics since 1987 and their twentieth overall.

Okay, enough with the history and the numbers. The only numbers and the only history that matters is that we lost four games to two. You know all that. You also know that game one was the wheelchair game, in which Paul Pierce was taken off the court in one, then returned in the third quarter to score 15 points and lead them to a 98–88 victory. When he hit consecutive three-pointers to give them the lead for good, I thought the building was going to collapse around us from all the noise the Boston fans were making. Even though we lost that first game, the thrill of being in the NBA Finals after so long an absence and after having been through so much personally was not diminished by the outcome. Standing in the new Garden and literally feeling my rib cage vibrating from all the noise and my own excitement made all the years of hard work more than worth it. That sea of green and white wasn't threatening to drown me, but buoy me to the surface and carry me. There is nothing like knowing that you are playing the game on the biggest stage in front of the largest audiences with everything on the line.

Game two was our turn to experience from another perspective the roller coaster of a big lead nearly vanishing. We had been down by 24 with less than eight minutes remaining in the fourth quarter. Our second unit was out there to start the fourth, with Jordan Farmar hitting a pair of threes and Ronny Turiaf making a couple of baskets in the first few minutes of the quarter. I came back in with about seven and a half minutes to go, and I could sense that the tide was turning after about a minute. The Celtics committed two turnovers, and Vladimir Radmanovic hit a three for us. I was fouled and hit both free throws to draw us within 16 at 96–80. We still had a long way to go, but we'd cut into the lead by 8 points in minutes. We weren't playing particularly amazing basketball, but we could all sense that an opportunity was there for us. With solid contributions from the role players, we knew that we didn't need to (and couldn't) rely solely on Kobe. We knew that we were onto something when Sasha Vujacic and I sandwiched three-pointers around a Ray Allen putback and Boston called a twenty-second time-out.

In the huddle, I looked the guys in the eye and could see the fire that had been lacking earlier in the ball game. As much as I'm sure fans are mystified about what happens when a team loses focus or seems to lack the energy or the firepower to do battle in a game, as players we're equally mystified. Believe me, if we knew that answer on how to turn it on and leave it on, we would do it. We're human beings playing a game, and as much as it is our skill that carries us, it is our belief in our skill that makes the difference between winning and losing. You could easily ask, "Well, why don't you believe in yourself all the time?" It's not as simple as believing. It's the combination of belief and skill and execution and a little bit of luck. Why do some shots rim out and others roll around the rim, then drop in? I'm not a physicist and I don't know the scientific answer to that, and I don't believe that some spiritual agency out there decides who wins or loses. I do know this: the reason we play the games and the reason we watch them and care so much about the outcome is because what goes on on the court mirrors what goes on in our lives. Why does one salesperson get the big account and another doesn't? Why do we invest in one company that we know has the best staff, the best price-to-earnings ratio, and then it goes into free fall for a while? It's all a combination of skill, execution, luck, and a whole lot more. Knowing the outcome is not guaranteed is what makes it fun and frustrating.

When we got within 2 at 104–102 with thirty-eight seconds left, none of us stopped believing that it was possible for us to pull the game out. We fouled the Celtics and they hit their shots and we lost by 6. We missed an opportunity to win, but we learned a lot about ourselves and what we were capable of. We put up 41 points in that fourth quarter, but we'd dug ourselves too deep of a hole. Shooting success can come and go, and we knew that we had to play better defense if we were going to get ourselves back in the series by winning all three games in Los Angeles.

The Celtics got a notable contribution in game two from their reserve forward Leon Powe, who scored 21 points in just fifteen minutes of action. He's a talented player, but no one would have expected that kind of wild-card contribution—another factor in the success or failure of a team. To have a guy like that step up in such a big way was crucial to their victory.

In game three, we limited the production of the Celtics' so-called Big Three. Paul Pierce had a horrible shooting night, making only 2 of 14 and Kevin Garnett only chipped in 12. With that kind of production, and a more intense defensive effort, those defense-loving fans went home happy, just as we did, with our 89–81 victory. It wasn't an artistic success, but in Hollywood terms, we opened big. We sustained that first-weekend box-office success in the first quarter of game four. We got out to a 35–14 lead, the largest first-quarter lead in finals history. We were playing nearly flawless basketball in front of one of the most boisterous crowds I'd ever played in front of. L.A. fans are often unfairly criticized for arriving late, leaving early, wanting more to be seen at the scene than to watch the game, but no one could say that about this bunch on that night—or ever as far as I'm concerned.

What happened in game four encapsulated everything that had gone on that season and to that point in the play-offs. I can't get into the semantics of it. Was it a collapse? Was it a monumental stumble? A great comeback? Whatever it was, it was as surreal to those of us playing the game as it was to those watching. Unfortunately, I was both playing in it and watching it. Being out there on the floor was a role I far preferred to watching it. At least I was out there for a time doing what I could to stem the rising tide of the Celtics' charge. We were up by 20 midway through the third quarter and still clicking on all cylinders.

What happened next is difficult to say. I've thought a lot about it, both because of how historic and important this was, and because I want to make sure it never happens again. Additionally, those kinds of dry spells seemed to plague us, though not to the extent they did in that game. I suppose that one way to look at it is that if it weren't for their remarkable turnaround, everyone would be asking a similar question of the Celtics. How could everything have gone so wrong for so long in that game? How could they have been outscored in historic numbers in the first quarter? Of course, I understand that how they performed down the stretch was important and remarkable, but the points in the first quarter count for the same value as they do in the fourth. Yet, I also understand that a more intense focus is placed on the last part of the game (and should be) than on the first parts. That's how you really measure yourself, and in any realistic sense we came up way short at the end of game four.

When the Celtics went on that 21–3 run to close out the third quarter and pull within 2, I was reminded of times when I would help my mom bring the groceries in. I hated having to make too many trips, so I'd often grab as many bags as I could at one time. It was hard to hold on to them all, but I was confident I could. When one of the bags started to slip or tear, I'd tell myself it was okay. I'd been in that situation before, I was able to get into the house and into the kitchen with them safely. I just needed to keep moving. As the bags slipped and tore even more, I'd pick up the pace and try to run. That put additional stress on the bags, and a few times things had come spilling out of them. I'd had the sense to lower them so the distance they fell wasn't too great, and that limited the damage.

That's how it was when I was sitting there or out on the court during that Celtics run. Even as we entered the fourth quarter, our attitude was "Hey, we're still ahead by two. We had our bad patch. No pressing. Just do your job and we'll be okay." No real straw broke the proverbial camel's back, and as much as has been made of P. J. Brown's thunderous dunk near the end of the third quarter, or Eddie House's jumper six minutes into the fourth that gave the Celtics the lead at 84–83, we were still thinking we were very much in the ball game, and we were.

Being a professional athlete requires you to be a realist and an optimist—pessimism can't play a part in your game—and knowing when to let each of those tendencies take over is an invaluable skill. We knew we weren't playing well, but we also knew that we had been playing great basketball before that. Who was to say we couldn't recapture what we'd lost? That's not an optimistic attitude, that is a realistic one. Yes, momentum factors into a game big-time, but who was to say that the Celtics were going to be able to sustain the energy and success they'd attained. They were playing out of their minds at that point, and we had to figure that they'd come down a notch or two down the stretch. That didn't quite happen.

I reentered the game with 2:10 left in the fourth quarter. Kevin Garnett had just hit an eight-foot jumper to put them up by 5 at 88–83. Immediately after that, Kobe had gone to the line to make two and made a driving layup. Everyone figured he'd try to take over, and getting to the basket for a foul or layup was to be expected. The teams had been trading baskets, and James Posey's three had kept their lead at 5 points with just slightly more than a minute to play. As he'd done so many times before, Kobe drove the lane, was met by the collapsing Celtics defense, and kicked the ball out to me beyond the arc. I let it go and sensed the shot was true. We were down by just 3 and the Lakers crowd went nuts. Unfortunately, those were the last points we'd score in the game.

I don't want to imply that we would have won had I played more minutes down the stretch, or that if I'd got more opportunities to score, we'd have won, but I did want to be out there and I did want those opportunities. I hated being on the bench watching that lead dwindle. Ray Allen had stolen one of my passes and converted a layup to bring the Celtics within 11 with three minutes to go in the third. We were outscored 10 to 1 after that, and I thought that I was being rested for the crucial fourth-quarter minutes. I wish that I could have been out there for more than those last two minutes. We'll never know how things might have turned out.

I'm proud that we came back in game five to win despite a near repeat of our game four performance. We led 43–24 before the Celtics came back on us to lead 62–60. We were a young team, and we'd learned a valuable lesson in game four, and we didn't let another horrible third quarter do us in. I knew I had to be more aggressive going to the basket, and it paid off with me making 8 of 11 free throw attempts that contributed to my 15 points. Our 103–98 victory was sweet, and as Coach Jackson said of us, "We're young enough and dumb enough to do this." By "this" he meant to be the first team to come back from a 3-1 deficit in the finals to win. It wasn't to be, and our 131–92 defeat was painful. The Celtics' Big Three played as advertised, and their vaunted defense took hold. We would all have liked to have put on a better effort, and whether we lost by 1 or by 39 didn't matter in the end. The Celtics were champs and we weren't.

As disappointed as I was at not winning the championship, I can't say that I was devastated by the loss as I would have been earlier in my career. Professionally, it was difficult to deal with, but personally, I didn't take losses to heart in the way that I had for so many years before. It may be hard to understand this, but as much as I enjoyed winning game five at home on Father's Day, I also enjoyed that my kids were at the game and came down onto the court afterward to be with me. That was the real victory, and even if we'd won games six and seven, I'd still say that. I take my job seriously, and I do everything I can to be a success at it, but keeping an eye out for what I need to do at home and how I can help the Lakers win has kept me in much better balance than ever before. In the past, I might have moped around and been miserable for weeks after the series ended. In this case, I had to put my mind on another goal immediately—Tatum's ongoing treatment. In the back of my mind, somewhere on the periphery instead of at the forefront, was the thought that the Lakers still had another mountain to climb and I wanted to be there with them, at the summit, looking down to see just how far we'd all come.

I couldn't dwell on our loss for too long. I still had family matters to attend to. Just as I do at the end of every season when I meet with the Lakers and review the season and preview the upcoming one, here's a bit about where the Fishers stood heading into 2008–09 season.

Since her procedure, Tatum has done remarkably well. Through the diligence of her doctors and the grace of God, the tumor has receded and she has approximately 50 percent of her vision in the affected eye. Later on as she gets older, she will have to do some therapy and training of the weaker eye so that the unaffected one won't dominate too much. Her prognosis is excellent, and she and her brother are getting to be even more of a handful each day. I haven't checked out their jump shots yet, but there's still plenty of time for all that.

My mother continues to be a strong and active and positive influence in my life. I sometimes kid her that I wish that she would retire. It seems no matter where I travel in the league, people ask me to give my mom their best. Recently, on a road trip to New York, David Stern, the NBA commissioner, asked me to send my mother his greeting. My mother is active in the Mothers of Professional Basket-

ball Players Association doing charity work. The organization intro-
duces new players and their families to the NBA life and eases their
transition. She's made some good friends and recently flew to Denver
to hang out with Chauncey Billup's mom while I was there with the
team. We talk at least once or twice a week, and lately she's even got
into sending text messages.

From what my male friends tell me, my dad and I are pretty typical of most fathers and sons. We don't speak as often as Mom and I
do, but that doesn't seem to trouble either of us. We say far less, but
when we do speak, it really matters. At my wedding, my dad spoke
to me before the ceremony. I was glad that he didn't give me the
birds-and-bees talk, especially since what he said was so heartfelt and
meaningful. He told me how proud he was of me, and that he was so
glad that I was going to be a family man. That meant so much to me.
He remarried about a year ago, and I'm happy that he seems happy
and more settled than he had been for a while. Candace encourages
me to ask about some of those issues from the past with my mom, but
I'm not sure I'm ready for that.

As for me, I'm enjoying life on and off the court so much, but I've
got a few thoughts about my next steps. Nothing definite, but I have
no immediate plans to retire. As long as I keep improving, as long as
my body holds out, I don't see any reason that I should hang it up
other than a desire to spend more time with my family. I sometimes
feel guilty about not being there full-time for Marshall. He's about to
head into high school, and because of my busy schedule, I'm kind of a
"special events" presence in his life—attending some football games,
birthday parties, graduation, and so on. I check in on him every day,
whether it's seeing that his homework is done or just to talk with him
or to play a video game or two. Candace, Marshall's father, and I easily manage a respectful relationship with one another, but I still wonder if Marshall has been shortchanged by not having someone in the
home full-time and as fully involved as my dad was.

When I do retire, I've done some planning ahead of time. I've
done some color commentary for the Women's National Basketball
Association team in Los Angeles—the Sparks—and enjoyed that. I

have some friends in the broadcasting industry, and they've told me that they see that as a natural fit for me. I'm not certain of what I want to do, but it will have to be fulfilling on a deep level. One reason I wanted to be the president of the Players Association is to leave the game in better shape than it was when I got here. Whatever is next for me in this life will have to fulfill that same mission—to better the lives of others. That was the important fundamental my mother and father taught me.

Epilogue

Mission Accomplished

Winning a championship is what it's all about. I've won them at nearly every level, and believe me, the feeling never gets old. Having won four of them in the NBA, I've been asked after each of them how it feels. After winning the second and the subsequent championships, I've been asked where the 2008–9 one ranks. That's a very difficult question. In the moment, just after the final buzzer has gone off and you and your teammates are awash in an overwhelming sensation of relief, joy, amazement, and vindication, it's hard to put it all in perspective. All I can say to those who've never won any kind of championship, those victories are like your children, and they are each special in their own way. That said, because we are talking about games and not children, when asked, I have said that this fourth championship was the most special to me. The reason is simple: When I look back at all the things that have taken place in my life—both personally and professionally—since winning that third championship back in 2001–2, this one is especially gratifying. I guess that the longer and tougher the road, the more grateful you are when you arrive at the destination, particularly when that destination puts you at the top.

I purposely use the word *vindication* in describing those feelings above because after having lost in the finals the year before, we had a lot of doubters who were convinced that we didn't have what it took to go all the way. That was another of the reasons that this one was so special. None of those doubters were in our locker room or in our front office, but I'd be lying if I said that I wasn't aware of their presence in the media and out there in "fandom." I don't think anyone can go through life without having people who doubt your abilities, your commitment, your mental strength, and in my case in this year's run to the championship, my age, my quickness, my shooting ability. Based on the results, and what I was able to contribute personally to the Lakers' winning the championship, that V word fits.

Along with being aware of what's being said about the Lakers and me on various media outlets, fan sites, blogs, and all the other ways that people are able to communicate these days, I was also made aware of another factor that was being discussed widely—the officiating in the games and to a lesser extent the idea put forth by conspiracy theorists that the NBA had a vested interest in seeing the finals come down to LeBron James's Cleveland Cavaliers taking on Kobe Bryant's Los Angeles Lakers. That was the marquee matchup the NBA wanted, and David Stern had issued orders to the league's officials to make sure that much desired pairing took place. Or so the crazy thinking went. That's like saying that I masterminded a conspiracy of my own. Some people could say that I knew that this book was in the works, and so, using my considerable powers of persuasion,

I engineered a one-man conspiracy to make certain that all the points about the fundamentals I was making played a large role in the outcome of individual games and ultimately the championship.

I'm kidding about the conspiracy, but as I've said several times in this book, it seems as though there were larger forces at work in my life. The events of the 2008–9 season, but more specifically the playoff series, all seemed to fit into a larger plan for my life and also for this book. Ifs, buts, would haves, should haves, and could haves are all a part of sports and our fascination with them, and no one can ever say how things might have turned out if such and such didn't happen. What I find ironic is that in the game that will go down in a lot of people's minds as the most pivotal in our series against the Orlando Magic, game four, I hit a three-pointer with 4.5 seconds to go to tie the game and to get us into overtime. While I'm really proud of that contribution and what it meant for our team, something happened prior to that shot that illustrates one of the points that I've been trying to make throughout this book. I'm referring, obviously to those of you who watched the game, about Dwight Howard missing two free throws just prior to our last possession when we tied it up. I mean no disrespect to Dwight. He's one of the bright young stars in the game and a terrific competitor. But—and here we go with those speculative what ifs, might haves, and could haves—if he had hit one or both of those foul shots, our task would have been immensely more difficult. I'm not a gambling man, but I would say that the odds of us tying that game with so little time left on the clock would have been considerably longer than they were with us down by three instead of by four or five. I'll talk more about that sequence in a bit, but for now let's just focus on the missed opportunity those unmade free throws represent.

I hope that by now you see my point. Who knows what would have happened in the series if we had lost that game four. I believe that we would have still won it all, but who knows what could have happened in terms of injuries, etc. The point I want to make is that as much as series and games and life turn on critical moments, as much as people will remember LeBron James hitting a buzzer-beating three against Orlando or my three to get us into overtime, it really is about those fundamentals. The reason we won the championship is because we executed when it mattered the most. Execution and fundamentals go hand in hand. You can't talk about the one without the other. Ask fans of the Denver Nuggets and the failure of their team to successfully inbound the ball on a couple of occasions. They're likely to point out the team's inability to successfully perform one of the most basic plays in basketball as a reason for their missing out on a championship parade. Too often, fundamentals are noticed when they aren't executed than when they are. That's just how it is in life, and you likely won't get a whole lot of individual attention for being fundamentally sound, but as is true in my case, you will get the ring eventually. You will feel the enormous sense of accomplishment that comes from knowing that your contributions lead to a team victory.

I can't put myself in Tiger Woods's shoes. I wish I could and hit a golf ball the way he does, and this is only speculation on my part. I believe that winning an individual championship like Tiger has must feel very different from what it feels like to win a team championship. One is not better, of course, just different. One of the challenges every team in every sport faces, and not just the Lakers, is how you blend different personalities, skills, and desires into a winning effort. Much was made of Kobe winning his first Shaq-less championship. To be honest, that wasn't something that Kobe and I ever discussed, even though we were in the same situation. Much was also made of Kobe's scowling focus and the ferocity and fatigue that marked the incredibly long journey he (longer for him because of the 2008 Olympics) and the rest of us undertook. Ultimately, motivation mattered less than our collective ability to do what it took to get the job done. As I said following game four and the two key three-pointers I hit, when I am out there on the court, I know that my teammates are counting on me to contribute in some way. One of the reasons I was so exultant after that game was that I knew that not only had we won, but I'd solidified the faith that my teammates and my coaches and the Lakers organization had in me. I never doubted myself, I never wondered whether my teammates had lost their faith in me, but I still felt an obligation toward them to do what it took to win.

Coming downcourt as the seconds ticked away, I didn't have time to think about anything other than the game. As I crossed the half-court line, my focus was as tight as the 2,350 or so square feet of floor on either side and in front of me. As I dribbled toward the three-point arc, and just before I let the ball go, my field of vision narrowed down to that rim. I've shot thousands of jump shots, been in that position mentally probably thousands of more times since I was a kid shooting hoops at Chuckie's house or at the Penick Boys Club or out on the playground. None of that mattered. It all came down to that moment, and the reason that shot was good was because I was in that moment exclusively. I put my faith in myself, my ability, and the countless hours of preparation I'd put into the game. I let go of the shot and was fully prepared to accept the consequences, good or bad, of my action. That's all you can ever hope to be able to do in this life. Give it your best shot, take the result, and move on. Fortunately, things went my way. I'm grateful and humbled by the fact that the result was positive. I'm enormously grateful and humbled by the fact that we went on to win the championship. I'm thrilled and ecstatic. I know what it feels like to be on the other side of that experience and I'll take winning over losing every time. That's why we play the game.

Truth is that the high I've experienced since we closed out the Magic hasn't worn off. But in another version of the if, could have, would have scenario, I can confidently say that if we hadn't have won the championship, I'd have experienced a different kind of postfinals high. I would have been home with my family spending more time with them than I can during the season. I'd have experienced a different kind of satisfaction. I'd not have had the sense of vindication that I experienced, and that would be just fine with me. The thing about family is that there are no doubters. They believe in you, trust in you, and love you unconditionally, win or lose, swish or brick. That's the most fundamental truth I know, and I'm glad that I get to live it everyday. Holding my wife and my kids in my arms is a better feeling than hoisting any kind of championship trophy. No, no one holds a parade in my honor for being a good husband and father, and I know that our priorities as a culture need some shifting so that maybe we can honor parents who do the right thing and bring home the championship for their families the same as we do for athletes. Let's just say that off-the-court success and on-the-court success aren't necessarily better or worse than the other. Let's just say that they are different in some ways, but the skills and values you need are the same. I'm going to keep striving for more victories in both places. This is no if, could have, or should have kind of a thing. I'm driven and I see no sign of that changing. My eye is firmly fixed on the rim, and no opportunity is going to pass me by.

Acknowledgments

Putting a book together is a lot like assembling a winning basketball organization. I have many people to thank for assistance along the way. I can't possibly name all of the family members, friends, teammates, coaches, teachers, and business associates who have contributed to my life in one way or another, but please know that you have my thanks. There are a few people whom I would like to thank specifically.

First I want to thank my family, especially my mother and father and my siblings, who have always supported me. Without Candace and our kids Drew, Tatum, Chloe, and Marshall, none of what I do would have much meaning. While you've been on the sideline cheering me on when I played, you've always been the center of the action in my life.

Many people have helped me in seeing this project through to completion. From the beginning Peter McGuigan and Foundry Literary + Media, Sandy Fox, my editor Zachary Schisgal and all the folks at Touchstone Fireside, along with my collaborator Gary Brozek have helped guide me through the process. Also, to Duran McGregory and Jamie Wior for all that you have done and continue to do.

Photo Credits

Page 1 photograph courtesy NBAE/Getty Images: Andrew D.
  Bernstein
Page 26 photograph courtesy NBAE/Getty Images: Jesse D.
  Garrabrant
Page 45 photograph courtesy NBAE/Getty Images: Noah Graham
Page 67 photograph courtesy NBAE/Getty Images: Garrett Ellwood
Page 96 photograph courtesy NBAE/Getty Images: Noah Graham
Page 123 photograph courtesy NBAE/Getty Images: Joe Murphy
Page 163 photograph courtesy NBAE/Getty Images: Harry How
Page 181 photograph courtesy NBAE/Getty Images: Andrew D.
  Bernstein
Page 222 photograph courtesy NBAE/Getty Images: Wendi
  Kaminski